Cross-Linguistic Transfer of Writing Strategies

SECOND LANGUAGE ACQUISITION

Series Editors: **Professor David Singleton**, *University of Pannonia, Hungary* and Fellow Emeritus, *Trinity College, Dublin, Ireland* and **Associate Professor Simone E. Pfenninger**, *University of Salzburg, Austria*

This series brings together titles dealing with a variety of aspects of language acquisition and processing in situations where a language or languages other than the native language is involved. Second language is thus interpreted in its broadest possible sense. The volumes included in the series all offer in their different ways, on the one hand, exposition and discussion of empirical findings and, on the other, some degree of theoretical reflection. In this latter connection, no particular theoretical stance is privileged in the series; nor is any relevant perspective – sociolinguistic, psycholinguistic, neurolinguistic, etc. – deemed out of place. The intended readership of the series includes final-year undergraduates working on second language acquisition projects, postgraduate students involved in second language acquisition research, and researchers, teachers and policy makers in general whose interests include a second language acquisition component.

All books in this series are externally peer-reviewed.

Full details of all the books in this series and of all our other publications can be found on http://www.multilingual-matters.com, or by writing to Multilingual Matters, St Nicholas House, 31–34 High Street, Bristol BS1 2AW, UK.

SECOND LANGUAGE ACQUISITION: 145

Cross-Linguistic Transfer of Writing Strategies

Interactions between Foreign Language and First Language Classrooms

Karen Forbes

MULTILINGUAL MATTERS
Bristol • Blue Ridge Summit

DOI https://doi.org/10.21832/FORBES9745
Library of Congress Cataloging in Publication Data
A catalog record for this book is available from the Library of Congress.
Names: Forbes, Karen, 1985- author.
Title: Cross-Linguistic Transfer of Writing Strategies: Interactions
   between Foreign Language and First Language Classrooms/Karen Forbes.
Description: Bristol, UK; Blue Ridge Summit: Multilingual Matters, 2020. |
   Series: Second Language Acquisition: 145 | Includes bibliographical
   references and index. | Summary: "In the context of increasingly
   multilingual global educational settings, this book provides a timely
   exploration of the phenomenon of cross-linguistic transfer of writing
   strategies (in particular, transfer from the foreign language to the
   first language) and presents a compelling case for a multilingual
   approach to writing pedagogy"– Provided by publisher.
Identifiers: LCCN 2020025474 (print) | LCCN 2020025475 (ebook) | ISBN
   9781788929745 (hardback) | ISBN 9781788929752 (pdf) | ISBN 9781788929769
   (epub) | ISBN 9781788929776 (kindle edition)
Subjects: LCSH: Language and languages–Study and teaching
   (Secondary)–Foreign speakers. | Rhetoric–Study and teaching
   (Secondary). | Academic writing–Study and teaching (Secondary). |
   Composition (Language arts) | Second language acquisition. | Multilingualism.
Classification: LCC P53.27 .F67 2020 (print) | LCC P53.27 (ebook) | DDC
   418.0071–dc23 LC record available at https://lccn.loc.gov/2020025474
LC ebook record available at https://lccn.loc.gov/2020025475

British Library Cataloguing in Publication Data
A catalogue entry for this book is available from the British Library.

ISBN-13: 978-1-78892-974-5 (hbk)
ISBN-13: 978-1-78892-973-8 (pbk)

Multilingual Matters
UK: St Nicholas House, 31–34 High Street, Bristol, BS1 2AW, UK.
USA: Ingram, Jackson, TN, USA.

Website: www.multilingual-matters.com
Twitter: Multi_Ling_Mat
Facebook: https://www.facebook.com/multilingualmatters
Blog: www.channelviewpublications.wordpress.com

Copyright © 2021 Karen Forbes.

All rights reserved. No part of this work may be reproduced in any form or by any means without permission in writing from the publisher.

The policy of Multilingual Matters/Channel View Publications is to use papers that are natural, renewable and recyclable products, made from wood grown in sustainable forests. In the manufacturing process of our books, and to further support our policy, preference is given to printers that have FSC and PEFC Chain of Custody certification. The FSC and/or PEFC logos will appear on those books where full certification has been granted to the printer concerned.

Typeset by SAN Publishing Services Pvt. Ltd

Contents

Acknowledgements		vii
1	Introduction	1
	An Introduction to the Research Context	5
	A Note on Terminology	6
	Aims and Outline of the Book	7
2	The Position of First Language and Foreign Language Learning in Schools	11
	Language(s) in the Curriculum	12
	L1 and FL Teachers' Conceptualisations of and Approaches to Language Teaching	19
	Student Conceptualisations of and Approaches to L1 and FL Writing	22
	Conclusion	27
3	An Overview of Strategy Research and the Role of Language Learning Strategy Instruction	28
	Strategy Research in the Field of L2 Acquisition	28
	Strategy Research in the Field of Composition Research	37
	Exploring the Effects of LLSI on Writing	47
	Conclusion	54
4	Considerations for Researching the Effects of a Cross-Linguistic Intervention of Language Learning Strategy Instruction	55
	Designing the X-LiST Study: Considerations of Research Design	55
	Getting Inside the 'Black Box': A Mixed-Methods Approach to Strategy Research	58
	The Ethics of Conducting Classroom-based LLSI Research	68
	Conclusion	69
5	Teaching for Transfer: Developing a Cross-Linguistic Approach to Language Learning Strategy Instruction	72
	Challenges in Implementing Cross-Linguistic LLSI	73
	General Considerations for Developing LLSI	74

	Developing a Cross-Linguistic Programme of LLSI: A Step-by-Step Guide	77
	Conclusion	89
6	An In-Depth Exploration of Patterns of Strategy Development in Foreign Language and First Language Writing	90
	Performance in Writing Tasks	90
	Pre-Task Planning	92
	Problem Solving While Writing	98
	Evaluation of Written Work	100
	Errors and Error Correction	104
	Conclusion	107
7	Exploring the Cross-Linguistic Transfer of Strategies	109
	The Phenomenon of Cross-Linguistic Transfer	109
	Evidence of Strategy Transfer from the X-LiST Study	116
	Multiple Directionalities of Transfer	118
	Conclusion	123
8	Negotiating Language Learning Strategy Instruction: Individual Trajectories	124
	The Strategic Writer (Carissa)	125
	The Experimenter (Chris)	130
	The Struggling Writer (Zoe)	136
	The Multilingual Writer (Mei)	141
	Conclusion	147
9	The Role of Learners' Individual Differences	149
	The Symbiotic Relationship between Proficiency and Strategy Use	149
	The Importance of Metacognitive Engagement	153
	Attitudes towards Writing	155
	Strategic Multilingualism	156
	Conclusion	159
10	Reflecting Back and Looking Forward: Implications and Conclusions	160
	Revisiting the Key Questions	161
	Limitations of the X-LiST Study	166
	Implications for Research and Practice	169
	Looking Forward: Areas for Future Research	172
	Final Reflections	173
Appendix A: Student Questionnaire		174
Appendix B: Writing Strategy Task Sheet (Carissa, German Task 2)		178
References		182
Subject Index		195
Author Index		197

Acknowledgements

Some say that raising a child takes a village, and I think the same can probably be said for writing a book! This has been a long time in the making, and the PhD study on which this book is based would never have happened without the unwavering support and wisdom of my long-suffering supervisor, colleague, mentor and friend, Linda Fisher. The fact that it was ultimately turned into a book is largely down to the encouragement of Michael Evans. Thank you both! I am also incredibly grateful to the Economic and Social Research Council for funding this project.

Thank you also to Yongcan Liu and to all of my current and former students who have acted as sounding boards for ideas over the years. And, of course, to my mum and dad for their constant encouragement and understanding.

I would also like to give special thanks to the anonymous reviewer for their incredibly valuable suggestions and to the wonderful team and series editors at Multilingual Matters for all of their guidance and patience and for making this process so smooth.

And most of all, I am indebted to the superb teachers and students who so willingly agreed to take part in this study – this would not have been possible without you.

Thank you also to De Gruyter for permission to build on aspects of the following paper in this book:

Forbes, K. and Fisher, L. (2020) Strategy development and cross-linguistic transfer in foreign and first language writing. *Applied Linguistics Review* 11 (2), 311–339. https://doi.org/10.1515/applirev-2018-0008

This book also draws on aspects of the following studies published under a Creative Commons Attribution license:

Forbes, K. (2018) 'In German I have to think about it more than I do in English': The foreign language classroom as a key context for developing transferable metacognitive strategies. In Å. Haukås, C. Bjørke and M. Dypedahl (eds) *Metacognition in Language Learning and Teaching* (pp. 139–156). Abingdon: Routledge.

Forbes, K. (2019a) Teaching for transfer between first and foreign language classroom contexts: Developing a framework for a strategy-based, cross-curricular approach to writing pedagogy. *Writing and Pedagogy* 11 (1), 101–126. doi:10.1558/wap.34601

Forbes, K. (2019b) The role of individual differences in the development and transfer of writing strategies between foreign and first language classrooms. *Research Papers in Education* 34 (4), 445–464. doi:10.1080/02671522.2018.1452963

1 Introduction

> *Wer fremde Sprachen nicht kennt, weiß nichts von seiner eigenen.*
> Those who know nothing of foreign languages,
> know nothing of their own.
> Goethe

The above quote by Goethe is one that has resonated with me in various ways over the years, first as a language learner, then as a secondary school teacher and more recently as a researcher. It seems to encapsulate the essence of the various reflections and experiences, both personal and professional, that ultimately led to the research at the heart of this book. I remember 'discovering' language only when I started to learn French at age 11. That may sound strange given that I had been a reasonably fluent speaker of English for many of those 11 years, but I had never thought about 'my' language in such an explicit way before – I simply took it for granted. At age 18, I remember sitting in my first linguistics lecture at university when we were told that on Mondays the focus would be on English language and grammar. As one of the few native English speakers in the room I sat back smugly thinking this would be easy, but when the first question was asked and dozens of hands shot up around me, I slumped down in my seat and realised just how little I knew. Later, as a teacher of French and Spanish in a secondary school in England, I thought a lot about how we position 'language' in schools and the great chasm that seems to exist between how we engage with and teach the first language (L1) versus foreign languages (FL). I had many a heated debate with my English teacher friend who insisted that I was the *language* teacher whereas she identified herself primarily as a teacher of *literature*. Yet, I always instinctively felt that, for me, learning French, German and Spanish in school made me a better speaker, writer and user of English. As I moved into educational research I looked for evidence to support this; yet, while there is a substantial body of work on how the L1 can transfer to or interfere with learning additional languages, there are fewer empirical studies that explore the potential positive effects that learning a second language (L2) or FL in school may have on the first.

The above reflections are purely anecdotal; however, they have far wider implications in the current climate of FL education in England and beyond. While the learning of English as an L2/FL is booming in many countries around the world and represents around a $50 billion a year industry (Statista, 2019), FL learning in Anglophone countries such as the United Kingdom, the United States of America, Australia and New Zealand has been in steady decline in recent years. Languages are considered as 'hard' and sometimes 'pointless' in light of the global status of English. Debates around migration and the 'nation' fuelled by political developments such as the Trump presidency in the United States and the Brexit referendum in the UK have led some to be suspicious of anything that represents the 'other' or the 'foreign'. Yet, it is vital to acknowledge that, even though English continues to be the lingua franca for much world trade and diplomacy, it alone is simply not enough (Commission on Language Learning, 2017). Teachers of FLs in these countries therefore often battle to justify the place of their subject in the curriculum. We highlight the social, cognitive and economic benefits of speaking another language; we emphasise the importance of developing communication skills and intercultural competence. However, what if we could provide further evidence to demonstrate that the benefits and value of FL learning in schools can extend beyond the subject to other areas of the curriculum? Indeed, the need for robust research evidence to answer such questions has recently been highlighted in a report by the British Academy (2019), which calls for more studies exploring the cross-curricular benefits of language learning.

In addition to reflecting on *why* we teach FLs, we also need to think about *how* we teach these languages. The reality is that some students do struggle, and we must therefore do what we can to make languages accessible and to help them to flourish. This led me to the field of language learning strategies, first as a teacher and later as a researcher. Language learning strategies will be discussed in depth in Chapter 3, but they are generally considered as a means of ensuring that language is stored, retained and able to be produced when necessary. Or, as Oxford (2017) effectively puts it:

> L2 learning strategies are complex, dynamic thoughts and actions, selected and used by learners with some degree of consciousness in specific contexts in order to regulate multiple aspects of themselves (such as cognitive, emotional, and social) for the purpose of (a) accomplishing language tasks; (b) improving language performance; and/or (c) enhancing long-term proficiency. (Oxford, 2017: 48)

Even though the field has been around since the 1970s, it continues to evolve, to innovate and to attract the attention of scholars worldwide. While the focus of early studies in this area was largely on identifying and classifying the various strategies that 'successful' learners use, attention later shifted to *how* such strategies can be taught and the effectiveness of various programmes of language learning strategy instruction (LLSI). In recent decades a substantial body of evidence has been produced which largely suggests that: (a) there is a positive relationship between strategy use and attainment in language learning; and (b) such strategies are indeed both 'teachable' and 'learnable' (see, for example, recent meta-analyses by Ardasheva *et al.*, 2017; Plonsky, 2019). There are, of course, a range of complex factors that will influence the extent to which individual students will develop and use language learning strategies, such as, for example, the educational context, their proficiency level in the language itself and their attitudes towards learning the language. However, there is a growing body of research that provides insights into what these factors may be and how teachers can account for them in the classroom.

While studies on LLSI have addressed a range of different skill areas such as speaking, listening, reading and vocabulary learning, the particular focus of this book is on writing. Developing the ability to communicate effectively in writing is a skill that permeates the entire school curriculum and one that is vitally important for future success in the workplace. Indeed, it is also frequently the medium used to assess learners in all subjects. However, within the context of secondary school classrooms, developing competence in writing represents a notable challenge for many learners. This is particularly true in an FL where it is 'arguably the most difficult of the modalities in which to achieve communicative competence' (Chamot, 2005: 121), but is often also the case in their L1 where it is equally recognised as 'an extremely complex skill that is not easily mastered' (Graham, 2015: 767). In addition, unlike speaking, which can be acquired naturally provided there is a sufficient level of input and exposure, writing is a skill that requires more conscious development. As such, it lends itself well to explicit strategy instruction in a range of language contexts.

However, while there is certainly evidence in the literature to suggest that effective strategy use can be of benefit to language learners across a range of skill areas (Ardasheva *et al.*, 2017; Cohen, 2011; Oxford, 2017; Plonsky, 2011), the majority of this research has taken place within a single context of either L1 or FL education and, as such, there has been less focus on the potential interactions between the two. In addition, it is often the case within the literature that any reference to transfer between these two contexts implies the one-way transfer of pre-existing skills and strategies *from* the L1 *to* the FL. However, the study at the heart of this book emerged from a hypothesis that the reverse may be equally valid; if the use of writing strategies is explicitly developed within the FL classroom (where students are arguably more explicitly aware of themselves as *language* learners), then it seems logical that this knowledge could not only benefit FL writing tasks, but might also positively affect L1 writing. Guo and

Huang (2018: 3) similarly highlight the need for studies that examine 'the actual transferability of writing strategies from one language to another'. Yet, it is also important to explore the potential of cross-curricular collaboration between L1 and FL teachers through, for example, parallel LLSI – an area in which, to date, there is a paucity of research (Gunning *et al.*, 2016). As suggested by Grenfell and Harris (2017):

> If students are being invited to reflect on and share approaches to their language learning in both their mother tongue and their foreign language classes, then it seems to us to be a wasted opportunity not to facilitate the transference of new understandings between both arenas by developing a common understanding and approach to teaching how to learn. (Grenfell & Harris, 2017: 217)

Such a focus on exploring interactions between different languages is also in line with more recent developments in the field of translanguaging. While this does not constitute the framework in which the current book is situated, it would be remiss not to acknowledge the potential intersections here at a theoretical level. At its core, translanguaging is a practice that involves the 'dynamic and functionally integrated use of different languages and language varieties' (Li, 2018: 15), for example, when learners switch between languages or draw on their full linguistic repertoire to convey meaning. This could include both spontaneous translanguaging (i.e. the fluid use of languages both in and out of school) and pedagogical translanguaging (i.e. designed instructional strategies that integrate two or more languages) (Cenoz & Gorter, 2017). Such practices are underpinned by the idea that multilinguals (or those in the process of learning another language) 'do not think unilingually in a politically named linguistic entity, even when they are in a "monolingual mode" and producing one nameable language only for a specific stretch of speech or text' (Li, 2018: 18). The underlying implication, therefore, is that having knowledge of additional languages may influence the way in which someone uses or thinks about language more broadly, including their L1. While translanguaging studies to date do not necessarily focus on such fluidity and interactions at the strategic level, what such a perspective shares with the focus of the current book is an interest in exploring interactions between the different languages in a learner's repertoire.

In light of both the personal experiences and the empirical evidence considered above, a number of questions therefore emerged which became the drivers for the study at the heart of this book. These include:

- How are L1 and FL learning positioned in schools?
- To what extent do the existing writing strategies used by students in L1 and FL classrooms differ?
- What happens when L1 and FL teachers collaborate to develop parallel LLSI? What are the stages in developing such an intervention?

- How does an intervention of LLSI in an FL classroom influence performance in writing and strategy development in the FL, and do any such effects transfer to writing tasks in another FL or the L1?
- What are the key factors relating to individual differences that influence students' development and transfer of language learning strategies?

By no means can I claim that this book will provide definitive answers to each of these questions. However, it is hoped that the results and insights provided will shed light on our understanding of the nature of and potential for the cross-linguistic transfer of language learning strategies which, to date, is a relatively unexplored area.

An Introduction to the Research Context

This book is based largely on data that emerged as part of the Cross-Linguistic Strategy Transfer study (hereafter referred to as the X-LiST study), a longitudinal, quasi-experimental study conducted in a secondary school in England. The key aim of this study was to explore how an explicit focus on strategy instruction in the FL German classroom influenced students' strategy development and performance in writing in German, and whether any such effects transferred to another FL (French) and/or to the L1 (English). The study involved FL teachers of German and French, L1 teachers of English and two intact classes of Year 9 students (age 13–14). This year group was chosen specifically because the students had completed at least two years of FL learning at secondary school; therefore, they were at a point where they were beginning to write longer pieces of text in the target language, an important practical consideration for this study. Crucially, this was also the final year of compulsory FL learning in school and therefore the students represented a wider range of ability levels and attitudes towards the subject than those who would self-select to continue the subject in Year 10 and beyond. It is also important to note that the school was situated in a semi-rural area in the East of England. Students who spoke a language other than English in the home represented only around 10% of the student population (which is around 4% below the national average for secondary schools at the time). As such, the main focus of the X-LiST study was on L1 English speaking students learning FLs in school. However, there were two bilingual students in the intervention group – one who spoke Mandarin at home and another who spoke Polish at home. There is a particular focus on these students in Chapters 8 and 9.

The majority of Year 9 students in the school studied both French and German as FLs. While they were all in their third year of learning both of these languages at secondary school level, some had also received an additional one or two years of French at primary school. However, it is important to note that any such input was minimal and did not have a notable impact on their level of proficiency. At the time, therefore, the secondary school curriculum did not assume any prior knowledge of the language. As such, it is fair to say that all of the participants were at a relatively similar stage of learning in both French and German. Two parallel mixed-ability classes were selected from the year group: one was designated as the intervention group which received an intervention of LLSI initially in the German classroom and later also in the English classroom, and the other as a comparison group which continued with the normal scheme of work in each subject. There were 22 participating students in the intervention group and 23 in the comparison group and both classes were comparable in terms of variables such as the spread of gender and academic performance.

A mixed-methods approach was adopted and data were collected from all students at various points over the course of the year through writing tasks (completed on task sheets to capture strategy use), assessment data and questionnaires. In addition to gathering data at a whole-class level, 12 students were also selected to participate in additional stimulated recall interviews and general interviews to allow for a more in-depth exploration of the role of individual differences in the development and transfer of students' strategy use between the different language contexts. These students were chosen to represent a range of gender, academic performance, attitudes towards the subjects and L1 background.

A Note on Terminology

Within the fields of both language learning strategies and research on writing more generally, the terms 'L1' and 'L2' are commonly used, yet it is important to recognise that such terms are highly context dependent and may prove problematic. The term L1 is typically used to refer to an individual's mother tongue; however, bilingual children may have more than one language as their 'first' language. Similarly, if children move to a different country during their schooling, their dominant or primary language may eventually shift from their mother tongue to the language of the country in which they are living and attending school.

The term L2 is equally complex. This is often used as an umbrella term for any languages learned after the L1 (Hammarberg, 2001), yet distinctions can also be made between a learner's L2 and third language (L3) according to the chronological order in which each language was encountered (Bardel, 2015). Such a distinction is considered important by some, as the L2 is typically learned by monolinguals, whereas the L3 or LX is learned by bi- or multilinguals who will therefore have already developed certain cognitive qualities that will differentiate them from the former group (Bardel & Falk, 2012). However, while this may have implications for languages learned at different stages, in the case of the X-LiST study the students started learning German and French at around the same age and were considered to be at a similar level of proficiency in both (as noted above). As a result of such parallel experiences, it would not make sense to impose a hierarchical distinction by referring to one as an L2 and another as an L3.

The term 'L2 learning' can also be used to refer to learners who are living and/or working in the target language environment, as distinct from 'FL learning' where learners receive a limited amount of exposure to the FL in an instructed, classroom environment, as is the case in the current study. Such a difference in sociocultural environments necessitates that L2 and FL development should be considered as different entities (Kecskes & Papp, 2000). Therefore, for the purpose of this book the term 'first language' or L1 will be used to refer to English, which is the native language and/or primary language of the vast majority of the participants (any exceptions to this will be clearly stated throughout), while German and French will be referred to as 'foreign languages' (FL). Reference to the L2 (or L3) will only be made when referring to other studies where these terms have been used by the authors.

Aims and Outline of the Book

The overarching aim of this book is primarily to provide insights into the phenomenon of cross-linguistic transfer of writing strategies (in particular, transfer *from* the FL *to* the L1) and, as such, to further highlight the potential contribution of FL teaching to the development of writing skills more generally. It is hoped that this may encourage more joined-up, cross-curricular, cross-linguistic thinking in relation to language in schools. The book is structured as follows.

Chapter 2 sets out important contextual information for the subsequent study by reviewing **the position of L1 and FL learning in schools** from a range of perspectives. First, key trends are explored at the national level such as provision for and uptake of FL learning. The relative positioning of both the L1 and FLs within the curriculum is then examined, with a particular focus on the perceived 'status' of each language and also the presence (or absence) of any explicit cross-curricular links made between different languages. While the main focus of this book is on the UK context, comparisons will also be made here to a range of other (predominantly) Anglophone countries, namely the United States, Canada, Australia and New Zealand. As stated earlier in this chapter, having English as the dominant official language in these countries means that, on the one hand, they may be seen to share a linguistically privileged position but, on the other hand, they also share similar struggles when it comes to the promotion and positioning of other languages in the curriculum. The focus then shifts to the individual level and, more specifically, to the perspectives of teachers and students which are explored by drawing on data from the X-LiST study. The aim here is to examine the various approaches and priorities of L1 and FL teachers when it comes to the teaching of writing and to consider the extent to which these views and practices are reflected in students' conceptualisations of writing and strategy use. Based on the evidence presented in this chapter, a case is made for the FL classroom as a key context for developing strategies which may also benefit the L1.

Chapter 3 brings together **a review of the literature** relating to strategy research in both FL and L1 contexts (i.e. within the fields of L2 acquisition and composition research, respectively); even though these two streams of research have undoubtedly influenced one another over the years, to date they have largely remained separate. The chapter begins by considering ongoing debates surrounding the definition of the term 'strategy' and then traces the evolution of research into language learning strategies from its origins in the 1970s to the present day. Key theoretical perspectives are identified which have influenced research in both L1 and L2/FL writing strategies. The focus then shifts to exploring the extent to which these strategies can be taught and learned in a classroom context. To this end, a series of empirical studies are reviewed and evaluated which consider the effect of an intervention of LLSI on performance in writing in L1 and FL contexts, respectively.

Chapter 4 explores issues related to the complex task of **researching strategy use**. The key aims are, on the one hand, to fully describe the research design of the X-LiST study and, on the other hand, to more broadly reflect on some of the key methodological issues inherent in strategy research. These include, for example, considerations of research design and reflections on the affordances and limitations of a range of methods that aim to capture data about learners' strategy use. Consideration is also given to the practicalities and ethics of designing and researching LLSI interventions in schools, in order to provide food for thought for other researchers in the field.

Chapter 5 focuses on the role of L1 and FL teachers in facilitating strategy development and transfer within and between different language contexts. While most existing studies on LLSI focus predominantly on the outcomes of such interventions, the aim here is to consider **the *process* of developing the cross-linguistic, pedagogical intervention** at the heart of the X-LiST study. While Phase A of the study involved strategy instruction in the German FL classroom only, Phase B involved parallel instruction in both German FL and English L1 lessons in order to encourage students to reflect on, develop and transfer their language learning strategies across contexts. The chapter begins by acknowledging some of the challenges inherent in setting up such collaborations and then explores how these challenges might be overcome. The key considerations and steps in the design and implementation of a cross-linguistic programme of LLSI are described and exemplified with reference to activities developed as part of the X-LiST study. The chapter ultimately calls for a more collaborative and multilingual approach to writing pedagogy where FL and L1 teachers are both recognised as teachers of *language* and, as such, work together to encourage and facilitate connection making.

Chapter 6 begins by presenting performance data from the X-LiST study which suggests the potential positive effects of LLSI on *both* L1 and FL writing. The focus then shifts to looking behind this performance data to provide **an in-depth exploration of the patterns of strategy development in FL and L1 writing which emerged in the X-LiST study.** Whole-class trends are explored over time to determine if and how the strategic writing approaches of students in the intervention group changed in German, French and English from Point 1 (before any intervention took place), to Point 2 (following a period of explicit LLSI in the German classroom only), to Point 3 (after parallel programmes of LLSI were implemented and mutually reinforced in both German and English). Strategy development is considered here largely in terms of planning strategies used *before* writing, problem-solving strategies used *while* writing and evaluation strategies employed *after* writing. As a more objective measure of the effectiveness of strategy use, instances of errors and error correction are also examined. The data presented in this chapter not only illustrate the strategic approaches used by students in both L1 and FL writing, but also provide an insight into the ways in which LLSI shapes their strategy development across different languages.

Chapter 7 aims to shed light on our understanding of **the nature of bi-directional transfer between a learners' L1 and FL strategy use.** The chapter first examines key literature related to the phenomenon of transfer. This begins with an overview of early conceptualisations of language transfer from the L1 to the FL, and then discusses more recent developments relating to multicompetence which have led to an increasing interest in reverse transfer from the FL to the L1. Multiple directionalities of transfer in relation to students' strategy development and use are then explored in more depth, drawing on data from the X-LiST study. At the beginning, students took different approaches to writing in English and the FLs and, as such, there was limited evidence of transfer of pre-existing strategies from the L1 to the FL. What did emerge throughout, however, were similar patterns of strategy development for both German and French, suggesting a high level of transfer *between* the two FLs. There were also instances of reverse transfer from the FL to the L1 which suggests that even beginner or low-proficiency FL learners can develop effective strategies in the FL classroom that can transfer to their L1 writing.

Chapters 8 and 9 shift the focus from more general trends in terms of performance and strategy development to the individual. The aim here is to identify and reflect on some of **the complex and dynamic factors that influence the way in which individual learners develop and transfer writing strategies.** To this end, Chapter 8 draws on qualitative data from the

X-LiST study to provide an in-depth exploration of the way in which four students negotiated their way through the intervention of LLSI and the extent to which they developed and transferred strategies between their FLs and L1. The four students were selected to represent a range of distinct writer 'profiles' that emerged from the data; these are referred to as 'the strategic writer', 'the experimenter', 'the struggling writer' and 'the multilingual writer'. Drawing on these case studies, Chapter 9 then explores the key factors related to individual differences that emerged, namely, students' level of proficiency in both the L1 and FLs, their metacognitive engagement with the task, their attitude towards writing and their strategic use of other languages.

Finally, Chapter 10 concludes the book by revisiting and reflecting on the key questions presented above in light of the data generated from the X-LiST study. Limitations of the study are considered and a range of implications relating to theory, methodology and pedagogy are suggested.

This chapter began with reference to the ubiquitous quote from Goethe that 'those who know nothing of foreign languages, know nothing of their own'. Even though this claim dates back to the early 19th century, the underlying sentiment continues to appeal to language learners, teachers and researchers alike. Nonetheless, there are still questions that remain unanswered about precisely *how* FL learning can influence the L1 at the level of strategy use. This is precisely what this book seeks to address. There is a growing need for such evidence not only to support the position of FL learning in the curriculum, but also to highlight the potential for cross-curricular collaboration between L1 and FL teachers.

2 The Position of First Language and Foreign Language Learning in Schools

As stated in Chapter 1, one of the key aims of this book is to provide insights into the phenomenon of cross-linguistic transfer of strategies and, in particular, to encourage more joined-up, cross-curricular thinking in schools by highlighting the potential contribution of FL teaching to the development of writing skills more generally. As such, it is important to begin by considering the ways in which L1 and FL learning are positioned in schools. As noted by Leonet *et al.* (2020: 42), 'it is common to find school policies that follow a strict separation of languages' at both the curricular and organisational levels. Such policies may, in turn, influence not only the potential for collaboration among language teachers, but also the extent to which students are able to make connections and transfer strategies between languages. This chapter, therefore, aims to set the backdrop by exploring the relative position of L1 and FLs from a range of perspectives: from decisions made at a national level concerning the position of languages in the curriculum, to the individual perspectives of teachers and students. While the primary focus of this book as a whole is on the UK context (and more specifically, England), comparisons will also be drawn in this chapter to the situation in a selection of other predominantly Anglophone nations such as the United States, Canada, Australia and New Zealand. While this seeks, on the one hand, to broaden the relevance of the topics discussed, a key objective is also to shine a light on some of the fundamental issues facing language learning in Anglophone countries given the international status and ubiquity of English (Duff, 2017). To this end, this chapter explores the relative positioning of languages (both English and FLs) within the curriculum across a range of countries before considering in more depth how teachers and students conceptualise and approach language (and more specifically, writing) in both the L1 and FL classroom contexts.

Language(s) in the Curriculum

An important first step is more closely to examine the decline in provision for and uptake of FL learning in schools. On the surface, such downward trends in recent years may seem to be indicative of a decline in interest on the part of the students. However, this may also be reflective of broader priorities at a national level (e.g. complacency due to the status of English as a global lingua franca) which will inevitably influence the relative position of subjects within school curricula. Those subjects that form a compulsory part of the curriculum are typically viewed as 'higher status' subjects and may consequently receive more resources (i.e. teaching hours). Such status, in turn, may influence students' later decisions about what subjects to continue to study when they have more choice. This section, therefore, explores the status of language(s) in the curriculum across a range of Anglophone countries, namely the UK, the United States, Canada, Australia and New Zealand. The focus here is very deliberately on language(s) more broadly; given that much discussion and debate in this area tends to focus on *either* L1 *or* FL education, the driving force of this book is to encourage and facilitate connection making between these various language contexts. To this end, the following will focus particularly on the presence (or absence) of any cross-curricular links made between these subjects at the level of the curriculum.

It should also be noted that this book is primarily set within a context where the majority of learners (a) have English as their L1 and (b) attend a school where English is the medium of instruction and where FLs are offered as subjects within the curriculum. This is indeed the case for many students in Anglophone countries. In England, for example, over 80% of secondary school students are currently recorded as being L1 speakers of English (DfE, 2019). Similar patterns are reflected at a national level in the United States (Kids Count Data Center, 2018), Canada (Statistics Canada, 2016), Australia (Australian Bureau of Statistics, 2016) and New Zealand (Edwards, 2012; McGee *et al.*, 2015). Yet, it is also important to acknowledge and value the increasing linguistic diversity in schools around the world and the significant number of students in the above countries who have languages other than English as their L1 (Evans *et al.*, 2020). Such multilingual students are considered in particular in Chapters 8 and 9 of this book and the key findings are no less relevant to them. Indeed, perhaps this makes it even more crucial for all teachers to reflect more explicitly on the linguistic skills and strategies that students bring with them to class.

United Kingdom

The United Kingdom is an interesting and diverse national context where responsibility for education is devolved to the various constituent countries of England, Scotland, Wales and Northern Ireland. While largely considered to be a 'monolingual' English speaking country, the presence of other indigenous languages influences language curricula in schools in various parts of the country. Scotland and Wales have adopted policies that are more in line with European recommendations that school students should have the opportunity to learn at least two other languages in addition to their L1 (Council of the European Union, 2002). The Scottish government, for example, promotes the '1+2' (L1 plus two additional languages) model of language teaching and learning in schools (Scottish Government Languages Working Group, 2012), and has committed to encouraging the learning of indigenous Scottish languages and dialects alongside other FLs beginning from the first year of primary school. The Welsh government has similarly set out a series of strategic objectives to improve and promote language learning by adopting a 'bilingual plus one' model, where students learn English, Welsh and an additional FL from primary school (Welsh Government, 2015). In Northern Ireland there are a small number of Irish-medium schools (predominantly primary schools), and some schools also offer an Irish-as-a-second-language option (Department of Education, 2008).

On the other hand, however, such multilingual European models have not been as widely adopted in England where provision varies greatly from school to school. This may be due, in part, to the lack of an additional widespread indigenous language, such as Scottish Gaelic or Welsh, and to the predominance of English as a global language. Yet, even the study of a single FL is facing challenges. In secondary schools in England there is increasing concern about the declining number of students who choose to study a language beyond the compulsory phase, currently fewer than 50% (Tinsley & Doležal, 2019). Even where the study of languages is a curricular entitlement (between the ages of seven and 14), there is a growing trend in the number of schools that exclude or excuse students from FL lessons in favour of receiving extra literacy support in English or because they are not considered to be 'successful' language learners. This practice of disapplication from FL learning in the first few years of secondary school restricts the learners' access to language study at a higher level.

English, conversely, has consistently enjoyed a higher status in schools as a 'core' or 'foundation' subject. A report by the schools' inspectorate in England (OFSTED, 2012: 4) begins with the statement that: 'there can be no more important subject than English in the school curriculum. English is a pre-eminent world language, it is at the heart of our culture and it is the language medium in which most of our students think and communicate.' However, as suggested by Burley and Pomphrey (2003), the high status of the English language in the school as a whole may paradoxically interfere with the way in which it is presented as a subject:

> Traditionally in the school curriculum in the UK, the English language maintains an unquestioned status as the medium of everyday communication and of the majority of teaching and learning activity in the school

curriculum. This has made it difficult to study English as a language in a sufficiently objective way, particularly for those for whom it is a first language and a teaching subject. (Burley & Pomphrey, 2003: 247–248)

While the previous National Curriculum Programme of Study for students aged 11–14 made some effort to encourage FL teachers to make links to students' literacy learning in English (QCA, 2007), this is conspicuous by its absence from the current curriculum in England which came into effect in September 2014 (DfE, 2014). It is also interesting to note that there are no similar guidelines encouraging English teachers to explore connections to students' FL learning. The potential for such links has also been highlighted by the Office for Standards in Education (OFSTED, 2013: 4) in their report on improving standards in literacy; this report recommends that the curriculum should offer the opportunity for students to 'develop writing skills through work that makes cross-curricular links with other subjects' and calls for long-term planning and more collaboration between teachers in different subject areas. It would seem that FL teachers, who are able to focus more explicitly on the development of language learning strategies, are in a unique position to contribute to the overall improvement in writing standards.

United States of America

In the United States, language instruction typically begins in middle school or high school, although provision for and uptake of FL learning in schools varies considerably across states. The share of elementary and secondary school students enrolled in language classes for the nation as a whole is 19.66%; however, this ranges from only 8.5% in New Mexico which does not have an FL requirement for graduation, to 51.2% in New Jersey which does (American Councils for International Education, 2017). There has also been a significant decline in FL instruction over the past decade (Commission on Language Learning, 2017; Pufahl & Rhodes, 2011), with fewer public schools offering classes in world languages.

The English language, however, is a key part of the curriculum and is considered to be 'a resource to be cherished and should continue to be an educational priority' (Commission on Language Learning, 2017: 1). A series of core academic standards have been established for the teaching of English language arts in schools (Schutz, 2011) which highlight the key role of language in developing critical thinking, problem-solving and analytical skills. They also provide 'a vision of what it means to be a literate person who is prepared for success in the 21st century' (Schutz, 2011: 3). Interestingly, the standards emphasise that there is a 'shared responsibility for students' literacy development' (Schutz, 2011: 4) across multiple disciplines, and links are made to literacy in history/social sciences, science and technical subjects, yet there is no mention of the potential contribution of FL learning to the development of literacy or language skills more generally.

It is important to note, however, that the above comments apply to schools where English is the sole medium of instruction and other languages are offered as (optional) curriculum subjects. Yet, it is important to acknowledge the increasing number of bilingual (or dual language) education programmes in schools across the United States (Kim *et al.*, 2015). While such programmes undoubtedly vary by structure and student populations, the two main models are: (a) one-way dual language programmes, where students predominantly come from one language group and receive instruction in both English and the partner language (which may be their native language); and (b) two-way dual language programmes, where there are roughly equal numbers of students from two language groups (i.e. English speakers and partner language speakers) who are integrated to receive instruction in both languages (Boyle *et al.*, 2015). The most commonly reported partner language in such dual education programmes is Spanish, which represented over 90% of the dual language programmes reported by schools in a survey completed by McGraw-Hill Education (2017).

There is also a growing body of evidence from dual language programmes which shows that learning a second language not only helps students to develop problem-solving skills, but also helps them to tackle the 'nuances and complexities' of their first language (Commission on Language Learning, 2017: 15). Such benefits are similarly acknowledged by Steele *et al.* (2017) who found that students randomly assigned to dual language programmes outperformed their peers in English reading by around 7 months in Grade 5 and 9 months in Grade 8. This provides further evidence in support of the strong link between literacy-related skills across languages. Yet, while the number of dual language education programmes in the United States has been growing in recent years, they still serve only a small proportion of the population. While exact figures are not available due to the range of terminology used and the wide variation in policies and implementation across states, estimates suggest that as few as 3% of elementary school students are currently enrolled in bilingual programmes (Goldenberg & Wagner, 2015). The predominant model in the United States therefore remains similar to the UK context, where English is typically used as the medium of instruction, with foreign languages offered as discrete subjects within the curriculum.

Canada

In Canada, education is the responsibility of the provinces and territories and, as such, there is no overarching curriculum at a national level. As a bilingual country, English and/or French are taught as L1s depending on the region and the particular school and, similar to the United States, there is also a range of schooling models in operation such as French immersion and bilingual education programmes (Dressler, 2018; Gorter & Cenoz, 2017). Taking the predominantly English-speaking province of British Columbia as an example, there is a requirement that all students must take an additional language as part of the curriculum in Grades 5–8 (Ministry of Education, 2004). For the majority of students in schools where English is the medium of instruction this language is French, although curricula are also available for American Sign Language, German, Italian, Japanese, Korean, Mandarin, Punjabi and Spanish.

It is encouraging to see that the FL curricula in British Columbia make explicit links to students' English language skills:

> As students gain proficiency in [the foreign language], they develop many competences essential to their continued success in life, including critical thinking, creative thinking, and communication skills. For example, learning an additional language is known to enhance students' learning and literacy in their first language, as well as contributing to their overall cognitive development. As they learn to communicate clearly and effectively in [the foreign language], students gain transferable skills and processes that contribute to their proficiency as communicators in English. (Ministry of Education, 2004)

Yet, interestingly, no such links are made to other languages within the English language arts curriculum. While it does refer to 'transferability of learning' as a goal, which includes helping students to 'develop language and thinking strategies that can be applied to new contexts', it does not specify which contexts.

Australia

Education in Australia is regulated by individual states and territories, but they are guided by an overarching national curriculum (Australian Curriculum Assessment and Reporting Authority, 2018). This identifies eight learning areas which include English and Languages. Within the latter, there are language-specific curricula for a range of world languages (e.g. French, German, Hindi) and there is also a separate framework for Aboriginal languages and Torres Strait Islander languages. Most states have some form of compulsory FL education at specific year levels up to Year 8 (age 13–14); however, in recent years language education in Australia has been in serious decline (Bense, 2014) and there is a concern that 'provision of languages in schools in Australia and uptake by students remain fragile at all phases of schooling' (Australian Curriculum Assessment and Reporting Authority, 2011, as cited in Bense, 2014: 487). This echoes similar concerns in other predominantly Anglophone countries.

As with the Canadian curriculum for FLs, references are also made in the Australian curriculum to the potential links between English and other languages (Australian Curriculum Assessment and Reporting Authority, 2018). Students are expected to engage in a 'reciprocal and dynamic process' whereby they 'move between the new language being learnt and their own existing language(s)' and reflect on the 'comparative dimensions' between these languages. It is also highly encouraging to see explicit recognition that 'learning languages develops overall literacy. It is in this sense "value added", strengthening literacy-related capabilities that are transferable across languages, both the language being learnt and all other languages that are part of the learner's repertoire.' Yet, as with similar contexts explored above, the onus here seems to lie solely on the FL teachers to make such connections. While the English curriculum acknowledges that 'Australia is a linguistically and culturally diverse country', there is no reference to the potential ways in which English teachers could draw on students' multilingual capabilities within the language classroom (whether these are students' home languages or FLs learned in school).

New Zealand

In New Zealand, English is an official language along with Te Reo Māori and New Zealand Sign Language. Even though FLs constitute a learning area in the New Zealand curriculum, it is one of the few countries where language learning is not compulsory at any stage of schooling. While many schools offer international languages as an option, such as Mandarin, French, German and Japanese, New Zealand has similarly experienced a decline in the proportion of students choosing to study a language. Over the past decade there has been a 14% decrease in the number of secondary students learning languages as a subject in school and for Asian language learning the decline has been 29% (New Zealand Association of Language Teachers, 2016: 1).

The curriculum as a whole highlights the importance of literacy and numeracy as key skills (Ministry of Education, 2017). In order to obtain the National Certificate of Educational Achievement at the end of secondary school, students must accumulate sufficient credits in each of these two areas which can be attained from a range of subjects. However, even though literacy credits are described as reflecting a student's writing, speaking and listening skills, credits in languages (with the exception of Te Reo Māori and Latin) do not count towards literacy credits. Given that the FL curriculum states that 'learning a language provides students with the cognitive tools and strategies to learn further languages and *to increase their understanding of their own language(s)*' (Ministry of Education, 2017: 24, my emphasis), it is surprising and concerning that such skills are not valued as contributing towards overall literacy development. Furthermore, while the English curricula explored above make no reference to possible links with FL learning, the English curriculum in New Zealand explicitly rejects such a link: 'Success in English is fundamental to success across the curriculum. All learning areas (with the possible exception of languages) require students to receive, process, and present ideas or information using the English language as a medium' (Ministry of Education, 2017: 18).

Curricular priorities

Even though there is a lot of diversity both within and between the various national contexts explored above, there are indeed also commonalities in relation to the positioning of language(s) within their respective curricula. They can all be considered as predominantly Anglophone countries (even if there are several languages that hold an official status) and, as such, the English language quite rightly holds a dominant place in the school curriculum. The position of FL learning, however, is less certain. Statutory entitlement (where it exists) is usually limited to just a few years of education during late primary or early secondary school, and uptake in language learning after (and in some cases, even during) the compulsory phase has been in steady decline in recent years. In such a climate of decreasing interest in studying FLs, there is therefore a growing need to promote the FL classroom as a key context for developing not only valuable communicative skills in the FL itself, but also important transferable skills related to language more generally. As stated by Kecskes and Papp (2000):

> Foreign language is not just another school subject. FL learning requires and develops a complexity of skills that can have very beneficial effects on the general development of every student. FLs should be taught not just for themselves but for the general educational enhancement and development of students. (Kecskes & Papp, 2000: 122)

Yet, this is not reflected in the curriculum documents examined above. What emerged is that, in each of these countries, English and FLs are conceptualised differently and presented very separately at the level of the curriculum. Where references to potential links between the two do exist (although they are few and far between), these are situated exclusively within the FL curricula where students may be encouraged to make links to their knowledge of English or other languages. There are no references in the English language curricula to the potential links that could be made by L1 teachers to the skills and strategies developed by students in other languages, even though, as stated by Grenfell and Harris (2017: 216), 'insights gained from the study of a foreign language can be used to reflect on the structure of the mother tongue and vice versa'. This could include (but is by no means limited to) encouraging students to reflect on the spelling and grammatical structure of languages, consideration of approaches to structuring texts in different languages, and drawing attention to the particular skills and strategies used and developed across languages.

It seems, therefore, as though opportunities have been lost to acknowledge the potential contribution of FL learning to the understanding and use of language in general.

L1 and FL Teachers' Conceptualisations of and Approaches to Language Teaching

While curriculum documents provide valuable insights into provision for and the relative status of school subjects at a national level, it is also crucial to consider how the teachers enacting these curricula conceptualise the subject(s) they teach. Of particular interest here is the way in which English and FL teachers perceive themselves as teachers of *language*. There is a growing evidence base that suggests that there is indeed, 'little common understanding between L1 and L2 teachers' (Grenfell & Harris, 2017: 187) which leads to distinct approaches and priorities when it comes to the teaching of language. In terms of priorities, Grenfell and Harris (2017: 189) suggest that while the main aim for FL teachers is to develop students' ability to communicate in the language (alongside developing their cultural awareness), English teachers, on the other hand, are not only concerned with language, 'but also with sociolinguistics and language variation, literary analysis and linguistic effects in texts, media concepts and drama'. This gap inevitably widens as students progress through their schooling and as the focus of the English curriculum shifts beyond basic literacy. This is consequently reflected in a difference in approach to language pedagogy in the classroom, where L1 teachers, who can often assume a certain level of proficiency among learners, are more likely to take a subconscious, synthetic, top-down approach, whereas FL teachers tend to take a more conscious, analytical, bottom-up approach (Kecskes & Papp, 2000).

Such issues were brought to the fore in the UK context in the mid-1990s with a study conducted by Mitchell *et al.* (1994) into English and Modern Language teachers' beliefs and practices with regard to knowledge about language (KAL). The researchers noted substantial levels of KAL-related activity among both L1 and FL teachers and found some evidence of its positive contribution to learning, particularly in relation to writing development. However, they also noted that such activity was often fragmented and episodic. They found that L1 and FL teachers seemed to be conveying divergent and 'largely unrelated messages' (Mitchell *et al.*, 1994: 14) about language to their students and called for more consistent policies and shared perspectives between teachers in the two departments.

This work was further developed in England by Cathy Pomphrey and colleagues, who conducted a series of studies exploring language awareness among trainee teachers of English and Modern Languages and subsequently implemented shared training sessions to promote cross-subject dialogue (Burley & Pomphrey, 2003, 2015; Pomphrey, 2004; Pomphrey & Burley, 2009; Pomphrey & Moger, 1999). What emerged, in line with the literature above, was that the subjects of English and FLs were perceived by the teachers as very separate areas with their own curriculum, subject culture and pedagogical practices:

> There seems to be a continued tension between English and Modern Languages teachers in terms of perceptions of their aims, roles, classroom activity, relationship with pupils and a whole gamut of other aspects which lead to different priorities in their teaching of language and thus prevent cross-subject dialogue from taking place. (Pomphrey & Moger, 1999: 224)

In terms of differing approaches to language teaching, the authors found that whereas FL teachers placed emphasis on working at word and then sentence level in a more linear way, English teachers viewed text-level work as the starting point and therefore took a more top-down approach. Perhaps as a result of this, the English student teachers expressed more anxiety over explicit knowledge about language than their FL counterparts, which the authors identified as a specific factor that may inhibit conversation and collaboration between the two groups. The subsequent shared training sessions, however, succeeded in providing a space for dialogue and intercomprehension among the trainee teachers. They reported gaining valuable insights into the perspectives and practices of their counterparts and some participants even reported a shift in their own view of language. According to one L1 teacher, for example, 'it is all too often the case that English in schools is no longer treated as a language that is still being learned even by native speakers' (Burley & Pomphrey, 2003: 253). Evidence, on the whole, suggests that these sessions strengthened participants' understanding of language more broadly and was particularly beneficial with respect to literacy. Yet, when followed up after their training year, the participants reported difficulty in establishing such cross-curricular links in their respective schools due, in part, to a lack of time and a lack of structures to support such collaboration.

Similar issues emerged within the X-LiST study. While the primary focus of the study was on the students, preliminary conversations were also arranged with two English teachers and two teachers of FLs (French and German) in order to gather some initial insights into their priorities and approaches in relation to teaching language and, in particular, writing. While notes were made during these conversations, they were not intended to constitute a formal part of the data collection process. Nonetheless, the information gathered proved useful in developing the subsequent intervention (as outlined in Chapter 5). In line with the previous studies cited above, there had been no previous collaboration between the L1 and FL teachers and they revealed a lack of awareness about the way in which writing was taught or viewed outside their particular subject area. However, collaboration and shared practice *was* evident between the two FL teachers. This is perhaps due to the similarity of the curricula and the fact that learners were at a relatively similar stage of learning in both French and German. Such collaboration was also facilitated structurally by the fact that the FL teachers shared the same department, teaching rooms and office space. When asked about how they approached writing tasks, the responses of the L1 and FL teachers varied considerably. In line with Grenfell and Harris (2017) and Burley and Pomphrey (2015), the FL teachers reported taking a more bottom-up approach to the teaching of writing and prioritised issues such as 'which tense they're going to be using', 'vocabulary' and 'the use of connectives'. The English teachers, on the other hand, prioritised more holistic issues relating to originality, style and appropriateness for the audience.

The above UK-based findings surrounding the different conceptualisations of language teaching among L1 and FL teachers are echoed in similar studies internationally. In the Norwegian context, for example, Haukås (2016) explored L3 teachers' beliefs about language and multilingualism. Although this study did not incorporate a focus on L1 teachers, what is of particular interest is that the L3 teachers of French, German and Spanish perceived themselves as very different from L2 teachers of English. This was attributed to a range of factors that resonate with the points raised above; for example, they believed that students' higher proficiency in and wider exposure to English led L2 teachers to take a more implicit approach to language instruction compared to L3 teachers. Evidence from Haukås' study similarly indicated a lack of existing collaboration between L1, L2 and L3 language teachers. A lack of collaboration between L1 and L2 teachers has also been documented by Gunning *et al.* (2016) in the context of Francophone Canada. They found that opportunities were limited by the isolation of L1 and L2 teachers and their lack of knowledge of each other's curriculum.

The aim of this section is by no means to insinuate that L1 and FL teachers should approach their teaching in the same way – obviously there are fundamental differences here in terms of students' proficiency levels and general expectations. However, the aim is rather to suggest that, in spite of these differences, both groups of teachers are ultimately working towards some shared goals, i.e. to enable their students to be able to use language, both written and spoken, to express themselves effectively. They are both, after all, teachers of *language*, and perhaps if they can learn from each other's' expertise and align some of their practices in a more cross-curricular way, this may also help students to make connections and transfer skills between their different languages. As suggested by Pomphrey and Moger (1999: 224), 'pupils' perceptions about language are unlikely to be very coherent if the underlying attitudes and perceptions of their teachers of English and Modern Languages differ so widely and the teachers are not engaged in dialogue about the differences'.

Student Conceptualisations of and Approaches to L1 and FL Writing

Having briefly considered how languages are positioned within the curriculum and the way in which L1 and FL teachers conceptualise language teaching, we now turn crucially to how such contextual and social factors may be reflected in (or indeed, shape) students' views. While there are a number of studies that explore students' beliefs about and attitudes towards FL learning in schools, few consider these in relation to L1 lessons. To this end, the X-LiST study started by exploring students' conceptualisations of writing through interviews and questionnaires (see Appendix A, and for more detail see Chapter 4). Given the difference between the core aims of English and FL curricula and those of the teachers, as noted above, it was important to begin by considering whether the students perceived the two language contexts as being similar or different. It was also hypothesised that such views may, in turn, influence their ability and willingness to make cross-curricular links and to transfer strategies from one context to another. This section will first draw on data from the initial interviews conducted with 12 Year 9 (aged 13–14) students to explore their perceptions of writing in the L1 and an FL. Secondly, consideration will be given to what they viewed as the most important features of writing in each subject. A brief overview will then be given of students' general approaches to writing in each language at the beginning of the study.

The distinct nature of L1 and FL writing

What emerged from the interviews is that students, unsurprisingly, perceived the nature of language and, more specifically, writing to be very different in their L1 and an FL. The key explanations for this related to the relative ease of writing in the L1 (what is referred to here as the 'native-speaker' factor), the diversity of task types and expectations between the L1 and FL classrooms and, perhaps most interestingly, the way in which the language of writing influenced their (meta)cognitive engagement with the task.

The 'native-speaker' factor

The general impression given by the students interviewed was that, regardless of the language, the nature of writing in one's native language(s), or most proficient language(s), is very different from writing in a more recently acquired FL. Such differing views seemed to be inherently linked to how they defined themselves as either an L1 or FL speaker/writer. Interestingly, one L1 English speaking student said he felt that writing in different languages would be the same: 'if you can speak the language, if I could speak say, Chinese and English, they would both be the same, the writing tasks and the speaking tasks would be exactly the same ... [but now] it's not the same, it's because we're not as advanced as I am in English in French' (Ben). The use of the 'if' clause here suggests that he did not yet view himself as being a legitimate 'speaker' (or indeed 'writer') of German or French and for him such tasks consequently remained distinct from English.

However, it is also worth noting that the advanced bilingual students who were interviewed similarly distinguished between writing in English (their L2, so to speak) and writing in German or French (as additional FLs), even though none of these constituted their L1. As Mei, an L1 Mandarin speaker, explained: 'cause I've been here for a long time I've adapted to like, English...it's just like, natural for me'. This was echoed by a Polish speaker in the same class who stated that writing in each of the subjects is 'different, because obviously I've studied English for longer...it just kind of flows in your head now that I've done it for such a long time'. However, he added the caveat that 'if I was meant to compare my Polish to English I'd say my Polish is a lot better, because I speak it at home' (Kacper). It seems as though their acquired proficiency in English has allowed these bilingual students to adopt the perspective of an 'L1 writer'. It therefore seems as if the 'native-speaker' factor (and by extension, level of proficiency) is key to determining students' overall conceptualisation of the nature of writing tasks.

Task type and expectations

Students' prevailing view of FL writing tasks was that they were much more rigid and confining than the English tasks. While English was considered to be 'more creative, they expect like, they expect you to use your imagination more' (Aleksandra), FL writing tasks were viewed as more restrictive. One boy commented that 'there's not much variety of tasks that we do in French and German, so it's just, writing' (Owen), a sentiment echoed by several of his peers who similarly suggested that 'with German you have to do what you have to do, like in the subjects they set you' (Zoe) and 'you know what you have to do and you just have to put it into a sentence' (Aleksandra). FL writing was also considered to be a means to an end rather than an expression of creativity, and while one of the higher achieving students recognised that this was 'good for learning more vocab' (Tom), on the whole, the view of FL writing tasks was that they were more restrictive and formulaic: 'it's like, you're never asked to write a story in German are you? You're always asked to write about yourself and what you've done and where you've been on holiday, past tense and stuff like that' (Annie). The FL tasks were therefore perceived as being more about the correct construction of individual sentences, rather than composition of a narrative text. This is very much in line with the views expressed by teachers outlined in the previous section and echoed by Grenfell and Harris (2017) and Burley and Pomphrey (2015).

Students reported enjoying writing in English more than in the FLs which also seems to be linked to the task types and expectations. In English, they overwhelmingly expressed a preference for creative writing tasks over essays or 'set tasks'. Reasons given for this included being able to 'use your imagination' (Ben) or enjoying 'thinking of a story and just writing it out' (Aleksandra) and also a preference for tasks based on personal experiences or opinions because there is less chance of 'getting it wrong' (Zoe). However, while the ability to express creative ideas freely in English seemed to lead to enjoyment of writing, conversely students' limited language ability in the FLs seemed to act as a barrier to enjoyment. They expressed frustration that 'you haven't got the ability to do, to write up your experiences cause you don't know how to say everything' (Chris) and that 'you can't describe as much and it gets a bit boring because you're repeating over and over again' (Aleksandra). Yet, even though some students did not enjoy writing in an FL due to a lack of proficiency, others reported feeling a sense of achievement when they completed a writing task, which they did not express in relation to English where they perhaps took it for granted. This was particularly evident among higher achieving learners who seemed to enjoy the challenge: 'I like, when you're writing in French or German, when you've written it all and seen how much you can actually do and like, that you are actually OK with this language' (Carissa).

'Thinking' in L1 and FL writing

Perhaps the most interesting theme that emerged from the interviews in relation to writing in L1 and an FL was students' awareness of the need to *think* more when writing in an FL. Table 2.1 provides an overview of some of the students' comments in relation to both language contexts.

There is an obvious link to be made here to the 'native-speaker' factor discussed above; however, it is important to recognise that even though

Table 2.1 Comments about 'thinking' in the FL and L1 classroom

Foreign languages	English
'In French you normally have to keep thinking what you need to write and how to spell it and things'	'I can just write more naturally'
'I think like, when you're doing French and German you're thinking more about the, like, the words'	'You don't have to think about it as much, cause like, you already know it'
'In German I concentrate and I make sure that it makes sense'	'In English I don't really have to think about it cause I've been doing it for like, 10 years'
'In German like, I don't know the whole language so I have to like…think about it more than I do in English'	'That's your born language so you know all the words'
'I use more adjectives […] than I do in English… because I'm thinking more about it'	'I don't need to think about it as long as I do with French or German'

these students *perceived* themselves as thinking less when writing in English, this was not necessarily the case. It may be that, due to their experience and level of proficiency in English, their thought processes had become proceduralised to the extent that they were no longer consciously aware that they were taking place. Therefore, this does not mean that they were not thinking in English, but rather that they were more conscious and metacognitively aware of their thought processes in the FL classroom. Yet, such comments provide some evidence to support the hypothesis that the FL classroom, where students are undoubtedly more aware of being engaged in thinking, is perhaps more conducive to the development of language-related metacognitive strategies than the L1 classroom (Forbes, 2018).

Students' views on what is important when writing in L1 and FL

Another useful indicator of students' conceptualisations of writing across different languages is what they consider to be the most important features. Forty-five Year 9 students were asked to complete a questionnaire which aimed to establish and track their view of writing in each subject (English, German and French). Using a Likert scale, students were asked to rate the importance of a range of criteria; some of these related to general features of writing, such as thinking of creative and interesting ideas, organising and structuring a text and overall accuracy, while others related to aspects of the writing process such as planning your work and revising/editing your work. General trends were then further explored within the individual interviews.

The first notable finding to emerge from the questionnaire data was that there were no significant differences between any of the importance ratings in German and French (following a series of Wilcoxon signed rank tests), which highlights the similarity in the ways in which students conceptualised writing in the two FLs. When comparing the FLs with English, however, the mean importance ratings for almost all of the criteria were higher in English, and this difference was significant in relation to five items: thinking of creative and interesting ideas, developing ideas, punctuation, fluency and overall accuracy. The fact that criteria such as thinking of creative ideas and developing ideas were rated as considerably more important in English can perhaps be explained by the differing task types as outlined above; given that tasks in English were seen to require more creativity and imagination, it seems logical that the expression of ideas would be considered more important than in German or French. It is perhaps more surprising that students considered overall accuracy to be more important in English, especially considering that they seemed to view writing in German and French as more about correct sentence construction. All in all, such views expressed on the questionnaires align with those expressed by some students in the interviews that English, as one of the 'core' subjects, is 'an important subject' (Chris), and by implication, more important than FLs.

In terms of the writing process, it is also worth noting that planning and revising/editing generally had the lowest ratings across each of the languages, although both were considered as slightly more important in English than in the two FLs. This also emerged in the interviews, where several students commented that, although they may engage in some planning in English, they did not feel it was as important in German or French because 'when it's like, the [foreign] languages I'm more focused on like, the words and stuff rather than like, the plot' (Carissa), or because 'you just find like, the words you wanna write and you write it down, you just go, you just do it as you go along really' (Annie). While some students expressed that they did not feel that planning was important in English because, for example, they were able to 'just write it down without having to plan it' (Katarina), on the whole they were more likely to feel that planning in English could be beneficial because of the longer length of tasks. However, one student, Mei, added the caveat that the importance of planning in English depended on what the task was and that it would be more important for something like an essay or newspaper report than for a creative story.

In relation to revising/editing, on the whole, students in the interviews agreed that this was generally quite important. Such comments, however, predominantly referred to correcting superficial errors rather than making any substantial revisions or editing content. One girl, for example, commented that she felt it was important to check her German writing for 'silly mistakes' (Katarina), while one of her peers similarly stated: 'I don't think like, there's any point in really just keep going through it and looking for like, really big mistakes. I just look like, for the little correction, like spelling mistakes I need to correct and stuff like that' (Claire). The views expressed here by the students very much align with the claims made above by Grenfell and Harris (2017) and Kecskes and Papp (2000) that the approach to writing in the FL classroom tends to be bottom-up, while in the English classroom the approach tends to be more top-down.

Students' approaches to writing in L1 and FL

While the data presented above provide an insight into students' *views* on writing, more objective data were also collected to explore their actual writing process and the strategies they use. While this will be discussed fully in Chapter 6, it is worth briefly summarising the key points from the analysis which suggest that they did indeed approach writing differently in English and the FLs at the beginning of the study:

- Students were much more likely to engage in any form of planning in English than in German or French, to produce much longer plans and

to use a wider range of planning strategies. While a common approach in English was for students to draft all or part of their work during the planning phase, in German and French very little written planning was produced and where there was some, this was generally limited to a small number of bullet points or vocabulary items.
- Students were much more likely to engage in problem-solving strategies, such as asking for help or referring to notes or a dictionary, when writing in German and French, which is not surprising given their much lower proficiency in the FLs.
- Students identified a wider range of evaluation strategies in English, even though they were aware that they were much more likely to make mistakes when writing in German or French.

Conclusion

The aim of this chapter was to consider the relative position of L1 and FLs from a range of perspectives: at the national level an overview was provided of curricula documents from a range of Anglophone countries, and at the level of the individual the perspectives of teachers and students were considered. Similar themes emerged at each of these levels which suggest considerable disparities between the ways in which English and FLs are positioned in the curriculum, taught by teachers and perceived by learners. Such segregation between these language-related subjects in schools may hinder students from making connections between these contexts which might, in turn, inhibit them from using the skills and strategies they develop in one to help in another. As such, one of the key objectives at the heart of this book is to encourage more joined-up ways of thinking about language across the curriculum by developing students' awareness and use of language learning strategies.

3 An Overview of Strategy Research and the Role of Language Learning Strategy Instruction

As discussed in Chapter 2, in spite of the underlying commonalities between some of the fundamental aims of L1 and FL teachers, there are often substantial differences in the way in which these subjects are taught and perceived in schools. It seems that L1 teachers take a more top-down, implicit approach to dealing with language in the classroom and, as such, students may be less consciously engaged in thinking about their approaches to language. It would seem logical, therefore, that FL teachers, who are able to focus more explicitly on the development of language learning strategies, are in a strong position to contribute to the overall improvement in writing standards more generally. The aim of this chapter is therefore to set the background for the X-LiST study by bringing together a review of the literature relating to strategy research in both L2/FL and L1 contexts, i.e. from the fields of second language acquisition and composition research, respectively. It begins by exploring the definitions and origins of language learning strategy research within the field of L2 acquisition, and then examines the theoretical perspectives that have influenced research in both L1 and L2/FL writing strategies. Empirical evidence that considers the effect of an intervention of language learning strategy instruction (LLSI) in both L1 and L2/FL classrooms is then reviewed. The focus of this chapter, therefore, is predominantly on reviewing the theoretical background and empirical evidence relating to strategies. Literature relating to research methods, the development of an intervention of LLSI and the phenomenon of transfer will be considered in Chapters 4, 5 and 7, respectively.

Strategy Research in the Field of L2 Acquisition

This section reviews literature and research relating to the field of strategy use in L2/FL learning. Issues surrounding the definition of the term 'strategy' are discussed and then the evolution of strategy research is considered alongside seminal studies that have sought to describe and classify strategy use.

Defining 'strategy'

Given that it constitutes one of the key terms in this book and, indeed, a field of study in itself, we should begin by considering what is meant by the term 'strategy' (although this is easier said than done). Looking first of all to more general sources, a strategy is defined by the Oxford English Dictionary (2019) as 'the art or practice of planning or directing the larger movements or long-term objectives of a battle, military campaign etc.', which reflects its etymological roots in the military sphere. On the surface, this seems rather far removed from the context of language learning, but on further reflection there is something here about directing, managing or orchestrating which seems apt – learning a language is indeed a long-term objective (and at times may also feel like a battle!). The subsequent, broader definition of a strategy as simply 'a plan, scheme, or course of action designed to achieve a particular objective, especially a long-term or overall aim', certainly seems very fitting.

Yet, within the field of applied linguistics, definition has proved a lot more elusive and research in this area has been characterised by an inability to conclusively agree on the meaning of the term 'strategy'. Indeed, the lack of consensus in arriving at a universally accepted definition has led to a plethora of other terms in the literature such as 'operation, routine, process, procedure, action, tactic, technique, plan and step' (Macaro, 2006: 324), which are used interchangeably by some, and by others to differentiate between nominal levels of specificity. In response to such ambiguity, Dörnyei and Skehan (2003: 611) have also suggested following the field of educational psychology by abandoning the term *strategy* in favour of *self-regulation*, which 'refers to the degree in which individuals are active participants in their own learning'. Yet, while this has been adopted more recently by some (e.g. Oxford, 2017), this shift has not yet fully occurred within the L2 field. As Cohen (2014) points out, such a change in terminology leaves unanswered the question of what learners do to self-regulate, which he suggests may, in fact, be to use strategies. In this sense, strategies can therefore be viewed as a useful tool to *facilitate* self-regulation. I suggest, therefore, for the sake of clarity in this book to use the general term *strategy*, while acknowledging that there are certainly meaningful links to be made to the broader self-regulation concept.

In the absence of a unified definition, there has been much debate over the years about the key characteristics of strategies for language learners. It has been generally accepted that L2 learning strategies are a means of ensuring that language is stored, retained and able to be produced when necessary; that is, they affect *learning* directly. They can be used by learners at varying levels of proficiency (Cohen, 2007) in response to problems when and where they arise (Grenfell & Macaro, 2007; Wenden, 1987), and to improve progress and accomplish language-related tasks in the L2 or FL (Macaro, 2001; Oxford & Schramm, 2007). They are 'optional' (Bialystok, 1978: 69), particular to the individual and can change and evolve over time (White *et al.*, 2007). Another key characteristic of learning strategies emphasised by Wenden (1987), Oxford (1990), Cohen (1998) and Grenfell and Harris (1999) is their close link with increasing learner autonomy, which has become a significant concern in modern classrooms.

One of the key areas of disagreement, however, lies in the level of consciousness of strategies and the potential distinction between a strategy and a process. While Wenden (1987: 7) previously had not distinguished between the two, and insisted that a strategy alone could be 'consciously deployed *or* automated', for many key researchers in the field it is precisely this element of consciousness and the learners' ability to identify it that distinguishes a *strategy* from an automatic or subconscious *process* (Anderson, 2005; Cohen, 2011, 2014; Griffiths, 2013; Oxford, 2011). Yet, as both Grenfell and Harris (2017) and Griffiths (2018) more recently suggest, any reference to consciousness is inherently problematic given the difficulty in ascertaining levels of awareness: 'strategies are both conscious *and* unconscious, and everything in between. The difficulty is with the descriptor, not the thing being described' (Grenfell & Harris, 2017: 37). Rather than considering the notions of strategy and process or consciousness and automaticity as being diametrically opposed, instead it seems more appropriate to consider these as existing at different ends of a continuum where the possibility exists for a conscious, deliberate strategy, through practice, to become a more automatic process. A useful analogy for comparison here may be learning to drive: at the beginning, the learner driver has to think very consciously about everything they do – moving into a new lane, for example, becomes a series of very deliberate steps involving checking mirrors, changing gear and indicating. In time, the same steps (or strategies) are still used (one hopes!), but the driver may be less aware of what these are and, consequently, less able to articulate these steps.

In a bid to make sense of the wide variation in strategy definitions and to bring 'order to the chaos', Oxford (2017: 48) conducted a content-analytic study of 33 key definitions provided by researchers in the field. This resulted in the following nuanced and encompassing definition:

> L2 learning strategies are complex, dynamic thoughts and actions, selected and used by learners with some degree of consciousness in specific contexts in order to regulate multiple aspects of themselves (such as cognitive, emotional and social) for the purpose of (a) accomplishing language tasks; (b) improving language performance or use; and/or (c) enhancing long-term proficiency. Strategies are mentally guided but may also have physical and therefore observable manifestations. Learners often use strategies flexibly and creatively; combine them in various ways, such as strategy clusters or strategy chains; and

orchestrate them to meet learning needs. Strategies are teachable. Learners in their contexts decide which strategies to use. Appropriateness of strategies depends on multiple personal and contextual factors. (Oxford, 2017: 48)

It is particularly encouraging to see the 'teachability' of strategies highlighted here and also recognition of the role of individual differences in influencing strategy use. What also emerges here is the shift away from thinking about strategies as being used separately and towards consideration of more complex combinations of strategy use. As noted by Cohen and Wang (2018, 2019), strategies are often used in pairs (i.e. where two strategies are used in combination), in sequence (i.e. where more than two strategies appear consecutively) or in clusters (i.e. where more than two strategies occur almost simultaneously and complement each other).

The origins of language learning strategy research

Having considered some of the definitional challenges inherent in strategy research, we now consider how strategy research has evolved from its origins in the 1970s. As stated by Grenfell and Macaro (2007: 11), 'if there is one article which can be seen to have announced the birth of language learner strategy research, then it was "What the 'good language learner' can teach us" by Joan Rubin in 1975'. This study marked a shift in focus from the teacher to the learners and the key aim was to examine what strategies successful language learners used, with a view to being able to use these to help less successful learners improve their proficiency: 'Commonly, the poorer student may notice that the better student always has the right answer but he never discovers why, never finds out what little "tricks" lead the better student to the right answer' (Rubin, 1975: 42).

In order to investigate these 'tricks' or strategies, Rubin observed and interviewed learners and teachers in addition to analysing learner diaries and self-reports. She succeeded in creating a list of strategies presumed to be important for a 'good' language learner. This included strategies that directly affect learning, such as deductive reasoning and memorisation, along with more social strategies that contribute indirectly to learning, such as seeking out native speakers to practise. This was certainly the first study of its kind and one that would come to be very influential in its field. Yet, in spite of the title of her study, we have to question what Rubin means by a 'good' language learner and, as Macaro (2001) suggests, we also have to question the validity of simply observing the strategies of a 'good' language learner with a view to imposing these on weaker students.

Rubin's study was closely followed by a study by Stern (1975), who compiled a list of ten strategies used by the 'good' language learner, which included categories such as planning, active, empathetic, semantic and internalisation strategies. His study was primarily based on his own experiences as a language learner and a teacher and as such has been criticised for being 'conceptual and speculative' (Grenfell & Macaro, 2007: 12), rather than being firmly rooted in empirical investigation. However, his work gave rise to the more in-depth study by Naimen, Fröhlich, Stern and Todesco in 1975, which aimed to further develop Rubin and Stern's preliminary work on learning strategies. For Naimen *et al.* (1975: 8), the learning process consisted 'of consciously employed strategies and techniques and unconscious mental processes'. And unlike Rubin, Naimen *et al.* also aimed to take into account factors such as age and previous language experience, and to address the affective aspects of language learning such as personality and cognitive style factors which are likely to influence the use of strategies.

The study by Naimen *et al.* (1975) focused on French classes at Grades 8, 10 and 12 in six schools in Toronto. They used a listening comprehension and imitation task to measure linguistic competence, completed interviews with 34 'good' language learners (as rated by interviewers or through recommendation) about language learning experiences and attitudes, interviewed teachers about the language behaviour of their students and undertook observations of the classroom environment. The authors organised their findings into five broad categories of learning strategies: the active task approach; realisation of language as a system; realisation of language as a means of communication and interaction; management of affective demands; and monitoring of L2 performance. The main oversight in this study, however, is that 'no relationships were identified between the use of learner strategies and learner variables, which is disappointing in view of the original goal of the study' (Graham, 1997: 38). Nonetheless, even though these relationships may not have been adequately determined, this study saw the beginning of other factors being linked to strategy use and to the suggestion that 'successful and highly motivated learners adopted more strategies, especially those involving planning, evaluation and monitoring' (Grenfell & Macaro, 2007: 15).

Classification of strategies: Developing a theoretical framework

During this early period of strategy research in the 1970s and early 1980s, studies had a tendency only to describe the general approach of 'good' language learners. Admittedly, there had been tentative attempts made by Rubin (1975) and Naimen *et al.* (1975) to begin to classify strategies, yet it was not until the late 1980s and early 1990s that the considerable variation in strategy type was fully acknowledged, and a need was identified for 'a clear and precise theoretical framework' (Grenfell & Macaro, 2007: 16).

Some early classifications drew on the distinction made by Selinker (1972) in his seminal paper on 'Interlanguage', between 'strategies of second-language learning' and 'strategies of second-language communication' as two of the five central processes involved in L2 learning. While the focus here is more on the former, it is worth briefly considering what is understood by communication strategies. Communication strategies, also referred to as language use strategies, are ways of predicting or repairing breakdowns in communication that arise due to limited knowledge of the L2 or limited expertise in a specific skill; they are therefore often a reaction to something that could not be foreseen. This aligns largely with the notion of strategic competence established by Canale and Swain (1980), who state that such 'coping strategies' are 'most likely to be acquired through experience in real life communication situations' rather than through classroom practice. Communication strategies, therefore, aim to improve *performance* rather than *competence* (Macaro, 2001). As such, studies in communication strategies often focus narrowly on speaking skills, such as finding ways to express a forgotten piece of vocabulary; however, they also have relevance to receptive skills, such as making sense of input when under the pressure of time. Research into communication strategies was pioneered by Faerch and Kasper (1983) with their study of a corpus of spoken and written language of 120 learners of English at Copenhagen University. They created a concrete taxonomy where each strategy is defined by its goal as a reduction strategy (such as avoidance), an achievement strategy (such as code-switching) or a repair strategy (such as a direct appeal to the interlocutor). Nonetheless, given the greater relevance to the instructed classroom context, the focus here remains centred on language *learning* strategies.

Two of the earliest and most influential taxonomies of language learning strategies were proposed by O'Malley and Chamot (1990) and Oxford (1990). While these were developed three decades ago, they have nonetheless been instrumental in building the foundations for future research and are therefore worth reviewing. The work of O'Malley and Chamot (1990) is clearly situated within a theoretical framework emerging from cognitive psychology and uniquely brought together research in L2 learning and the cognitive psychology of John Anderson. Anderson (1985) distinguished between declarative knowledge, what we know *about*, which is often learned in an explicit manner and can be acquired quite quickly, and procedural knowledge, what we know *how to do*, which is unanalysed, automatic knowledge, often requiring extensive practice. When applied to the field of strategy research, declarative knowledge can be considered as simply knowing about the strategies in one's repertoire, while procedural knowledge becomes 'the knowhow, the ability to enact or execute a strategy in the context of a particular task' (Gu, 2019: 23). O'Malley and Chamot (1990: 18) posit that the role of learning strategies within this framework is 'to make explicit what otherwise may occur without the learner's awareness'. They further develop this by suggesting that strategies that begin as declarative knowledge can become proceduralised with practice. This relates to the above debate surrounding conscious strategy use versus automatic processes.

Following a series of empirical studies on strategy use by FL students and English as a second language (ESL) students, O'Malley and Chamot were able to classify strategies into three groups according to their function: cognitive, metacognitive and social-affective. They state that cognitive strategies 'operate directly on incoming information, manipulating it in ways that enhance learning' (O'Malley & Chamot, 1990: 44). They are therefore related closely to the *processing* of language, for example, inferencing, deductive reasoning and translation strategies. The theoretical rationale behind the next category of metacognitive strategies was undoubtedly influenced by the work of Brown (1987) and Flavell (1979), who distinguished between normal cognitive processes and the overarching, reflective functions that control and monitor these processes (Desautel, 2009). Within the framework of language learner strategies, metacognitive strategies are defined as those that 'involve thinking about the learning process, planning for learning, monitoring of comprehension or production while it is taking place, and self-evaluation after the learning activity has been completed' (O'Malley & Chamot, 1990: 8).

The final category described by O'Malley and Chamot (1990: 45) is that of social-affective strategies, which are defined as 'either interaction with another person or ideational control over affect'. The affective strategies are linked with motivation and attitudes, whereas the social strategies could take the form of questioning for clarification, cooperation with others or, in the case of Rubin's (1975) study, creating opportunities for practice by seeking out native speakers. Dörnyei and Skehan (2003: 609) consider this category to be the 'odd one out' which 'appears to have been introduced simply to accommodate all the strategies that did not fit in the first two types, but which could not be left out either'. However, while these strategies are perhaps not as directly related to the cognitive framework adopted by the authors, there is little doubt that issues of motivation and attitude will inevitably have an impact on learning.

A contemporary taxonomy of language learning strategies was developed by Oxford (1990), who compiled a list of 62 language learning strategies divided into two main groups: direct and indirect strategies. The direct strategies involve direct manipulation of the target language and are further divided into memory, cognitive and compensatory strategies, while the indirect strategies consist of metacognitive, affective and social strategies. The basis for several of the distinctions made here (e.g. between direct and indirect, and cognitive and memory strategies) have been questioned and have since been largely discarded. Nonetheless, this taxonomy was useful for placing more emphasis on social and affective strategies such as cooperation with others.

Oxford (2011: 7) later presented a revised taxonomy identified as the Strategic Self-Regulation (S_2R) model of language learning, where 'learners actively and constructively use strategies to manage their own learning'. The S$_2$R model consists of three main groups: cognitive strategies, which 'help the learner construct, transform and apply L2 knowledge'; affective strategies, which 'help the learner create positive emotions and attitudes and stay motivated'; and sociocultural interactive (SI) strategies, which 'help the learner with communication, sociocultural contexts and identity' (Oxford, 2011: 14). These groups are in turn controlled by metacognitive strategies, meta-affective strategies and meta-SI strategies, respectively. These 'metastrategies' 'by virtue of their executive-control and management function, help the learner know whether and how to deploy a given strategy and in determining whether the strategy is working or has worked as intended' (Oxford, 2011: 18). Oxford (2011) criticised researchers such as Macaro (2006) for downplaying the importance of affective strategies by suggesting that they are simply a part of metacognition. She argued that the term *metacognitive*, as it had previously been defined, had therefore confusingly also applied to the control of strategies in the social and affective realms, not just to the control of strategies within the cognitive dimension, and so coined the terms meta-affective and meta-SI strategies in order to fill this gap. The introduction of these new concepts therefore emphasises the importance of learners' awareness of their own learning and their learning environment. However, similar issues remain in relation to the difficulty in delineating the boundaries between each of the various (meta)strategies.

This framework was further revised by Oxford in 2017 with the addition of motivational and metamotivational strategies. Here she draws on complexity theory to emphasise the dynamism of strategy use in context and presents each of the categories as fluid and overlapping. As she suggests: 'Let us be as scientific and precise as possible about categories and at the same time recognize that [...] strategies refuse to be tightly bound and are actually very flexible' (Oxford, 2017: 164). This goes some way to addressing criticism raised about the various endeavours that have been made over the years to classify strategies. Dörnyei (2005), for example, criticised the seemingly arbitrary classification of strategies and the blurring of distinctions between overlapping categories. More recently, Griffiths (2018: 63) has also claimed that, in practice, it is often 'not easy to exclusively classify a particular strategy into one group or another', while Zhang and Zhang (2013) have questioned the need for developing a unitary classification of strategies at all.

This has led to a more recent shift away from attempts to artificially force strategies into seemingly mutually exclusive categories and towards the recognition that a single strategy can operate at different levels of abstraction and can have multiple functions that are much more fluid in nature. Cohen and Wang (2018: 169), for example, note that classification of strategies according to function (e.g. metacognitive, cognitive, social, etc.) to date has been done in a relatively monolithic way with the tacit understanding that a strategy 'possesses just one function'. Based on a micro-analysis of the performance of a small group of Chinese learners of English on a vocabulary task, they found that the functions of any given strategy are much more fluid in nature and can fluctuate on a moment-to-moment basis. For example, in using the strategy of checking an inference with a more knowledgeable speaker of English, the social, cognitive and affective functions were sometimes activated almost simultaneously.

Situating the X-LiST study: Exploring the metacognitive function of strategies in writing

The various frameworks for describing and understanding strategies, as considered above, have been instrumental in furthering our understanding of strategy use and, indeed, in identifying a focus for the study at the heart of this book which has a particular interest in the metacognitive *function* of strategies. It is fully acknowledged that it is neither useful nor possible to isolate this metacognitive dimension and there will inevitably be intersections with, for example, cognitive and social functions. Nonetheless, there are several reasons for focusing in particular on the metacognitive dimension. First, it is important to note that O'Malley and Chamot (1990: 6) early on discovered a correlation between learners' success and metacognition, stating that 'students without metacognitive approaches are essentially learners without direction and ability to review their progress, accomplishments, and future learning directions', a link that has also been repeatedly acknowledged over the years by, for example, Ardasheva *et al.* (2017), Cohen (2011), Graham (2006), Griffiths (2013) and Lee and Mak (2018).

Secondly, the metacognitive function of strategies has been identified as a vital component of any form of strategy use. It is the metacognitive element that helps maintain strategy use over time and helps in transferring strategies to new tasks. This is an important objective of strategy instruction within the classroom and a key concern throughout the X-LiST study. Over time there has also been a shift in interest from the frequency or quantity of strategy use, to the quality of strategy use and the use of combinations of strategies in pairs, sequence or clusters, as noted above. This has resulted in an increasing interest in metacognition which has been shown to play 'an important role in activating the cognitive function, and generally in orchestrating strategy use more effectively' (Cohen & Wang, 2018: 180). It has also been acknowledged that strategies are not necessarily inherently 'good' or 'bad', but can be applied effectively or ineffectively (Grenfell & Harris, 1999; Griffiths, 2018) and it is the metacognitive element that helps learners to select and use strategies appropriate to them as individuals, and to the particular task at hand.

Thirdly, the decision to focus primarily on the metacognitive function of strategy use is influenced by practical concerns. From the research explored above, it seems as though metacognitive strategies may be more conscious and easier to articulate than purely cognitive strategies, and in terms of conducting empirical research with secondary school aged students this is an important consideration. Similarly, Macaro (2001) makes an interesting distinction between 'natural' strategies which, he suggests, exist at the more 'cognitive' end of the spectrum, and 'taught' strategies which are more aligned with the 'metacognitive' end. The implication here is that metacognitive strategies, which involve more awareness on the part of both learners and teachers, lend themselves more easily to explicit, classroom-based strategy instruction.

Within the X-LiST study, such strategies were explored within the skill area of writing. Much of the research carried out in the field of strategy use in L2 education to date has focused on the receptive skills of reading and listening; yet, I would agree with Chamot (2005: 121), that 'writing in a second language is arguably the most difficult of the modalities in which to achieve communicative competence', and therefore that students would benefit from developing strategies to aid them with such a cognitively demanding task. Vygotsky (1962) similarly argued from an L1 perspective that writing requires a high level of abstraction and demands both conscious work and deliberate action. As such, it is important to note that writing, even in a student's L1, is a skill that has to be learned, not one that is acquired naturally like speaking. As noted by Steve Graham (2015: 767) in relation to L1 writing development, it is an 'extremely complex skill that is not easily mastered'. Additionally, in contrast to the inherently transient nature of speaking, 'while composing in a second language, learners may be obliged to monitor their language production in a way that is not necessary or feasible under the time constraints of comprehending or conversing in the second language' (Cumming, 1990: 483). The luxury of time to monitor language production here is also conducive to the investigation and development of metacognitive strategy use (Williams, 2012).

Strategy Research in the Field of Composition Research

After having examined strategy research more generally within the field of L2 acquisition, it is important to recognise that the study of writing strategies in particular is also situated 'within a wider research movement known as "process writing", which emerged in the field of L1 composition research with the aim of gaining insights into the mental actions writers engage in while composing' (Manchón et al., 2007: 229). This section will consider two key theoretical perspectives that have been influential in shaping our understanding of writing and writing development: the cognitive perspective, which stresses the importance of developing students' writing skills, strategies and knowledge, and the social perspective, which emphasises the importance of context in writing development (Graham, 2015).

Writing in L1: Origins of the cognitive perspective

Process writing emerged in the 1980s following an approach where the focus had been predominantly on the text (the 'product') and was pioneered by Hayes and Flower (1980) with their cognitive process model. This influential model was developed primarily from think-aloud protocols, where participants are asked to talk through their thoughts while writing, and views the process of composing as a writer-centric, goal-orientated, problem-solving task. Flower and Hayes (1981: 369) explain a model for writing in the L1 that involves 'the basic processes of Planning, Translating, and Reviewing, which are under the control of a Monitor'. Within the model, the process of planning includes an element of goal-setting, and 'embodies tentative decisions about what topics shall be covered in what order, and thus, aids the writer in using stored information efficiently' (Flower & Hayes, 1984: 143). Translating is essentially the process of putting these ideas into visible language; however, 'if the writer must devote conscious attention to demands such as spelling and grammar, the task of translating can interfere with the more global process of planning what one wants to say'. The final process of reviewing is when writers evaluate and revise what they have written, and may in turn lead to re-planning or re-drafting, perhaps in response to peer or teacher feedback which, 'with its potential to transform a writer's text, has a really important role in process writing' (Gordon, 2008: 245). This model was later revised by Hayes (1996), who 'supplemented descriptions of cognitive processes with broader discussions of content, motivation, affect, and memory' (McCutchen, 2006: 115).

When considering the above cognitive process model by Flower and Hayes (1981), consisting of planning, translating and reviewing processes, it is difficult not to draw comparisons with O'Malley and Chamot's (1990) later definition of metacognitive strategies as planning, monitoring and evaluating strategies. However, this once again raises questions of terminology; as previously examined, the term 'process', used to describe this very approach, can imply an action that is automatic and subconscious. Therefore, it may seem logical to consider Flower and Hayes' categories of planning, translating and reviewing to be more cognitive processes, whereas it is the 'monitor' in their model that acts as the higher order, conscious, metacognitive control mechanism for these processes. As stated by Flower and Hayes (1981: 374), 'as the writers compose, they also monitor their current process and progress. The monitor functions as a writing strategist which determines when the writer moves from one process to the next'. Hayes (2012: 373) also later clarified that the monitor was originally intended 'to account for an individual difference among writers'. It seems, therefore, as though the monitor in Flower and Hayes' model fulfils a predominantly metacognitive function.

Another important feature of Flower and Hayes' (1981: 375) cognitive process model is that they reject the linear conception of writing as progressing mechanically from one stage to the next, and propose instead that writing is recursive and that 'a given process may be called upon at any time and embedded within another process or even within another instance of itself'. It is then the responsibility of the metacognitive monitor to allow the writer to move effectively between these various processes and perhaps to combine them, just as metacognitive strategies can be used to manage clusters of strategies simultaneously as discussed above. This view is consistent with O'Malley and Chamot's (1990: 42) statement that 'language generators move back and forth between the planning or construction stage and the articulation or transformation stage as they actively develop the meaning they wish to express through speech or writing'.

However, although Flower and Hayes (1981) set the precedent for a more strategic approach to writing instruction, they have been criticised for attempting to describe features common to all writers in a single model (Grabe & Kaplan, 1996; Hyland, 2002). Building on their work within the context of L1 writing, Bereiter and Scardamalia (1987) posited the need for not one, but *two* process models in order to account for differences between what they describe as 'immature' and 'mature' writers. They identify these as the knowledge-telling and knowledge-transforming models, respectively. Here we can once again draw parallels with the early studies into L2 strategy use, where the aim of research by Rubin (1975) and Naimen *et al.* (1975) was similarly to identify what 'good' learners do, with a view to helping others progress to a more expert-like competence.

The knowledge-telling model represents the basic, linear approach of immature or novice writers who convert writing tasks into problems of telling what they know about a subject. Knowledge-telling 'involves little metacognitive control' (Harris *et al.*, 2010: 234) and, as such, writers engage in minimal planning and revision. Any revision that does take place has a tendency to be more superficial, such as correcting spelling errors, rather than making changes to the organisation or content of the text. If they encounter a problem, they avoid it or simplify it instead of attempting to solve it. Such novice writers 'are largely unable to control and direct their own writing process, and they often encounter considerable confusion as to which behaviour or strategy should be employed to solve a particular writing problem' (Pennington & So, 1993: 42).

The knowledge-transforming model, on the other hand, represents expert writing that considers composing as a more complex 'form of problem-solving' (Scardamalia & Bereiter, 1986: 792). It incorporates the simpler model, yet here the writers additionally engage in global planning and higher order reasoning and use more complex strategies which 'reprocess and reshape what is on one's mind instead of only expressing it' (Collins, 1998: 110). However, the knowledge-telling and knowledge-transforming models are not dichotomous. In line with Flower and Hayes (1981), Bereiter and Scardamalia (1987) similarly view writing as a recursive process, and as such it is possible to move back and forth between the two models.

Like Bereiter and Scardamalia (1987), Berninger and Swanson (1994) also aimed to create a modified version of Flower and Hayes' (1981) model. Theirs is considered by some to be 'vastly superior' (Alamargot & Fayol, 2009: 28) to other models, as it accounts for developing writers and acknowledges the central role of metacognition. They suggest that metacognition about writing tends to have a stronger relationship with the quality of writing in secondary school aged children rather than in younger children. Yet, with secondary school students they interestingly found that 'metacognitions about translating or reviewing/revising are more related to quality of writing than are metacognitions about planning' (Berninger & Swanson, 1994: 76). As a result, they conclude that metacognitive skills or executive functions play a central role in developing writing, yet they are less clear on how such skills can be developed. Like Hayes and Flower (1980) and Bereiter and Scardamalia (1987), they also 'fail to tackle the question of instruction and its possible effects on composition processes and performances, as though the evolution we observe were somehow "natural"' (Alamargot & Fayol, 2009: 29).

Writing in the L1: The sociocognitive shift

This trend of viewing writing as a process inevitably led to changes in pedagogy, where the role of the teacher became primarily 'to help students develop viable strategies for getting started, for drafting, for revising, and for editing' (Silva, 1990: 15). However, from the mid-1990s, this approach received criticism for being too writer-centric and neglecting the sociocultural context and more emic perspectives of writing. For social constructionists, writing was viewed as 'a social act that can only occur within a specific context and for a specific audience' (Roca de Larios & Murphy, 2001: 26), a view arising from the Vygotskyan notion that cognitive development results from social interaction. The focus then shifted from the writer to the reader and this led to the development of the genre approach. Here, texts in a particular genre are analysed and modelled by the teacher before students proceed to write their own text, and 'the language focus, and form of a text stem from the community for which it is written' (Johns, 1990: 27). It was against this backdrop of genre theory that the National Literacy Strategy was developed and implemented in England, perpetuating the influence of text types on writing in the English classroom (DfEE, 1998).

However, the divide that emerged between the cognitive and sociocultural perspectives and the resulting apparent incompatibility between the two was considered unhelpful (Carter, 1990; Pittard & Martlew, 2000) as it 'could deny opportunities for synergy that might lead to more powerful and useful theory and research on learner strategies' (Oxford & Schramm,

2007: 49). It was therefore acknowledged that writing should be considered as 'a *sociocognitive* activity which involves skills in planning and drafting as well as knowledge of language, contexts, and audiences' (Hyland, 2002: 23). In light of the current study, it is important to further consider how such a sociocognitive perspective relates to research into the teaching and learning of writing. It was influenced primarily by Bandura's (1986: 18) social cognitive theory, which is based on the premise that:

> People are neither driven by inner forces nor automatically shaped and controlled by external stimuli. Rather, human functioning is explained in terms of a model of triadic reciprocality in which behaviour, cognitive and other personal factors, and environmental events all operate as interacting determinants of each other.

It is also influenced by Lave and Wenger's (1991) theory of situated cognition in which the context and action of learning are inextricably linked to the learning itself. Interestingly, Allal (2000: 147) later made a case to also include an element of 'situated metacognition', which is specifically 'geared toward promoting the acquisition of self-regulation mechanisms'.

This sociocognitive perspective on writing has in turn influenced pedagogy and research in both L1 and L2/FL contexts. In relation to pedagogy, increasing attention has been paid to the role of individual differences in writing and strategy use such as gender, learning styles, learner beliefs and motivation and language(s) spoken. Teachers within a sociocognitive framework are often recognised as 'co-authors' of students' writing (Prior, 2006: 58), which allows for the 'co-construction of learning strategies by teachers and students by avoiding any attempt to simply give strategies to struggling writers, or to otherwise superimpose our strategies on their writing efforts' (Collins, 1998: 48). Similarly, students are encouraged to write for an audience other than the class teacher and, as such, increased importance has been given to peer feedback as a way of developing revision strategies. In terms of research, a need has been identified 'to adopt an inter-disciplinary framework, which is cognisant of linguistic, cognitive and sociocultural perspectives, in order to reflect with validity the complexity of classrooms as teaching and learning contexts' (Myhill *et al.*, 2012: 144). This is particularly evident in the methodological shift from a focus on a writer's individual cognitive processes by means of verbal protocols in artificial conditions, to a consideration of writing in an authentic social environment such as a classroom, reflected in the design of the X-LiST study which will be fully outlined in the following chapter.

Such sociocultural influences can be seen in more recent studies on L1 writing processes and strategies, such as those by Myhill and Jones (2007) and Myhill (2009) which deal with secondary school aged students in the UK. Myhill (2009) sought to investigate writers' compositional processes, whereas Myhill and Jones (2007) focused more specifically on students' reflections on their revision processes. Both studies involved Year 9 and Year 11 students (38 and 34, respectively) from state secondary schools in England and used observation and stimulated recall interviews as the primary sources of data collection. Their decision to observe students writing in a naturalistic classroom setting marks a significant shift from previous reliance on verbal protocols as a means of gathering data on composing processes. Myhill (2009) found that different writing profiles emerged for different writers, particularly in terms of the time spent pausing in relation to the time spent writing. In line with previous models of L1 composing, there was evidence that the high-achieving writers were engaged in more advanced planning, editing and revision during writing than the less confident writers. Yet, the findings also indicated relationships between composing patterns adopted and success in writing, as lower achieving writers tended to have longer bursts of writing, whereas the higher achieving writers spent the most time writing relative to their pausing. In relation to the same study, Myhill also reported elsewhere that weaker writers had a tendency to write long, overcomplicated sentences that were sometimes hard to follow (Myhill, 2006b), and they also used a more limited range of linking strategies than more able writers (Myhill, 2007).

When considering revision processes, Myhill and Jones (2007) discovered that even though students engaged in multiple revising activities during writing, they tended to conceptualise revision as a task that is primarily undertaken as a post-production reviewing activity, which reveals an interesting discrepancy between what students think they do and what they actually do. This is perhaps due to pedagogical practices that have typically presented writing as a chronological process of planning, drafting, writing and editing, as encapsulated in the National Literacy Strategy and the Key Stage 3 Framework for English. They therefore conclude by making a strong case for helping students develop a better metacognitive understanding of their own writing processes: 'we may well develop better writers not by doing more writing but by generating more thinking about writing' (Myhill, 2006b: 28).

Exploring writing strategies/processes in the L2/FL

It has been acknowledged that much research on writing in the L2 or FL 'is based directly on theoretical and instructional trends in writing-as-a-process theory' (Grabe & Kaplan, 1996: 84) in the L1, as explored above. As a result, it was initially presumed that such research on L1 writers could simply be generalised to an L2 context. However, as research specific to L2 writers gradually emerged, this assumption was soon challenged. Zamel (1983) is considered to be 'one of the most articulate advocates for allowing the insights of L1 research to guide research and pedagogy in L2 writing' (Ferris, 2003: 15) and, along with Raimes (1987) and Cumming (1989), was instrumental in shifting the focus onto the particular processes and strategies used by L2 writers. Zamel (1983) sought to investigate the composing processes of advanced L2 English students and, although her study is not explicitly set within the theoretical framework of L2 learning strategy research, she does make some reference to 'strategies', and seems to use this term synonymously with 'processes'. Raimes (1987), on the other hand, aimed not only to describe the writing strategies of L2 writers, but also to then consider them alongside those of L1 writers, as she felt that existing research had 'stressed the similarities between L1 and L2 writers without much attention to the differences between the two' (Raimes, 1987: 439–440). Cumming (1989) subsequently set out to build on this research by assessing the L2 writing performance of young adult learners of English in relation to both their writing expertise and their L2 proficiency.

The participants of all three studies were groups of advanced university-level ESL students in America or Canada (six, eight and 23, respectively) and, as with Bereiter and Scardamalia (1987) in their L1 research, they grouped their participants according to their level of proficiency (however, we know little about the basis for these groupings). In order to learn more about their composing processes, Raimes (1987) and Cumming (1989) required their students to compose aloud while writing in English, which was the prevailing method of data collection among L1 composition researchers at the time. Raimes (1987) then followed this with an unstructured interview, alongside language proficiency tests and structured interviews with each participant about their background and attitude to L1 and L2 writing. Cumming (1989), with his larger sample size, applied multivariate statistical analyses to his data, allowing him to present a more robust study of the effect of writing expertise and L2 proficiency. However, Zamel (1983) instead opted to observe her students while they were writing and then conduct retrospective interviews, as she felt that having to verbalise their thoughts while writing would alter the way in which they completed the task.

Yet, in spite of their differing approaches, the three studies reached some similar conclusions regarding the nature of L2 writing. In line with L1 studies, Zamel (1983), Raimes (1987) and Cumming (1989) found that skilled L2 writers spent more time planning, revising, rehearsing and editing at the discourse level. Similarly, the less skilled writers tended to plan less and to view writing as a series of words and sentences rather than as a global text (Raimes, 1987; Zamel, 1983). These studies have undoubtedly been instrumental in focusing attention on L2 writers; however, they focus exclusively on writing in the L2 and any comparisons made with the L1 come from generalisations taken from the L1 literature. A need was therefore identified for comparative studies that examined the writing processes and strategies of the *same* writers in the L1 and L2 in order to more effectively explore the similarities and differences between the two.

Comparative studies of L1 and L2/FL writers

Many studies comparing the strategies and processes of the same L1 and L2/FL writers deal with students learning English as the L2 or FL, but from a variety of L1 backgrounds, for example: Japanese (Uzawa, 1996; Wolfersberger, 2003), Chinese (Arndt, 1987; Guo & Huang, 2018), Dutch (Schoonen *et al.*, 2003), Danish (Albrechtsen, 1997), Polish (Skibniewski, 1988, 1990) and Spanish (Jones & Tetroe, 1987; Roca de Larios *et al.*, 2006). However, Whalen and Menard (1995) deal with Anglophone learners of French and Pennington and So (1993) with Singaporean students learning Japanese. In most of the above studies the participants are more advanced undergraduate or postgraduate learners, with the exception of Albrechtsen (1997) where the single participant is 15 years old, and Schoonen *et al.* (2003) where the participants are secondary school students aged 13–16. All studies used think-aloud protocols as their primary method of data collection apart from Pennington and So (1993) who opted for observation and retrospective interviews.

In line with Zamel (1983) and Raimes (1987), many of these studies likewise highlighted the similarities between the strategies and approaches of the same writers in their L1 and L2 (Albrechtsen, 1997; Arndt, 1987; Guo & Huang, 2018; Jones & Tetroe, 1987; Pennington & So, 1993; Skibniewski, 1988, 1990; Uzawa, 1996). In both contexts, for example, skilled writers were shown to compose differently from novice writers. Whalen and Menard (1995) specifically noted the similarity in the *quality* of planning in the L1 and L2, Jones and Tetroe (1987) found that the planning process, particularly at the level of abstraction, was similar in both languages, while Uzawa (1996) detected similar attention patterns in the two languages. Findings from the study by Guo and Huang (2018) indicated that over 90% of the writing strategies used by participants in their L1 and L2 were the same. Such similarities would seem to indicate that strategies developed in the L1 can, to some extent, be transferred to the L2 (Arndt, 1987; Jones & Tetroe, 1987; Skibniewski, 1988; Uzawa, 1996; Whalen & Ménard, 1995).

However, in spite of these outward similarities, 'it should not be presumed that the act of writing in one's first language is the same as the act of writing in one's second language' (Kroll, 1990: 2), as L1 and L2 writers often 'hold different cognitive models' (Devine *et al.*, 1993: 203). Due to the fact that these studies compared the L1 and L2 strategies of the *same* writers, some salient differences also emerged. On the whole, when composing in the L2, writers tended to use more cognitive strategies (Guo & Huang, 2018), to plan less (Albrechtsen, 1997) and to generate fewer goals (Skibniewski, 1988) and found it more difficult to incorporate planned ideas into the text (Jones & Tetroe, 1987). They tended to do more surface-level revision and spent twice as much time dealing with formulation problems in the L2 than in the L1 (Roca de

Larios *et al.*, 2006). Whalen and Menard (1995) also noted significant differences in the discourse-level processing between the L1 and L2, in that in the L1, writers used more strategies at the pragmatic and textual levels, whereas in the L2 they used more strategies at the linguistic (morphosyntactic and lexical) level. As a result of focusing more on 'lower-level' problems such as word searching and grammatical structures, Schoonen *et al.* (2003: 171) suggest that this leaves little or no capacity for 'higher-level' or strategic aspects of writing such as organisation and that, as a result, 'the discourse and metacognitive knowledge that L2 writers are able to exploit in their L1 writing may remain unused, or underused, in their L2 writing'.

As such, the obvious explanation for such differences in L1 and L2 writing would seem to be a lack of L2 proficiency; however, it has been suggested by Jones and Tetroe (1987) that this alone does not visibly affect the processes of composing. Instead they have posited that the quality of L2 texts is perhaps more strongly associated with the development of effective writing strategies, or what Cumming (1989) similarly refers to as a general 'writing expertise', used 'to compensate for the limitations imposed by their imperfect knowledge of the language' (Jones & Tetroe, 1987: 36). In line with this, Schoonen *et al.* (2003) found that L2 writing proficiency was highly correlated with L1 writing proficiency, more so than with either L2 linguistic knowledge or the accessibility of this knowledge, which would support the existence of a general writing competence across languages. This would in turn suggest that many of those strategies that relate to L2 writing proficiency may indeed 'transfer from the first language' as Jones and Tetroe (1987: 55) suggest, yet although this may be the case, they may not necessarily be used as effectively in the L2 (Wolfersberger, 2003).

Use of the L1 as a strategy when writing in the L2/FL

What may be considered as one of the most interesting differences between L1 and L2/FL writers is that the latter are, by definition, multilingual. In order to meet the additional challenges of writing in an L2, these writers have the unique opportunity to use the 'resources of both first and second languages together for various strategic purposes while composing' (Cumming, 2001: 6). Jones and Tetroe (1987) were among the first to explore this use of the L1 as a strategy in itself and although they were able to make only tentative conclusions about how less skilled writers were more successful when they used their L1 in planning, their study paved the way for more detailed research in this area.

Friedlander (1990) similarly explored the use of the L1 and L2 in the planning of a text. He conducted his study with 28 Chinese speaking ESL students at a university in America and found that performance was enhanced when the language of planning matched the language of topic knowledge, e.g. planning in Chinese when writing about a Chinese festival. Within the match condition, the students wrote longer and higher quality plans and essays. These findings were echoed in a study by Wang and Wen (2002), who found that their participants, who were university-level English as a foreign language (EFL) students in China, were more likely to rely on their L1 than their L2 when generating and organising ideas. This supports the statement that 'the strategy of planning in the L1 often helps produce better results in L2 writing but this depends on the nature of the task, the familiarity of the topic, the differences between the L1 and the L2, and other factors' (Oxford, 2011: 248).

In addition to the strategic use of the L1 when planning, Kobayashi and Rinnert (1992), Cohen and Brooks-Carson (2001) and Tavakoli *et al.* (2014) also examined the strategic use of the L1 through translation. In each study the university-level participants were asked to write one task directly into the target language and a second task initially in their native or dominant language to then be translated into the target language. Interestingly, both Cohen and Brooks-Carson (2001) and Tavakoli *et al.* (2014) found that students, particularly the higher proficiency students, performed better in the direct task and preferred the direct writing task. Conversely in the Kobayashi and Rinnert (1992) study, the translation tasks were rated higher in terms of length and syntactic complexity, yet in spite of this the majority of participants still preferred the direct task. In the latter study the researchers found that it was the lower proficiency writers who tended to benefit most from translation, whereas the higher proficiency writers did not, and were more likely to make errors that interfaced with meaning in the translation task. However, in each of these studies we must question the fundamental difference between the two tasks in terms of the use of the L1. The direct task was supposedly designed to encourage students to think entirely in the L2; however, this was not necessarily the case. In the direct composition task, participants in each of the studies reported initially thinking in the L1 before mentally translating into the L2; therefore translation was taking place in both tasks.

This raises an interesting point in relation to language of thought. Learners in the early stages of learning an L2 are generally not yet in a position to be able to think directly *in* the L2, but rather they think *about* the L2 through the medium of the L1. However, more advanced language learners, bilinguals and multilinguals, are more likely to have a sufficient level of proficiency to enable them to think in two or more languages, which Cohen (1995) refers to as 'diglossic' thinking. Selecting a particular language of thought may be unplanned and incidental, or deliberate and strategic, whereby learners purposefully draw on their knowledge of existing languages while learning the target language. Such choices may be influenced by social factors such as language status, interpersonal factors such as setting and audience, and individual factors such as language preference, proficiency and motivation (Brisk, 2011). However, due to the mentalistic and often subconscious nature of thought, it is difficult to empirically ascertain the role of a multilingual's various languages in it (Cohen, 1995: 18).

The results of the above studies suggest that L2 writers on the whole, whether they do so deliberately or not, will tend to use their L1 strategically when completing tasks in the L2. In some cases this is done more effectively than in others; therefore, as Macaro (2001: 237) suggests, 'both positive and negative transfer from the first language will trigger a need for specific strategy training. This need is particularly prevalent in the development of writing skills'. Interestingly, in spite of its importance, it is precisely this element of strategy instruction which, to date, has attracted less attention in the literature.

Exploring the Effects of LLSI on Writing

As examined above, much of the research that has been conducted in relation to writing strategies has been primarily concerned with the identification, description and comparison of strategies used by L1 and L2 writers and, in particular, the difference in strategies used by 'good' and 'poor' learners. However, there has been comparatively less research on the influence of instruction on strategy use and many questions still remain: Does strategy use lead to more effective writing? To what extent can strategies be 'taught' and 'learned' in a classroom context? While the number of studies exploring the effect of LLSI has been growing in recent years, the majority of this research has been conducted with adults or with advanced learners at tertiary level (Harklau, 2011) and predominantly deals with the learning of English (Manchón & de Haan, 2008); much less is known about the context of secondary school learners in Anglophone settings such as the UK (Harris, 2019). Indeed, this holds true across the field of L2 acquisition more broadly (Cenoz & Gorter, 2019). Existing research has also had a tendency to look at a sample of learners at a particular point in time rather than trying to measure changes over a longer period (Griffiths, 2018). The aim of this section, therefore, is to review key empirical studies that consider the effect of an intervention of LLSI on performance in writing in both L1 and L2/FL contexts. While the focus here is predominantly on the outcomes of the studies examined, the structure and content of LLSI in itself will be fully examined in Chapter 5.

L1 intervention studies: Influence of strategy instruction on performance in writing

Strategy instruction within the L1 context generally involves 'teachers explaining the purpose and rationale of the strategy, modelling how to use it, and providing students with assistance in applying the strategy with the goal of independent and effective application' (Graham, 2015: 769). The most prominent and well-researched model of L1 writing strategy instruction is undoubtedly the programme of self-regulated strategy development (SRSD) developed in the United States by Steve Graham and Karen Harris. This approach has been adapted to a wide range of students, from young elementary school learners to adults and, as such, is recognised as having 'developed into the "standard" in strategy instruction' (Koster et al., 2015: 267).

The SRSD model focuses on planning, composing and revising strategies and involves six recursive stages of instruction which can be reordered, changed and repeated as needed. These are: developing background knowledge, discussing the strategy, modelling the strategy, memorising the strategy, supporting the strategy and independent practice. These are further supported by four strategies for self-regulation which are explicitly taught and practised through the writing process: goal-setting, self-instructions, self-monitoring and self-reinforcement (Mason et al., 2011). SRSD makes use of mnemonics such as PLAN (Pay attention to the prompt, List main ideas, Add supporting details, Number major points) and WRITE (Work from your plan, Remember your goals, Include transition words, Try to use different kinds of sentence, Exciting words). Further discussion of the content and stages of instruction in strategy-based interventions can be found in Chapter 5. As indicated in the very name of this model, the L1 literature seems to align itself much more with the concept of self-regulation rather than metacognition; however, there are many overlaps. The self-regulation element within SRSD studies is generally considered as enabling the management of multiple processes and the transfer of strategies to new contexts and as facilitating learning from experience (MacArthur et al., 2015), which is almost synonymous with the metacognitive function of strategies referred to in other studies.

There is a rapidly growing body of evidence that suggests that explicit strategy instruction in the L1 classroom has positive effects on the quality of students' writing at all levels of schooling (Graham, 2015). At the primary school/elementary school level, Graham et al. (2012) conducted a meta-analysis of 20 studies involving true or quasi-experiments which examined the effectiveness of writing strategy instruction (14 of which implemented SRSD). They concluded that all of the studies produced positive effects and that strategy instruction enhanced the quality of students' writing with a large effect size of 1.02. This is supported by a more focused meta-analysis of 32 writing intervention studies involving students in Grades 4–6, which similarly demonstrated that writing strategy instruction has positive effects for upper elementary school aged learners (Koster et al., 2015).

Perhaps more relevant to the current study is the study conducted by De La Paz and Graham (2002) into the effects of instruction in predominantly metacognitive writing strategies on 58 middle school aged students.

This study was conducted in the United States within an L1 English context and entailed a six-week period of strategy instruction integrated into the curriculum by classroom teachers. They placed particular emphasis on planning, considering it to be 'a critical element in skilled writing' (De La Paz & Graham, 2002: 687), and also taught strategies for drafting and revising texts alongside the skills and knowledge the students needed in order to apply such strategies to their own work. Findings indicate that the work of the experimental group after the intervention was of an overall higher quality; they created longer texts using a greater range of vocabulary and their plans were more developed. The researchers also set an essay task one month after instruction had ended and found that the effects were maintained by the experimental group. However, De La Paz and Graham (2002) did not take account of students' existing strategy use and based their findings on students' written work alone. It is therefore not clear which particular strategies in the intervention students actually used or found most effective.

While the vast majority of existing studies in this area have been conducted in North America, the SRSD approach has also been implemented in other countries. As part of a wider focus on literacy catch-up during the primary to secondary school transition in England, the Education Endowment Foundation funded a pragmatic randomised controlled trial to evaluate an intervention of SRSD with students in Years 6 and 7 across 23 schools in the North East of England (Torgerson *et al.*, 2014). The programme was adapted slightly for the English context, as some of the teachers commented that the original programme of instruction was 'too American'. In line with previous SRSD studies, this project had a large positive effect on writing outcomes, with participating students making approximately nine months' additional progress compared to similar students who did not participate in the intervention.

Some studies have used a similar approach in non-Anglophone contexts. In their project based in the Netherlands, Bouwer *et al.* (2018: 59) developed a programme of writing strategy instruction referred to as 'Tekster', which aimed to help upper elementary school students (Grades 4–6) 'develop the knowledge and skills required to manage the cognitive overload that often occurs when composing' in L1 Dutch. Teachers were trained to deliver a series of 16 'Tekster' sessions over an eight-week period to more than 1400 students across 60 classrooms. The main focus of the intervention was to teach students 'a general writing strategy, as well as the self-regulation skills needed to use the strategy successfully' (Bouwer *et al.*, 2018: 60) and it incorporated elements of observational learning, explicit instruction, guided practice and the gradual release of responsibility. It is therefore highly reminiscent of the SRSD model and, as with other studies into L1 writing strategy development explored above, evidence here similarly indicated that the intervention led to statistically significant improvements in the quality of students' writing. It is valuable to see such an approach applied to L1 writing instruction in languages other than English, and the scale of such a study, along with an integrated focus on three genres of writing (narrative, persuasive and descriptive), allows the authors to make some claims of generalisability.

The SRSD approach has also been identified as being effective for school-aged students with specific learning disabilities or difficulties, such as attention-deficit hyperactivity disorder (ADHD), Asperger's syndrome, and emotional or behavioural disorders. These students can struggle particularly with transcription (e.g. handwriting, typing, spelling), concentration, generating content and remembering ideas to include, which further adds to the cognitive challenge of the writing process. A series of studies and meta-analyses have demonstrated that explicit instruction in SRSD can improve the writing performance of these students across a range of genres and also positively influence their motivation towards writing (Cramer & Mason, 2014; Gillespie & Graham, 2014; Graham & Harris, 2003; Mason *et al.*, 2011; What Works Clearinghouse, 2017). These findings hold true for students across all levels of schooling and for whole-class, small group and one-to-one instruction. Gillespie and Graham (2014: 468) comment that such positive effects of strategy instruction support the theoretical contention that the writing difficulties experienced by students with learning disabilities 'are due to strategic difficulties with planning, revising and editing. When they are taught strategies for carrying out these processes, students with [learning disabilities] show considerable improvement in the quality of their writing'. However, the authors also point out that, in order to be effective, such teaching needs to be explicit and to include opportunities for practice.

L2/FL intervention studies: Influence of strategy instruction on performance in writing

While there is a growing evidence base for the positive effects of strategy instruction, such as SRSD, on the development of writing skills in the L1, Steve Graham (2015: 771) comments that 'very little writing intervention research has been conducted with students learning to write in a second language'. This has been reiterated by scholars within the field of SLA: Griffiths (2018: 168), for example, notes that strategy instruction in general 'remains an under-researched area', while Plonsky (2011: 1000) comments particularly on the scarcity of studies into the effects of LLSI on writing. It is important, therefore, to review the existing (albeit limited) evidence on the potential effects of strategy instruction on writing in an L2/FL context.

In recent years a series of meta-analyses have been conducted in the field of language learning strategies which have been instrumental in furthering our understanding of the current evidence base. Plonsky (2011) conducted a meta-analysis of 61 studies (contributing a total of 95 unique samples) into L2 strategy instruction and detected a small to medium overall effect of strategy instruction (0.49). However, it is important to note that the effectiveness of strategy instruction was moderated by a range of factors such as the learning context and length of intervention. In particular, there was a substantial difference in the effects obtained among high school participants (0.23) compared to university-aged learners (0.55). However, the author notes that this difference may partly be the result of range restriction, i.e. university-aged students are typically a more 'homogeneous group' which produces less group variance and, by extension, yields larger effect sizes (Plonsky, 2011: 1014). Effects were also greater in an L2 context (0.84) compared to an FL context (0.46), which is unsurprising given the increased exposure to language in the L2 context. Among the six samples that focused specifically on writing, the effect size was relatively small (0.42), and is referred to as 'modest' in comparison to effects found in other skill areas such as speaking (0.97), reading (0.74) and vocabulary (0.64).

However, Plonsky (2019) more recently conducted an update of this meta-analysis which saw 16 additional studies added to the sample. Here, the mean overall effect size increased to 0.66 with the effect size for writing increasing to 0.59. Such results are encouraging and perhaps suggest an increase in our understanding of how to design and carry out programmes of LLSI. Plonsky (2019: 10) also notes here that 'although cognitive strategies are taught more often than metacognitive strategies, the effects of LLSI involving the latter yield much larger effects'. Such patterns are in line with findings from another recent meta-analysis conducted by Ardasheva *et al.* (2017). The researchers here found that strategy instruction positively influences both FL and L2 learning with medium to large overall effects which were almost two times larger than those reported by Plonsky in his 2011 study. The authors note that the difference may be due to the greater emphasis of more recent interventions of strategy instruction on self-regulation and, particularly, on the metacognitive component. The overall trends revealed by the above meta-analyses suggest that strategy instruction is indeed 'a viable instructional tool for second/foreign language classrooms' (Ardasheva *et al.*, 2017: 544).

While the above research suggests some encouraging trends with regard to the positive effects of strategy instruction on writing and, in particular, with regard to the importance of the metacognitive component, it is also crucial to consider some of these studies in more depth. One of the most relevant to the current study is the Oxford Writing Strategies Project conducted by Macaro (2001), which focused on the teaching of writing strategies to improve the performance of 14–15 year old learners of French in six schools in the UK. Sengupta (2000) similarly focused on secondary school learners in Hong Kong and on the effects of instruction in one particular metacognitive strategy, revision, on students' performance and perceptions of writing in English. In the context of primary schools in Singapore, Bai (2015) has conducted one of the few studies that focuses on younger learners of English (age 10–11). Other relevant studies into writing strategy instruction have been conducted with university-level students. Olivares-Cuhat (2002), for example, examined the effect of LLSI on achievement among a group of students taking a Spanish writing course in the United States, which included both L1 and L2 Spanish speakers. Also considered are studies that have been conducted into the effect of LLSI on the writing achievement of EFL learners at universities in Japan (Sasaki, 2000, 2002) and Vietnam (Nguyen & Gu, 2013), and of English for academic purposes (EAP) students in Sri Lanka (De Silva, 2015; De Silva & Graham, 2015).

All of the above studies incorporated varying levels of explicit strategy instruction within their design, ranging from several weeks (Nguyen & Gu, 2013; Olivares-Cuhat, 2002), to six months (De Silva, 2015; Macaro, 2001; Sasaki, 2000, 2002), to a full year (Sengupta, 2000). However, few gave a clear explanation of the format and content of the intervention. In his study, Macaro (2001: 108) acknowledged that 'intervention without a prior stage of strategy elicitation of those particular learners (and therefore description) is invalid', and therefore gathered valuable baseline data on his participants' existing metacognitive strategy use and used this to design his intervention. Examples of strategies detected and explicitly developed in his project include: preparation strategies such as brainstorming, resourcing strategies such as using a dictionary, monitoring strategies such as checking relevance and content, and evaluation strategies such as back-translating and reflecting on decisions made, similar to those introduced in the studies by De Silva (2015) and Nguyen and Gu (2013). Olivares-Cuhat (2002), conversely, took a different approach. She focused on two classes, each following a different textbook – one that mentioned learning strategies overtly, the other implicitly. However, despite being framed as an intervention study, neither group received true LLSI as the strategies were not actively taught or reinforced by the instructors.

The studies also employed diverse methodologies in order to explore their research questions. All of the studies in question examined the writing tasks produced by their students on a pre- and post-intervention basis, and in addition to this Macaro (2001) used think-aloud protocols while De Silva (2015) and Sasaki (2000, 2002) conducted stimulated recall interviews. De Silva (2015), Macaro (2001), Olivares-Cuhat (2002) and Sengupta (2000) also made use of questionnaires on a pre- and post-intervention basis in order to gather data about students' strategy use, although it is important to remember that such reports can only be considered as students' *perceptions* of their strategy use.

In terms of their findings, Macaro (2001) discovered that the experimental group made significant gains over the control group, particularly in terms of grammatical accuracy. The experimental group also reported changing their approach to writing and became more independent of the teacher as a result of the strategy instruction. Focusing on slightly younger learners, Bai (2015: 103) also found that the intervention of writing strategy instruction led to a significant improvement in both writing ability and strategy use, and consequently notes a 'strong causal link between frequency of strategy use and writing competence'. Similar findings emerged from the study by De Silva (2015) and De Silva and Graham (2015), where the experimental group learners developed their strategy use as a result of the LLSI and their performance increased significantly. However, it is interesting to note that the effect was higher for the low-attainment group than for the high-attainment group, perhaps as a result of a ceiling effect for the higher attaining students. In line with this, both Sengupta (2000) and Nguyen and Gu (2013) also reported gains in performance among the students who received LLSI, with the latter authors noting that strategies related to planning were the most often exercised, followed by those related to evaluation and monitoring.

As could be expected, Olivares-Cuhat (2002) found that the L1 writers in her study outperformed the L2 writers, yet she made no link between the use of metacognitive strategies and achievement. However, she did conclude that the choice of textbook did not appear to influence performance, which questions the relevance of inserting strategies into textbooks without reinforcing them with explicit instruction and opportunities for practice. Interestingly, Sasaki (2000) found that after six months of writing instruction, neither the quality of the students' compositions nor their writing fluency appeared to have improved significantly, although more gains were made by the 'novice' writers than the 'expert' writers. Even more surprisingly, the number of strategies used by the novice group decreased by almost half after the period of instruction, although some of the students started using more 'skilled' writer strategies such as rereading and global planning. This reinforces that idea that it is not necessarily the *quantity* of strategies used that is important, but the *quality* of their use. One possible explanation for these findings is that some of the strategies used by the novice writers perhaps became proceduralised over the course of the intervention and the writers themselves were therefore less conscious of them.

What is evident from this section is that writing strategy instruction can have positive effects on writing in both L1 and L2/FL classrooms. However, as noted above, the vast majority of this research exploring LLSI has taken place *either* in the L1 classroom *or* in the L2/FL classroom and there has been less focus on how strategies explicitly developed in one of these contexts may transfer to and (positively) influence the other. It was the identification of this gap that led to the development of the X-LiST study.

Conclusion

The primary aim of this chapter was to review the literature relating to strategy research in both L1 and L2/FL contexts. What emerged is that research agendas on writing strategies within the fields of L1 composition research and L2 acquisition have evolved in a relatively parallel manner since the 1970s. Both began with a focus on identifying, describing and then classifying a range of strategies, before shifting attention to exploring the extent to which these strategies can be taught and learned in a classroom context and the subsequent links between strategy use and performance. However, while these two streams of research have undoubtedly influenced one another over the years, it is fair to say that that the L1 literature has influenced L2/FL research to a greater extent than the reverse. The empirical studies reviewed suggest that explicit LLSI does indeed have the potential to positively influence writing performance in both L1 and FL classrooms. However, to date, such studies have had a tendency to focus on only one of these contexts rather than exploring the potential for interaction and transfer between the two. The following two chapters, therefore, will fully outline the research design and development of the intervention in the X-LiST study, which was designed precisely to explore the nature and the effects of such cross-linguistic interactions.

4 Considerations for Researching the Effects of a Cross-Linguistic Intervention of Language Learning Strategy Instruction

As indicated at the beginning of this book, the overarching aim of the X-LiST study was to explore how an explicit focus on strategy instruction in the FL German classroom influenced students' strategy development and performance in writing in German, and whether any such effects transferred to another FL (French) and/or to the L1 (English). The purpose of this chapter is, first and foremost, to provide a detailed overview of the research design of the longitudinal, quasi-experimental X-LiST study which was conducted in a secondary school in England. This will also incorporate more general reflections throughout on a number of key methodological considerations for researching strategy development and use. As evidenced by previous studies, researching strategy use is highly complex due to the mentalistic nature of such processes. However, there are additional considerations which also need to be taken into account here given the cross-linguistic nature of the X-LiST study and the need to create appropriate tasks and methods for collecting data in both the L1 and the FLs. There are also important considerations surrounding the logistics and indeed the ethics of conducting any form of intervention research in schools. The sections that follow will therefore in turn consider aspects of the research design, methods for data collection and ethics. Limitations will be acknowledged where appropriate in this chapter; however, there will be further reflection on these in Chapter 10.

Designing the X-LiST Study: Considerations of Research Design

In order to research the key questions at the heart of the X-LiST study, it was necessary to adopt a longitudinal, quasi-experimental design which comprised three data collection points and two phases of intervention over the course of one academic year (as shown in Figure 4.1). The longitudinal nature of the study was key for several reasons. From a practical point of

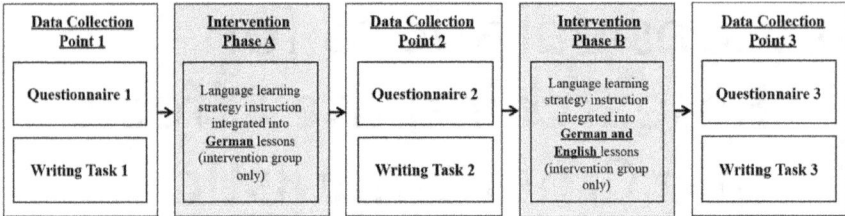

Figure 4.1 Research design of the X-LiST study

view, the process of implementing the various stages of LLSI (as outlined in Chapter 5) takes time, in particular, to allow sufficient opportunities for students to practise and experiment with their strategy use. From a research perspective, Kobayashi and Rinnert (2007: 87) suggest that a longitudinal design 'can help us capture the dynamics of beliefs and strategies over time', a sentiment that has been echoed by Graham and Macaro (2008) and Grenfell and Harris (2013). The shifts and variation in practice that emerged in relation to individual student trajectories (as shown in Chapter 8) confirm such dynamism.

A quasi-experimental design was adopted in order to evaluate the effect of the intervention of LLSI itself. Within educational research, an experiment is typically characterised by the researcher actively manipulating or changing aspects of what is studied, usually in the form of an intervention, in order to investigate the effect of a particular variable using pre- and post-tests. In this case, the intervention is the LLSI and the key 'variables' under investigation are students' strategy use and the written work they produce. However, in order to qualify as a 'true' experiment, participants would have to be randomly allocated to either an experimental or a control group, which is rarely possible (or desirable) within the context of a school. As such, studies typically involve intact class groups and are therefore considered as *quasi*-experimental. Two parallel mixed-ability Year 9 classes were then selected as the intervention group and the comparison group, respectively. The comparison group was established in order to strengthen the validity of the research; Dörnyei (2007: 117), for example, warns against employing a 'one-group pre-test post-test design', given that this 'cannot exclude other possible sources of change'. As this study took place over the course of an academic year, the students would have inevitably developed their language skills during this time as part of normal classroom progression (one would hope!). The findings from the comparison group therefore helped to establish the extent to which any changes that took place could be attributed to the strategy intervention. Given the cross-linguistic dimension of the X-LiST study, it was similarly important to ensure that the students were taught in the same intact groups for all three languages (English, German and French). If they had been in different groupings for each subject, then it would not have been possible to measure the effects of the strategy instruction in one subject on another at a whole-class level. Nonetheless, it is important to acknowledge a limitation here in relation to sample size given that there were just 22 participating students in the intervention group and 23 in the comparison group. Yet, studies which involve any form of pedagogical intervention necessitate considerable commitment on the part of the teacher(s), researcher(s) and students, and therefore typically tend to contain fewer participants. As such, outcomes here can only be seen as reflecting the trends within these particular classes. Working with a small sample, however, also has its advantages as it allows for a more in-depth exploration of the development and transfer of strategies at both a whole-class and an individual level.

It is also important to note that while the intervention group students completed tasks in all three languages, the comparison group students only completed the English and German tasks. While this undoubtedly must be acknowledged as a limitation of the study, there are several reasons for this omission. First, the X-LiST study was initially only designed to explore the interactions between strategy use in L1 English and a single FL (in this case, German). However, during negotiations with the school, the French teacher of the intervention group also expressed an interest in the study. She said that while she would not be able to incorporate the LLSI into her lessons with that particular class, she was certainly willing to set writing tasks during the three data collection points. It was felt that this would provide a valuable additional dimension to the study as it would allow for exploration of transfer to another FL context. Unfortunately, however, the regular French teacher for the comparison group was absent for some time at the beginning of the school year and it was therefore not possible to gain consent and to collect French data from this group. It was not envisaged at the time that the 'bonus' French data collected would end up playing such a central role in the study and this is certainly a consideration to bear in mind for future studies.

At Point 1 of the study (see Figure 4.1), crucial baseline data were collected to explore which writing strategies learners used in English and the FLs. First of all, questionnaires were administered to investigate students' conceptualisations of and attitudes towards writing in German, French and English more generally, and then the students were asked to complete a writing task in each language. Each task was followed by stimulated recall interviews with a smaller group of 12 students. This information was used to develop the intervention of LLSI to be carried out in the German classroom of the intervention group over the course of four months in partnership with the classroom teacher (Phase A). As discussed further in Chapter 5, the LLSI was designed to be integrated into the existing scheme of work and involved the introduction of tasks and activities to aid the planning, monitoring and evaluation of written work and to encourage students to reflect on and assess their personal learning strategies.

Next, a second set of measures were taken in order to investigate whether or not this explicit focus on strategy use in German lessons affected the students' approach to writing in German, and also whether they transferred these strategies to their French or English writing without any explicit encouragement to do so. During Phase B of the intervention, which also took place over the course of four months, the LLSI continued in the German classroom; however, it was also explicitly reinforced in the English classroom of the intervention group. Similar activities and resources were used by both teachers in order to encourage learners to transfer the skills and strategies they developed in one curriculum area to another. A third and final set of data was then collected to explore any further changes that took place as a result of this additional explicit strategy instruction in English. Using such a multi-phase design not only allowed for progress and strategy use to be tracked over the period of an academic year (which helps counter several threats to internal validity), but also meant that data could be routinely analysed throughout the study in order to ensure that the learning strategies introduced during the intervention were appropriate to the needs of the students.

Getting Inside the 'Black Box': A Mixed-Methods Approach to Strategy Research

As stated by Grenfell and Harris (1999: 54), 'it is not easy to get inside the "black box" of the human brain and find out what is going on there. We work with what we can get, which, despite the limitations, provides food for thought'. As a predominantly mentalistic process, it is particularly challenging for researchers to get an insight into the strategies learners use. Given that much of this cannot be observed, we therefore rely heavily on self-report. This involves individuals providing their 'subjective evaluations and reports of their thoughts, feelings, behaviours or experiences' (Smyth & Terry, 2011: 878). One of the most common methods of data collection in studies of strategy use is the questionnaire and, in particular, the Strategy Inventory for Language Learning (SILL) developed by Oxford (1990). This Likert-type questionnaire has been well validated and translated into many languages and is used in a wide range of countries around the world. It aims to gain insights into learners' typical strategy use and consists of generalised statements about their language learning habits, such as the frequency with which they write notes in the target language or use rhymes to memorise new words. However, as the statements are often somewhat removed from the event being described, participants may not remember what strategies they used in the past, which may in turn produce data of questionable validity. Similarly, presenting learners with a predetermined list of strategies restricts the possible responses to those strategies that the researcher has already identified. While such questionnaires undoubtedly have their uses, there is increasing awareness among the research community that the complexity of a learner's strategy use cannot be fully understood by quantitative data alone. Although such data may give an indication of *what* strategies learners use, a qualitative element is essential in order to further explore *why* students select specific strategies for particular tasks, *how* these impact on their writing and *how* they are able to transfer strategies from one language to another. As such, Oxford ceased to use the SILL in her own work over a decade ago (see Oxford, 2017).

A mixed-methods approach was therefore adopted for the X-LiST study, where quantitative data were gathered, for example, through attitudinal questionnaires and attainment scores alongside qualitative data collected through stimulated recall interview recordings and general interviews. This allowed data to be gathered at both a whole-class and an individual level; while the writing tasks and questionnaires were gathered from all of the students in the two classes, the stimulated recall interviews and general interviews were conducted with a smaller group of 12 students who were selected as embedded cases. These students were chosen to represent a range of gender, academic performance level, attitude towards the subjects and L1 background. This allowed general trends to be identified at a whole-class level (as reported in Chapters 6 and 7), but it was the closer examination of data at an individual level that revealed the complex and interrelated factors that influenced students' development and transfer of strategies (see Chapters 8 and 9). As stated by Yin (2012):

> …the explanations contained in a case study usually can enrich the understanding of a cause-and-effect relationship beyond what can be discerned by using experiments or quasi-experiments alone. Whereas these other methods may be able to formally test a cause-and-effect relationship and establish whether there appears to be one, a case study can explain the relationship as well as its absence. Therefore, experiments and case studies – as with other distinctive research methods – may be considered complementary methods. (Yin, 2012: 89)

Just as the case is made above for the need to adopt a mixed-methods approach to strategy research, it is similarly useful to draw on both psychological and social perspectives. As suggested by Oxford and Schramm (2007: 49), exploring strategy use from solely a cognitive or a sociocultural perspective 'could deny opportunities for synergy that might lead to more powerful and useful theory and research on learner strategies'. As such, the X-LiST study took a sociocognitive approach to the study of strategy development and transfer which influenced both the research design and the pedagogical intervention. At the level of the research design, the study was conducted in an authentic classroom environment in order to enable a better understanding of how students develop and transfer writing strategies in a real-world setting. The data therefore generated a more authentic representation of the complexities of the learning environment. At a pedagogical level this was manifest in the co-construction of strategy use by teachers and students (see Chapter 5).

The following sections will present and reflect on the various methods used in the X-LiST study to investigate students' conceptualisations of writing and their strategy use. However, given that each of the methods below involves some form of self-report, we must remember that any data obtained can only ever be considered as students' *perceptions* of their strategy use. We have to acknowledge that they may also have been using strategies that they were not consciously aware of or that had become proceduralised and performed automatically (and, by extension, were not available for self-report).

Investigating students' conceptualisations of writing: Questionnaires and follow-up interviews

As suggested above, questionnaires were not used in the X-LiST study for the purpose of collecting data about strategy use in itself, but rather to gather more general insights into students' conceptualisations of writing in each of the languages at a whole-class level (see Appendix A). As discussed in Chapter 2, it was important to begin the study by exploring how students viewed writing in German, French and English as it was felt that such views might influence the extent to which they were willing and able to make connections between these subjects. The questionnaires were also completed at the two subsequent data collection points in order to track changes over time.

The first four questions related to: (a) students' level of confidence when writing in German, French and English; (b) their perception of their ability in each language; (c) how difficult they found writing tasks; and (d) how much they enjoyed writing in each subject. Each question asked students to respond on a 4-point Likert scale. No central point was provided in order to force respondents to make a decision about how they felt (Taber, 2007). The remaining section of the questionnaire asked students to consider how important they felt certain criteria were in each language and how they would rate their own performance in each of these areas. The criteria were selected as they represented key common aspects identified in the curricula and mark schemes across the three languages, such as planning your work, thinking of creative/interesting ideas, fluency and overall accuracy.

With classroom-based research such as the X-LiST study, it is also important to consider when and where questionnaires are administered. If they are to be completed in the language classroom under the watchful eye of the respective teacher, this may influence the extent to which students feel that they can give open and honest responses; they may, for example, feel that they want to give the 'right' answer (e.g. I really enjoy writing in German!) in order to please the teacher, particularly if the questionnaires are not anonymous. If questionnaires can be completed in a more 'neutral' environment and administered by either the researcher or a teacher of another subject (such as a form tutor), then this may mean that students are less likely to associate the questionnaires directly with a specific language and are more likely to give honest responses. The questionnaires were first analysed descriptively by calculating the mean ratings per question for each class at each point in time. A series of Wilcoxon signed rank tests were then performed in order to gain further insights into the data, for example, to compare responses between ratings in German and English at each time point in order to examine the extent to which attitudes became more similar over time.

Yet, while the questionnaires alone provided a valuable overview of attitudes at a whole-class level, in order to explore responses in more depth each iteration of the questionnaires was followed up by interviews with a smaller sample of students, a common combination in mixed-methods studies more generally (Teddlie & Tashakkori, 2009) and in strategy research more specifically (Macaro, 2001). Follow-up semi-structured interviews were therefore conducted with the case study students in order to further explore their rationale for their questionnaire responses, reasons for any changes in views or writing practices over the course of the year and reflections on any similarities or differences in how they feel they approach writing tasks in German, French and English.

Capturing strategy use: Writing tasks and strategy task sheets

At each of the three data collection points, the students in both the intervention group and the comparison group were asked to complete a writing task during their English, German and French lessons. It was important to carefully consider the selection of appropriate task topics given the different types of writing, levels of proficiency and expectations in English and the FLs. As it would not have been feasible to adapt the same topic to all of the languages, narrative-style (rather than analytical) tasks were chosen in order to enable fairer comparisons of strategy use across the different subjects. From an ethical point of view, it was also important to ensure that the topic and nature of the tasks fitted in with the existing schemes of work in order to minimise disruption to the students' learning and maximise the relevance of the intervention. Examples of tasks include a piece of travel writing (English), a text about hobbies and interests (German) and writing a story about the journey of a drop of water (French – as part of a topic on the environment). Each of the tasks allowed some scope for students to be creative, although it must be acknowledged that students' ability to express themselves creatively in the FL tasks was inevitably limited by their lower proficiency level and restricted range of vocabulary. This can be seen in the extracts below from the three tasks by Carissa, a high-performing and strategic learner in the intervention group. The extracts are presented verbatim and therefore include errors and edits.

Extract from English task 1: Writing about a trip to Norway

Our Chalet was beautiful, complete with a log fire~~s~~, exposed wooden beams and those funny uneven stairs with steps on either side. (~~For~~ ᴬˢ a seven year old this was the most mentally challenging 'thing' I had come across in in all of my life). Norway was beautiful. The air was crisp, clean and fresh. The vast expanse of ~~so~~ snow was littered with pine trees, and the footprints of black birds (and mountain boots.)

That night there was a new moon, so the perfect opportunity to see the northern lights. A group of around fifteen all huddled around a fire in a hut, waiting for it to be dark enough to see the infamous display. An old man with a long white beard (not Father Christmas) was telling us all of myths and folk~~e~~lore of the area while we drank hot ~~drinks.~~ squash.

'Everybody come out side' he said. I layed down in the snow, and looked up to the starry sky. ~~As blu w~~ Waves of blue and green flooded across the sky ~~;~~ ; the colour would fade, and you'd think that was it before another burst of colour washed over the sky. I was mesmerised, such a scientific name as Aurora Borealis didn't seem to suit the ~~wonderous~~ stunning display as this. ~~The next day A~~ ᴺᵃᵗᵘʳᵉ'ˢ fire work display, the heavens opening, raining down with colour, dying the sky with vivid turquoizes and azures, greens and dark inky blues.

Extract from German task 2: Writing about hobbies and interests

'Ich finde meine Hobbies absolut fantastisch! Mein lieblingsHobby ist tanzen weil es lustig und nützlich ist. Die Lehrerin ist total super, und ich habe viel Freunde <u>wer</u> (not sure if correct) tanzen. Es ist lusig, und es ist gesund. ~~Ich tanze~~ Wenn es Mittwoch oder Samstag ist, ich tanze. Ich bin nicht so sportlick, aber ich tanze und ich liebe Schwimmen. Ich ~~to~~ finde Schwimmen lustig weil es einfach ist. Wenn es sonnig ist, bade ich manchmal am Strand, aber wenn es regnet gehe ich ins Hallenbad. Zur Schule ich spiele Netball und Hockey, aber ich hasse es. Schwimmen ist nützlicher und lustiger als Netball. Auch, ich finde Ski fahren super. Lästes Jahr ~~habe~~ ᵇⁱⁿ ich ~~zum~~ ⁿᵃᶜʰ Amerika ~~gefa~~ ski gefahren. Es war total fantastisch und sehr lustig.

Translation: I think my hobbies are absolutely fantastic! My favourite hobby is dancing because it's fun and useful. The teacher is really great and I have lots of friends who dance. It's fun and it's healthy. I dance on Wednesdays and Saturdays. I'm not very sporty, but I dance and I like swimming. I think swimming is fun because it's easy. When it's sunny I sometimes swim at the beach, but when it's raining I go to the swimming pool. At school I play netball and hockey, but I hate it. Swimming is more useful and fun than netball. Also I think it's great to go skiing. Last year I went skiing in America. It was really fantastic and a lot of fun.

> *Extract from French task 3: Writing about the journey of a water drop*
>
> *Bonjour, je m'appelle Gary la Goutte, et je suis une goutte d'eau. Je vais parler de mon voyage. Je suis dans la mer. L'eau est salée. La mer est très grande et bleu! Je suis dans la Ocean Atlantique. Voici une petit poisson – Bonjour! C'est assez chaud – ~~le soleil~~ il y a du soleil. Puis, je m'evapore et je suis dans la ciel. Je suis la vapeur. Pour commencer c'est plus froid. Je me condens~~er~~je je suis un nuage. Je peux voir la mer, les chutes d'eau, les rivieres, les fleuves et les montagnes. C'est très très belle. Je suis dans la nuage pour trois heures. Je pense que c'est ~~bien~~ ^{fantastique} dans la nuage. Je me précipe. AARGHHH! Je suis dans le ciel, non! Je suis sur le sol. Je me infiltre le sol. Je suis souterrain et je ne peux pas voir la ciel.*
>
> Translation: Hello, my name is Gary the Drop and I am a drop of water. I am going to talk about my journey. I am in the sea. The water is salty. The sea is very big and blue! I am in the Atlantic Ocean. Here comes a little fish – hello! It's quite warm and sunny. Then, I evaporate and I am in the sky. I am vapour. Firstly, it's colder. I condense, I am a cloud. I can see the sea, the waterfalls, the rivers, the streams and the mountains. It's very very beautiful. I am in the cloud for three hours. I think that it's fantastic in the cloud. I'm turning into rain. AARGHHH! I am in the sky, no! I am in the ground. I'm soaking into the ground. I am underground and I can't see the sky.

The difference in Carissa's proficiency level and ability to express herself in English compared to the FLs is evident here and this illustrates the impossibility of implementing truly parallel writing tasks in this particular context. Yet, in spite of this, there are clearly attempts to be creative and express humour in the FL tasks (as evident in the French task shown above). In addition, while the nature of the FL tasks may at first glance be considered as being more perfunctory, they nonetheless remained a challenge for the students given their stage of learning. As such, they were required to draw on a range of strategies in order to complete the tasks and this, in turn, generated valuable data.

In order to capture information about their strategy use, the students completed each of the tasks on a writing strategy task sheet, based on a method used by Macaro (2001) in the Oxford writing strategies study:

> As they were carrying out a writing task, the students could see on the page opposite the kinds of questions that they were going to be asked to respond to regarding strategy use when they had completed the task. So they could be thinking about their strategy use while writing but without the interrupting and possible distracting effect of actually writing about strategy use (in L1) while they were writing [...] in L2. (Macaro, 2001: 60)

The task sheets were divided into three main sections (see Appendix B for a completed example). First, a space was provided for students to use for optional pre-task planning and at the end of this section they were asked to note the length of time they spent planning (if applicable). This was included to make it easier to differentiate any pre-task written planning from the writing task itself. The next section consisted of space for students to complete the main writing task. Instructions were given at the top of the sheet which asked students to underline as they went along anything they looked up in a dictionary or in the textbook, and if they got stuck or sought help from the teacher or a peer. There was a blank margin down the right-hand side for them to add any notes, such as which resources were used for help or if they wanted to say something but couldn't. Students could complete this at the time of writing if they wished, or if they did not want to interrupt the flow of writing they were encouraged to use an asterisk or other symbol to remind them to add the details later. In order to see the extent to which students corrected, edited or rephrased their work, they were also asked not to completely erase any mistakes or changes they made, but simply to put a line through them.

The final section of the task sheet consisted of a series of questions about the evaluation process. Students were asked to indicate whether they had checked over their writing and, if so, whether they did this at the end or as they went along. While the use of such closed-ended questions may lead students to give what they thought was the 'right' answer, these were followed up with a series of open-ended questions which asked them to specify what they checked and whether they made any changes, the answers to which could be more easily verified by looking at their writing tasks. Students were then asked to explain what they had found easy and difficult about the task and how well they thought they had done in the task in order to provide an indication of their level of confidence and perception of their ability in relation to each task. As the writing strategy task sheets required students to report their strategy use relating to a specific and contemporaneous task, it was felt in this instance that this would provide a more accurate reflection of their behaviour than a more general questionnaire such as the SILL. Additionally, students were given the space to add their own thoughts and notes and were not restricted to selecting from a predetermined list. The use of the task sheets also allowed for the writing tasks to be completed simultaneously by the whole class under normal classroom conditions, an important practical consideration.

It is also important to be aware of the possibility that the students who took part in the X-LiST study may simply have reported what they felt they were expected to report given the focus of the intervention and the particular prompts used in the writing task sheets. It could therefore be argued that any increase in their reported use of strategies was the result of raised awareness of use, or ideas being planted in the minds of the participants. Yet, as Cohen *et al.* (1998: 147) state, 'the power of suggestion alone is not usually enough to produce strategy use' and furthermore, exactly the same prompts and elicitation techniques were used with the comparison group students.

After the writing tasks had been completed, they were scored out of 20 by two teachers according to the departmental mark scheme for written work. They were then typed verbatim into word-processing software and coded using NVivo[1] qualitative data analysis software. The coding scheme was organised into five main categories in line with those identified in the literature, as shown below, while the more fine-grained sub-codes emerged from the data. The majority of the codes were applicable to tasks completed in any language; however, there were a small number that were only applicable to the FL tasks (for example, translation of vocabulary items).

(a) Planning: related to any pre-task planning completed by students and covering a range of features of planning, such as content items (e.g. bullet points of topics to be covered), language features (e.g. past tense, rhetorical questions) and approaches to planning such as drafting (at sentence, paragraph or text level) and language of planning.
(b) Monitoring: designed to capture problem-solving strategies used by students while writing, such as the use of reference materials or asking for help from peers or the teacher. These codes were predominantly applied to the notes or annotations made by students on the writing task sheets.
(c) Errors and error correction: errors made and corrected were coded in order to provide an objective measure of the effectiveness of a range of strategies used by students in order to improve the accuracy of their work. Errors made and corrected were coded in four categories: grammar, punctuation, spelling and vocabulary.
(d) Evaluation: consideration of whether the students checked their work and, if so, what and how they checked. This was based on responses to the questions at the end of the task sheet.
(e) Post-task thoughts: related to comments at the end of the task sheet about what students found easy or difficult and how they felt they had done in the task.

Following the coding process, a table of frequency counts was created for each code, for each class, in each language and at each data collection point. This was then exported into SPSS[2] software for statistical analysis. Non-parametric tests were conducted due to the small sample size and non-normal distribution of data; for example, Mann Whitney U tests were used to compare the distribution of task scores between the intervention group and comparison group and Friedman's ANOVA tests were used to compare the difference in the distribution of errors within a group over the three time points.

Gathering insights into strategy use: Stimulated recall interviews

As noted above, research into language learning strategy use involves the identification and investigation of highly mentalistic and internal processes – a complex endeavour. Given that such strategies and processes generally cannot be observed, we therefore must rely on what learners can tell us. While the primary focus of this section is on the use of stimulated recall interviews to elicit such information, it is first worth acknowledging think-aloud protocols as one of the predominant methods that has been employed in studies into strategies and writing processes (e.g. Albrechtsen, 1997; Cumming, 1989; Flower & Hayes, 1981; Jones & Tetroe, 1987; Uzawa, 1996; Whalen & Ménard, 1995).

Thinking aloud has been defined as 'a voluntary activity in which learners, having been asked to tackle a relevant task, talk their thoughts out loud, while they are engaging with that task. A think-aloud protocol is a recording or record of that reporting, compiled at the time' (Cowan, 2019: 1). Thinking aloud as a research method was popularised in the field of cognitive science by Newell and Simon (1972) as a means of investigating general problem-solving processes and was later applied to the study of writing by Flower and Hayes (1981). The primary motivation for the use of concurrent think-aloud protocols in the studies cited above is that they allow participants to verbalise their thoughts immediately as they occur, while they are still in short-term memory, and are therefore regarded as being a more accurate reflection of thought processes and strategies. However, in spite of such advantages, stimulated recall interviews were felt to be a more appropriate method of data collection in the X-LiST study for the reasons outlined below.

Stimulated recall, on the other hand, is defined as 'a prompted interview, for example, watching a video of an event, listening to an audio recording of an event, or even seeing a piece of writing just completed' (Gass & Mackey, 2017: 10), and is conducted after (rather than during) a task (however, usually within two days) in order to 'explore learners' thought processes or strategies employed during a task by asking learners to reflect on their thoughts after they have carried out a task' (Gass & Mackey, 2017: 22). The theoretical foundation for stimulated recall relies on 'an information processing approach whereby the use of and access to memory structures is enhanced, if not guaranteed, by a prompt that aids in the recall of information' (Gass & Mackey, 2017: 22). The assumption, therefore, is that it is easier for writers to remember and describe the strategies they used when they have a particular experience in mind, which in turn is more reliable than asking them for a general description of strategy use. While this remains a form of self-report and is therefore inherently subjective, the act of asking learners to reflect on and refer to specific tasks can help strengthen validity.

While there may be less of a precedent for using stimulated recall interviews in previous studies into strategy use, there are still a number of researchers who have used them successfully (e.g. Lei, 2008; Sasaki, 2000, 2002). Sasaki (2000, 2002), for example, in her initial study of the writing processes of adult Japanese learners of English, video-recorded the hand movements of her participants while they were writing and then used this as a prompt for stimulated recall. In the latter study she used two cameras, with the second focused on the participants themselves. However, she admitted that the presence of the video cameras 'might arguably have entailed some reactivity problems' (Sasaki, 2002: 53) which are likely to be heightened further when dealing with young adolescent participants. Hence, in the X-LiST study the completed writing strategy task sheets were used as the stimulus in order to provide a concrete experience for the learners to reflect on.

Another important consideration when dealing with young, school-aged learners is that stimulated recall interviews are less disruptive and less likely to alter the thought process itself than thinking aloud. Thinking aloud is undoubtedly cognitively demanding and tiring; it requires participants to think, speak and write at the same time and occasionally they may also be expected to verbalise their thoughts in a language other than that in which they are thinking or writing. In their respective studies, Macaro (2001) and Uzawa (1996), for example, discovered that the ability to perform such a task varies considerably from one participant to another. Whalen and Ménard (1995: 387) similarly reported that ten of their 22 original participants 'could not produce text and verbalise their thought processes simultaneously. They became discouraged and claimed to be "blocked" by verbalizing during the writing task' and as a result they had to be excluded from the study. Stratman and Hamp-Lyons (1994) also found that the act of thinking aloud negatively affected the participants' ability to identify and correct errors in their text. It has been suggested that in order to reduce the risk of participants being unable to complete the think-alouds, training should be given in advance. However, this is not only time consuming but, given the focus of the current study, any demonstration of the process on the part of the researcher may produce preconceptions about the strategies that should be used and may therefore bias the data.

Taking into consideration the aims of the X-LiST study, the age of the participants and the classroom environment in which the writing tasks would take place, stimulated recall interviews provided a more reliable, appropriate and effective method of data collection than thinking aloud. While the latter may elicit more immediate data about *what* strategies participants were using at a particular moment, retrospective recalls allow learners to add more qualitative data about *why* they used particular strategies and *how* they were able to transfer them from one language context to another. There are limitations, however. The reliability of data generated from stimulated recall interviews has been criticised due to the time lapse between the task itself and the recall. Bowles (2010: 14), for example, suggests that 'retrospective verbal reports may not accurately reflect participants' thought processes because they simply may not recall what they were thinking as they completed the given task'. Similarly, Gass and Mackey (2017) draw attention to the possible contamination of memory during the intervening period. In order to minimise any such adverse effects, the stimulated recall interviews were conducted as soon as possible after the task had been completed (usually on the same day). Prompts were used to guide the students which addressed the following key areas:

- Thoughts and targets, e.g. main goals before starting the task;
- Planning, e.g. purpose of plan (if applicable), approach to planning, use of plan while writing;
- Writing, e.g. problems encountered and solved, resources used, approaches to translation;
- Evaluating, e.g. approach to evaluation, changes made, goals achieved.

The transcripts of the stimulated recall interviews were analysed using a thematic coding approach (Robson & McCartan, 2016). An initial set of codes was generated in line with the writing task coding scheme outlined above and incorporated references to strategies within the key areas of planning, monitoring and evaluation of the particular task in question. Other key codes were then added where students had made more general comments about their strategy use. This included comparisons between their approaches to writing and attitudes towards writing in different languages, and comments relating to a change in their approach over time and the transfer of strategies from one context to another. The codes were created in such a way as to ensure that links could easily be made between the interview data and the writing tasks – a consideration that was particularly important for the analysis of strategy use at an individual level.

The Ethics of Conducting Classroom-based LLSI Research

As stated in the guidelines set out by the British Educational Research Association (2018: 5), 'all education research should be conducted within an ethic of respect for: the person; knowledge; democratic values; the quality of educational research; and academic freedom'. The issue of voluntary, informed consent is therefore an important one, yet it is one that we often take for granted and it is worth considering the additional complexity that comes with conducting classroom-based interventions. In the X-LiST study, all participating students and teachers, along with school leaders and parents, were fully informed about the nature of the study and what their involvement would entail from the beginning – this was not problematic. However, given the fact that the intervention of LLSI was to be interwoven into regular timetabled lessons led by their class teacher, the issue of 'voluntary consent' and, by extension, the students' right to withdraw, was called into question. They could not simply 'opt out' of all of their English or German lessons (much to the dismay of some!) and therefore technically could not withdraw from the intervention itself. However, they were certainly able to opt out of contributing to any data collected purely for research purposes (such as the questionnaires and interviews).

We can justify this to some extent by claiming that the intervention sought to support their learning and their performance in writing and, as such, made sound pedagogical sense. It was, after all, informed by a substantial body of research evidence in the field of language learning strategies. Yet, this raises another question regarding the ethics of establishing a comparison group. If we truly believe that introducing a particular series of activities into lessons will benefit learners, is it ethical to deliberately deny this to another group for the purpose of conducting research? Perhaps not. However, in this case, as in the case of many quasi-experimental intervention studies, it was not clear what the effects of LLSI would be in this context – and in particular, it was not known what the interactions would be between the LLSI in the L1 and FL classrooms. It seemed prudent, therefore, to begin by investigating this thoroughly with one group, but with the knowledge that the resources and expertise generated could be extended to other classes after the data collection process had finished.

When considering ethics in more depth, Stutchbury (2017) outlines a helpful framework for making sense of ethical issues in school-based research which includes four layers or dimensions: external/ecological, consequential/utilitarian, deontological and relational/individual. While this framework is intended to apply to educational research more broadly, it can also be applied more specifically to research into language learning strategies. Table 4.1 provides an overview of the four dimensions along with some more specific considerations relating to LLSI. The questions outlined here provide a useful starting point for reflecting on the ethical considerations involved in such intervention studies.

Conclusion

The primary aim of this chapter was to fully describe the research design adopted in the X-LiST study and, by extension, to reflect more generally on a range of methodological considerations for researching the effects of a cross-linguistic intervention of LLSI. What emerged as particularly valuable here was the mixed-methods approach taken. While mixed-methods studies are undoubtedly becoming more common, Oxford (2017: 314) suggests that they are still 'not as frequently found in the L2 learning field as they should be'. I would argue that any exploration of LLSI should take advantage of both quantitative and qualitative approaches in order to effectively consider both *what* strategies learners use and also *how* they use them. This is particularly valuable for identifying the ways in which individual differences influence learners' trajectories through an intervention of strategy instruction. However, while each of the methods discussed in this chapter provided useful insights into the

Table 4.1 Ethical dimensions of classroom-based research into language learning strategies

Layer	Definition	Considerations for LLSI
External/ ecological	Consideration of the context of the research, the culture of the institution in which it is taking place, and the relationship between the part of the institution in which you are working and the institution as a whole.	• Will the research follow all relevant codes of practice and work within any legal requirements (e.g. data protection responsibilities, criminal record checks)? • Have relevant gatekeepers (e.g. the head teacher, classroom teacher, parents) given informed consent for the research to take place? • What are the current curricula, schemes of work and priorities for the target class? • To what extent is the research agenda compatible with this? • Is LLSI already an implicit or explicit component of normal pedagogy in the language classroom? • How might the implementation of LLSI be viewed by others in the institution?
Consequential/ utilitarian	Reflection on the potential consequences of the research on a school, teachers, students, or anyone else who may be affected by the results or process of carrying out the research.	• What are the potential benefits for the learners, the teachers, the school and the wider language learning community? • Has the intervention been developed in such a way that it is relevant to students and integrated so as to minimise any disruption to their learning? • Have the language teachers been consulted in developing and/or delivering the intervention materials to ensure they are appropriate? • How can findings and resources be disseminated to other practitioners and researchers (e.g. through subject associations)?
Deontological	Consideration of the way in which the research is carried out; acting with honesty and integrity.	• Have participants given their informed consent in advance and do they have the option to withdraw at any stage if they wish? • Have all participants been treated fairly? What are the implications for any comparison groups who do not have access to the intervention materials at the time of the study? • To what extent are the teachers/learners involved being asked to do additional work solely for the purpose of the research study? How can this be minimised? • What are the considerations in relation to language of instruction of the LLSI or the language used to interview or liaise with participants? • Will participants be ensured confidentiality and anonymity in any reporting of the findings?
Relational/ individual	Concern with the relationships at the heart of the research.	• How can an atmosphere of genuine trust/collaboration/respect be established with all participants? • Have any unnecessary or unreasonable demands on participants' time been avoided?

Source: Adapted from Stutchbury (2017)

learners' development and transfer of strategies, we must always be mindful of the limitations and, as Grenfell and Harris (1999: 54) suggest, 'we work with what we can get'. This chapter also drew attention to the ethical dimension of conducting classroom-based intervention studies which can sometimes be overlooked.

Notes

(1) NVivo 10 for Mac, produced by QSR International, Victoria, Australia.
(2) SPSS (Statistical Package for the Social Sciences) 22 for Mac, produced by SPSS, Inc., Chicago, USA.

5 Teaching for Transfer: Developing a Cross-Linguistic Approach to Language Learning Strategy Instruction

Having considered some of the key methodological considerations for researching the effects of a cross-linguistic intervention of LLSI, it is now important to turn our attention to the development of the intervention itself. Even though language learning strategies have long been considered as beneficial and 'teachable' (Oxford & Nyikos, 1989: 291), studies still tend to focus primarily on the outcomes of interventions of LLSI and pay little attention to *what* the LLSI consisted of and *how* it was delivered by the teachers (Gu, 2019). Griffiths (2018: 166) has similarly suggested that 'the pedagogical perspective has been seen as the essential *raison d'être* underlying debates on and research into the language learning strategy concept', yet, paradoxically, strategy instruction in itself remains 'an under-researched area' (Griffiths, 2018: 168). In addition, as has been noted previously in this book, any existing research in this area tends to focus on the teaching of strategies within either an L1 or an FL context. As such, there is 'a paucity of cross-linguistic studies' exploring the implementation of parallel L1 and FL strategy instruction (Gunning *et al.*, 2016: 76).

The aim of this chapter, therefore, is to outline the process of developing the pedagogical intervention at the heart of the X-LiST study; this involved the introduction of tasks and activities to aid students in planning, monitoring and evaluating their written work in both their FLs and their L1. While Phase A of the study entailed strategy instruction only in the German FL classroom, Phase B involved parallel instruction in both the German FL and English L1 classrooms in order to encourage students to reflect on, develop, and transfer their language learning strategies across contexts. Both phases were conducted with the intervention group only and each phase lasted for four months. The aim of Phase B, in particular, was to make the common aims and practices of L1 and FL teaching more explicit and to encourage connection-making among both students and teachers. To this end, this chapter will build on Forbes (2019a) by addressing some of the challenges inherent in developing a cross-linguistic, cross-curricular approach to LLSI and will then outline the key considerations and steps in the design and implementation of such a programme, exemplified throughout with reference to activities from the X-LiST study.

Challenges in Implementing Cross-Linguistic LLSI

It is important to begin this chapter by acknowledging some of the challenges and potential barriers to establishing collaboration between L1 and FL teachers. Such challenges exist at the level of the curriculum, the school and the individual and relate to some of the issues surrounding the difference in the status of and approaches to L1 and FL teaching set out in Chapter 2. At the curriculum level, Harris (2006) notes the distinction between the aims and priorities of English and FL teachers in the UK context, a gap exacerbated by government policies and a lack of time to plan cross-curricular activities. As such, teachers are often unfamiliar with the content or specific terminology used in another subject area and any potential collaboration may also be hindered by the L1 teacher's limitation in another language. Such challenges were similarly recognised by Gunning *et al.* (2016). In their study into developing connections between L1 French and L2 English teachers in Francophone Canada, they attributed early difficulties to a mutual lack of familiarity with one another's curricula.

At an institutional level, Perkins and Salomon (1988) similarly commented that the way in which certain skills are partitioned off from each other in schools as different subjects can impede students' ability to transfer them from one context to another. While this statement was made over 30 years ago, the sentiment still holds true today in many contexts. FL teachers are often grouped together in one department, while L1 teachers constitute a different, and often physically separate, department. While this can increase cohesion within particular subject areas (e.g. between French and German teachers), Grenfell and Harris (2017: 191) caution that it can 'block opportunities for boundary crossing, preventing teachers from learning from different communities of practice'. Furthermore, practical constraints within the school such as a lack of time and a lack of flexibility to change schemes of work and lesson plans can also constitute a considerable barrier to collaboration. Where such practical constraints can be overcome, for example, where teachers are provided with the time and space to engage in cross-curricular planning, this can lead to benefits for both teachers and students alike (Lyster *et al.*, 2013). At the level of the individual, evidence presented in Chapter 2 suggests that the above considerations also contribute to a difference in the way in which both learners and teachers view L1 and FL contexts which, in itself, can inhibit connection-making and transfer. However, rather than being deterred by such challenges, it is important to consider how they might be overcome. The following sections will therefore provide something of a step-by-step guide for designing and implementing a cross-linguistic programme of LLSI.

General Considerations for Developing LLSI

This section will reflect on some key questions that should be considered before developing a programme of LLSI. While many of these are relevant to any form of LLSI (e.g. within the context of a single language classroom), issues that are particularly pertinent to the design of cross-linguistic LLSI will be highlighted.

What is the aim of LLSI?

We must first ask ourselves what we are aiming to accomplish. Do we want to improve students' performance in a particular skill area? Do we wish to help our learners to become more independent? Are we seeking to make challenging tasks seem more manageable for them? All of the above? While performance and attainment are undoubtedly a concern among many teachers, the overall role of strategy instruction tends to extend beyond the language classroom itself. While students often encounter FL learning for the first time within a school setting, in reality, much language learning goes on later in life. Students therefore need to be equipped with the necessary skills and strategies to enable them to undertake this successfully. As such, for Gunning *et al.* (2016: 161), 'the ultimate goal of LLSI is for students to use strategies to autonomously manage their learning'. In a similar vein, Gu (2019) highlights 'learning to learn', the flexibility to adapt and the ability to learn strategically, as vital in a rapidly changing world. If the intention, therefore, is for learners to be able to utilise strategies beyond the particular task at hand, then encouraging transfer between contexts (and, by extension, metacognition) is key.

Who are the learners?

Given the crucial role of individual differences that will be highlighted later in this book (see Chapter 9), it is important to carefully consider *who* our learners are and, by extension, their respective proficiency levels in each of the languages involved in the LLSI. Proficiency level must be taken into consideration in several ways. First, when learners have very different levels of proficiency in their L1 and FL (and indeed, between different FLs) this will inevitably influence not only the extent to which they are able to develop strategies, but also the type of strategies they may need and use. Secondly, learners within any given class will all vary in terms of their proficiency in that particular language, which in turn will shape their strategy use. While one of the key objectives of LLSI is for learners to become more independent strategy users, it will take some learners longer than others to reach this stage. Such flexibility and differentiation (for example, in the form of varied levels of scaffolding) must be taken into account.

What skill area(s) is/are the focus?

Given that developing and implementing a programme of LLSI takes time and commitment on the part of both teachers and learners, it is often useful to begin by focusing on one particular skill area and then to gradually extend the range of strategies over time. Graham and Macaro (2007: 155), for example, admitted that their aim to implement a programme of LLSI simultaneously for both listening and writing strategies with a group of advanced-level secondary school learners in the UK was perhaps 'too ambitious'. Yet there is an additional layer of complexity when dealing with LLSI in two (or more) languages. This relates to identifying a skill area and a focus which is (a) relevant to all languages and (b) adaptable to the various classroom contexts and levels involved. Within the context of the X-LiST study, it was evident that developing competence in writing represented a challenge for many of the learners, particularly in an FL but often also in their L1. In addition, given that writing is a skill that needs to be explicitly learned, even in the L1, the associated strategies were thought to lend themselves well to classroom-based instruction. However, as outlined above and in Chapter 2, the teaching of English and the teaching of FLs in schools in England are often treated very differently and teachers have distinct approaches and priorities. As such, it was important to begin by examining the curricula and schemes of work in order to identify topics, tasks or outcomes where there might be possible areas of intersection.

In the X-LiST study, for example, students in English were expected to produce narrative-style tasks (which include creative writing) alongside more analytical tasks such as essays on novels or plays. In the FLs, however, where students were operating at a significantly lower level of proficiency, writing exercises predominantly took the form of more focused narrative-style tasks related to specific topics, such as writing about oneself or a past holiday. Yet, when looking at the mark schemes used in each subject, some similarities emerged in terms of overall aims and outcomes. Teachers in both subject areas focused on both content and accurate use of language; while English teachers looked for writing that was 'engaging' and made 'proper use of structure', FL teachers also sought evidence of a 'sound ability to convey information clearly' and a 'well organized structure'. Both mark schemes also highlighted the importance of the accurate use of spelling, punctuation and grammar. It seems, therefore, that teachers in both contexts were working towards some shared aims and goals related to writing, even if such links were not made explicit. Nevertheless, the selection of appropriate writing tasks that would enable links to be drawn between the various languages remained a challenge in the X-LiST study. As it would not have been feasible (or appropriate) to adapt the same task to all of the languages, given the discrepancy between L1 and FL proficiency, it was deemed suitable to ensure that each of the tasks was of the same style, i.e. narrative. Further reflection on the writing tasks along with some examples can be found in Chapter 4.

Should LLSI be integrated into normal classroom teaching or taught separately?

Early critics of strategy instruction (e.g. Kellerman, 1991; Rees-Miller, 1993) suggested that LLSI in the L2/FL classroom was unnecessary and took away from time that would be better spent simply teaching the language. However, this implies to some extent that the two are mutually exclusive, which does not have to be the case. It has long been recognised by supporters of strategy instruction that LLSI should be integrated closely with regular instruction. The primary reason for this is that it is helpful in highlighting the direct relevance and application of strategies to the language learning process (O'Malley & Chamot, 1990); that is, learners will 'quickly lose interest in *how* to learn if it is not perceived as being directly relevant to *what* they want to learn' (Griffiths, 2018: 206). Grenfell and Harris (2017) similarly highlight the importance of embedding LLSI into regular lessons in order to provide multiple opportunities for learners to proceduralise them in different tasks.

Should strategies be explicitly or implicitly embedded into activities and materials?

Another key element of LLSI is the need for such instruction to be made explicit. First, being clear about what strategies are being taught and what they are for is important for raising students' awareness of their own strategy use and facilitating the development of their strategic competence (Gu, 2019). However, in addition, explicit instruction is also vital for encouraging transfer. As suggested by Griffiths (2018: 179), 'if students do not understand what they are doing and why, they will not transfer the new strategies they have learnt beyond the immediate task to new ones'. From a transfer of learning perspective (Perkins & Salomon, 1988), explicit instruction has also been highlighted as being particularly pertinent for stimulating transfer between tasks or contexts that are superficially different, such as engaging in writing in English compared to an FL. In order to promote such transfer, LLSI should therefore not only explicitly address *how* to use a particular strategy or skill, but also *when* to use it.

What language should be used for strategy instruction?

Within the literature on strategy instruction in the L2/FL classroom there has been much debate about whether the LLSI should be in the L1 or the target language, particularly where beginner learners are concerned. While for some researchers the use of the L1 is considered justifiable 'if it means that the learners can reflect on and discuss in some depth their learning, their strategies, their needs and goals' (Grenfell & Harris, 2017: 154–155), others maintain that LLSI can be successfully conducted in the target language with the help of pictograms, posters and mascots (e.g. Gunning *et al.*, 2019). However, there is an extra layer of complexity where cross-linguistic LLSI is concerned. Should the L1 and FLs teachers conduct the strategy instruction in their respective languages, or should the L1 be used by both sets of teachers (presuming, of course, that the FL teachers also have knowledge of the students' L1)? For the purposes of the X-LiST study the latter option was chosen. This was partly due to the students' low level of German; however, it was also felt that if the LLSI was conducted in the same language across each of the subjects and if terminology remained relatively consistent, it might be easier for the students to make connections and to transfer the strategies between contexts.

Developing a Cross-Linguistic Programme of LLSI: A Step-by-Step Guide

A range of models of explicit LLSI have been proposed within both the L1 and L2/FL education literature. One of the most well-known is the cognitive academic language learning approach (CALLA) developed by Anna Chamot and colleagues. This was originally devised to support the academic achievement of migrant students learning through their L2 (e.g. English as an additional language (EAL) students) and is a cognitive-social model based on sociocultural theory along with constructivist theories and Anderson's skill acquisition theory (Chamot, 2009). As discussed in Chapter 3, the most prominent and well-researched model of L1 writing strategy instruction is the self-regulated strategy development (SRSD) programme developed by Steve Graham, Karen Harris and colleagues in the United States. However, while many other models have been developed in a range of different contexts, they all follow a similar sequence of four steps, as shown in Figure 5.1. These steps are not necessarily linear, but should instead be considered as recursive, 'so that teachers and students always have the option of revisiting prior instructional phases as needed' (Chamot, 2008: 271).

Table 5.1 outlines the way in which these four key steps are addressed across a range of well-known models of LLSI and highlights the similarities between them. For one, they all have a shared goal, which is to

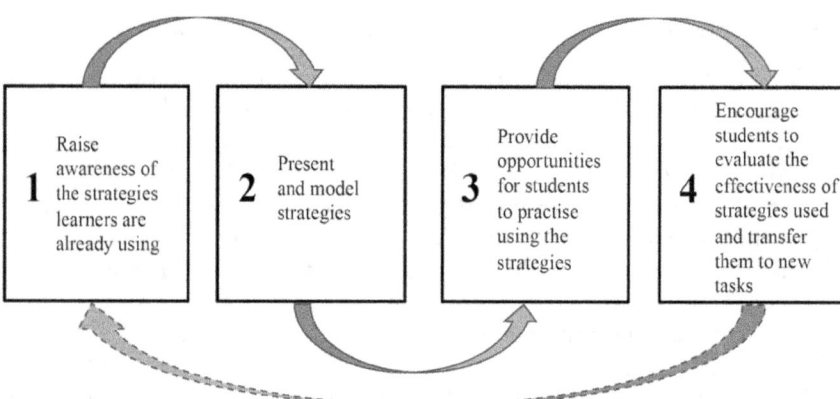

Figure 5.1 Stages of the LLSI cycle

encourage students to become more metacognitively aware language learners and more autonomous strategy users. In addition, to achieve this they all feature a progression from declarative knowledge, through teacher presentation and modelling, to procedural knowledge through practice. This section will therefore consider the rationale behind each of the four steps in turn and provide examples from the X-LiST study to exemplify how they were incorporated into both the L1 and FL classrooms.

Step 1: Raise awareness of the strategies learners are already using

It is widely recognised that an important first step in any form of strategy research 'is to help learners recognise which strategies they already use' (Cohen, 1998: 69) and this furthermore serves a pedagogical purpose as 'a foundation for deciding which strategies to teach' (Oxford, 2011: 140). There are a range of techniques that can be used by the teacher in order to accomplish this: at a whole-class level it is possible to use discussions or questionnaires; alternatively, students could be placed in smaller groups to complete a task that will require the use of strategies (which they will subsequently reflect on and share). The particular techniques used to elicit learners' strategy use and the language used to do so will depend on their proficiency level and also on practicalities such as class size. What is imperative here, however, is that the students are encouraged to identify their own strategies as part of the awareness-raising process. This is particularly important when working across different curriculum subject areas where tasks and challenges will vary. Similarly, given the students' higher level of proficiency in their L1, it is likely that they will be less consciously aware of their strategy use in this language. Paradoxically, therefore, such elicitation and awareness-raising may actually prove more difficult in the L1 classroom.

Table 5.1 Models of strategy instruction

	Step 1. Raise awareness of the strategies learners are already using	Step 2. Present and model strategies	Step 3. Provide opportunities for students to practise using the strategies	Step 4. Encourage students to evaluate the effectiveness of strategies used and transfer them to new tasks
Styles and Strategies Based Instruction (SSBI) (Cohen et al., 2005)	*Strategy preparation* Find out how much students know about strategies. *Strategy awareness-raising* of the learning process and existing strategies.	*Strategy instruction* Teachers describe, model and give examples of strategies.	*Strategy practice* To reinforce strategies that have been discussed.	*Personalisation of strategies* Learners evaluate how they are using the strategies and look at ways they can use them in other contexts.
Cognitive Academic Language Learning Approach (CALLA) (Chamot, 2005; Chamot et al., 1999)	*Preparation* The teacher finds out students' existing learning strategies for familiar activities and identifies gaps that need to be addressed.	*Presentation* The teacher models and explains strategies and asks if students have used them.	*Practice* Students practise new strategies; teacher gradually removes scaffolding.	*Evaluation* Students evaluate their own strategy use immediately after practice. *Expansion* Students combine and transfer strategies to new tasks.
Strategic Self-Regulation (S2R) Model (Oxford, 2011)	*Prepare* Identify current strategies; raise initial awareness. *Continue to raise awareness* Learners brainstorm and discuss strategies after completing a task.	*Model and name strategies* Teacher names, models and explains new strategies, stressing the potential benefits.	*Practice* Learners use, combine and monitor strategies.	*Evaluate and transfer Expand and adapt* Learners continue to increase ownership By monitoring and evaluating success.

Macaro (2001)	Raise the awareness of students Exploration of possible strategies available	Modelling by teacher and/or by other students	Combining strategies for a specific purpose or specific task Application of strategies with scaffolded support	Initial evaluation by students Gradual removal of scaffolding Evaluation by students (and teacher)
Grenfell and Harris (1999)	Awareness-raising For example, brainstorming strategies for checking work and discussing the value of checking over written work.	Modelling Teacher prompts learners to focus on style, content, accuracy, etc.	General practice and action planning Learners select strategies to help with their particular difficulties. Focused practice and teacher fades out the reminders	Evaluating strategy acquisition and recommencing the cycle
Self-Regulated Strategy Development (SRSD) Model (Mason et al., 2011)	Develop background knowledge Discuss the strategies	Model the strategies Memorise the strategies	Support use of writing and self-regulation strategies	Independent performance

In the X-LiST study the initial German writing task, which was completed by all of the participants at the beginning of the year, was used as a stimulus for a whole-class discussion about which strategies the students used and how they used them. The teacher asked the students to raise their hand if, for example, they had done any pre-task planning, used a dictionary, asked for help or checked over their work afterwards. This enabled learners to see that they and their peers had engaged with a combination of different skills and strategies to complete the task. The students then spent several minutes discussing their task in pairs, and were asked to explain to each other some of the specific strategies they used, why they used them and whether they found them helpful. The students and teacher then co-constructed a list of some of the existing writing strategies used by the class which included, for example, planning ideas using bullet points, looking up keywords, scanning their textbook for useful phrases, asking a friend or the teacher for help, re-reading their work and checking spelling. This was later mirrored in the English classroom during Phase B of the intervention. This process not only provided a starting point for the development of the intervention, but also raised the students' awareness of what a strategy is and what they do. This type of awareness-raising activity was revisited regularly throughout the course of the year in both the German and English classrooms in order to encourage learners to continually monitor and develop their strategy use.

Step 2: Teacher presents and models strategies

The second step involves the teacher presenting, modelling and explaining a range of writing strategies. While this step may seem, on the surface, to be a very deductive and teacher-centred method, the strategies selected should rather emerge from the collaborative discussions with learners during Step 1. The act of modelling on the part of the teacher is 'critical for establishing the metacognitive processes needed for effective strategy use' (Mason *et al.*, 2011: 24), and this is often achieved by 'thinking aloud' in order to make explicit the internal processes that so often go unnoticed. However, Gunning *et al.* (2019) caution that the process of thinking aloud must be carefully planned so that the language used is simple and the steps taken are logically sequenced. Strategies can also be presented using acronyms to make them memorable for students. Mason *et al.* (2011), for example, present clusters of planning strategies such as POW (Pick my idea, Organise my notes, Write and say more) and evaluation strategies such as SCAN (does it make Sense, is it Connected to my belief, can you Add more, Note errors).

In the X-LiST study not all strategies were presented at once, but they were grouped into planning, monitoring and evaluation strategies and built up gradually. Figure 5.2 provides an overview of the main strategies

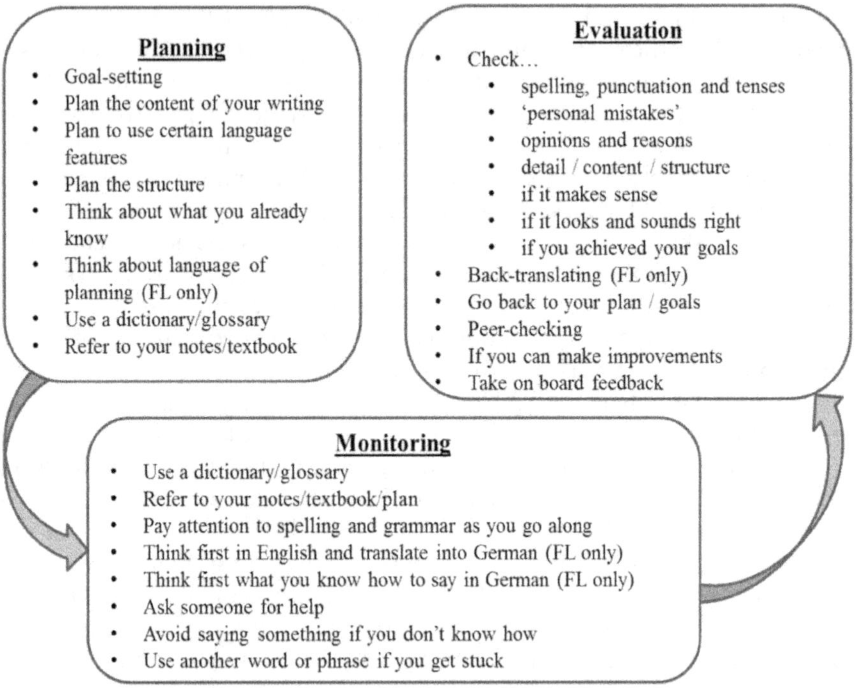

Planning
- Goal-setting
- Plan the content of your writing
- Plan to use certain language features
- Plan the structure
- Think about what you already know
- Think about language of planning (FL only)
- Use a dictionary/glossary
- Refer to your notes/textbook

Evaluation
- Check…
  - spelling, punctuation and tenses
  - 'personal mistakes'
  - opinions and reasons
  - detail / content / structure
  - if it makes sense
  - if it looks and sounds right
  - if you achieved your goals
- Back-translating (FL only)
- Go back to your plan / goals
- Peer-checking
- If you can make improvements
- Take on board feedback

Monitoring
- Use a dictionary/glossary
- Refer to your notes/textbook/plan
- Pay attention to spelling and grammar as you go along
- Think first in English and translate into German (FL only)
- Think first what you know how to say in German (FL only)
- Ask someone for help
- Avoid saying something if you don't know how
- Use another word or phrase if you get stuck

Figure 5.2 Overview of the main writing strategies developed
Source: Forbes, 2019a: 115

focused on within each group. It is fully acknowledged that some of the 'strategies' listed here are indeed more skill-like than strategy-like. For example, 'using a dictionary' is a skill that requires students to operationalise a combination of strategies: they may first employ metacognitive strategies to plan where to look; then they will activate a range of strategies with a cognitive function to process the material contained in the dictionary entry; and they may perhaps also use affective strategies to deal with frustration if they cannot find the appropriate meaning (Cohen & Wang, 2018). However, while some of this complexity indeed emerged in the stimulated recall interview data (as is evident in the case studies presented in Chapter 8), the more general terms in Figure 5.2 were used for the sake of clarity and accessibility given that the intervention was with 13–14 year-olds. When the LLSI was introduced into the English classroom, similar resources and terminology were used in order to encourage the students to think about transferring relevant strategies from one context to another. Inevitably, there were some strategies that were of particular relevance to the FLs, such as the use of back-translating as an evaluation strategy; however, on the whole the majority were relevant to both the L1 and FL.

Throughout the process of presenting strategies and thinking aloud, the teacher was always explicit about the rationale behind using the strategy; as underlined by Cohen (1998: 93), 'it is necessary for teachers to inform their learners fully as to the strategies that they are being taught and the value and purpose of employing these strategies'. However, it was also important to make it clear to the students that they would not necessarily find every strategy helpful, nor would every strategy be appropriate for every task. Within a sociocognitive framework, teachers are often recognised as 'co-authors' of students' writing (Prior, 2006: 58) which allows for the 'co-construction of learning strategies' (Collins, 1998: 48). Therefore, it is important for teachers to avoid any attempts to impose the 'right' strategies on learners and instead to provide them with a range of strategies and the skills to be able to assess which strategies would aid them as an individual to complete a particular task.

Step 3: Students practise using the strategies

The next step typically takes the longest and in order to provide a structure, Gunning *et al.* (2019) recommend breaking this up into three stages: (1) guided practice, (2) independent practice (when scaffolding is gradually removed by the teacher) and (3) individual progression and experimentation with strategy use. Given that strategies are not used in isolation, this final stage also provides an opportunity for the students individually to practise different combinations of strategy use. This, however, raises additional challenges for the teacher. As suggested by Griffiths:

> From a pedagogical perspective, [...] strategy orchestration is not an easy skill to teach. This is because the particular combination of strategies which will suit a given student is highly individual, and may vary according to numerous factors such as age, nationality, gender, affective states and so on [...] In other words, it is not possible to provide a pre-set formula for effective orchestration. Learners need to experiment for themselves to determine the combination which produced the best results given the unique blend of individual, situational and target variables. Nevertheless, discussion of the orchestration issue may well be helpful to assist students to work through the possibilities and arrive at a harmonious outcome. (2018: 184)

Opportunities for extensive practice are therefore key and, as suggested by Grenfell and Harris (2017), working across more than one language classroom can therefore provide additional benefits. Examples of some of the activities introduced in both the German and English classroom as part of the X-LiST study are outlined below.

Planning activity

Links between the development of effective planning strategies and improvement in the quality of writing have been reported in a number of studies in both FL (e.g. Sasaki, 2002) and L1 (e.g. De La Paz & Graham,

2002) contexts. A scaffolding sheet was therefore designed to help students plan for a German writing task on the topic of school. While this was presented as a single 'activity', it involved the use of a wide range of strategies. The students were guided to set themselves goals for the task, consider the main content ideas and language features they would include (such as particular tenses or structures), find key words and phrases in German, and think about the overall structure of their text (see Example 5.1). A similar sheet was used to help them to plan for an English writing task. While in the L1 version the students were not asked to find key phrases in the same way as they had done for German, they were prompted to think about using particular language features such as alliteration, metaphors and a variety of adjectives.

Evaluation activity

Following a German writing task on holidays, the students were given a scaffolding sheet to guide them through checking their work (see Example 5.2) and to prompt them to use a range of evaluation strategies. This asked whether they had specifically checked particular aspects of their work, such as spelling, relevance and verb tenses, and also asked them to indicate whether they had made any changes as a result of checking their work. This aimed to encourage the students to engage more actively with checking over their work and, combined with feedback from the teacher, enabled them to see which aspects of evaluation they perhaps needed more practice with. The scaffolding sheet also prompted the students to check back to their plan to make sure they had included everything they needed, to ask a peer to check over their work, and to think about what they could add to improve their work, rather than just correcting what had already been written. A similar sheet was used in the English classroom, but this was adapted slightly to capture aspects of particular relevance to this context. For example, following an argumentative essay task, the students were additionally asked to reflect on their use of persuasive language.

Error correction activity

As suggested by Macaro (2001: 219), strategy training should go beyond the planning, monitoring and evaluation stages and should also incorporate what are referred to as 'moving on' strategies, which 'update the mental models of the target language as a result of feedback'. This was incorporated into the X-LiST study by means of an error correction activity in German (see Example 5.3). This aimed to encourage the students to engage more actively with teacher feedback following a writing task, and to enable them to feed this forward into future tasks by improving their ability to detect and correct errors. Errors were underlined and the students were asked to identify the 'type' of error and then to correct it. In their workbooks, the students were then asked

Planning : German Writing

Goal-setting
What are your main aims for this writing task? What do you want to focus on/improve?

1.
2.
3.

Brainstorming

Content areas	Language features
e.g. favourite subject	e.g. past tense, comparatives

Key words and phrases to include

Structure/organisation

Example 5.1 Planning activity

Strategies for checking over your work

Things to check for…	Did I check this? ✓/✗	Did I make any changes as a result of checking this? ✓/✗
Spelling	☐	☐
Punctuation	☐	☐
Relevance	☐	☐
Structure	☐	☐
Style	☐	☐
Have I included enough detail?	☐	☐
Does it makes sense?	☐	☐
Does it look right?	☐	☐
Does it sound right?	☐	☐
Other: ……………………………………	☐	☐

Things to ask yourself…	Did I ask myself this? ✓/✗
Did I achieve my goals for this piece of work?	☐
Did I check back to see if I included everything on my plan?	☐
Did I stop to think if there was any way I could make my work even better rather than just checking what I had already written?	☐
Did I ask anyone else to check it over as well?	☐

Example 5.2 Evaluation activity

Correcting mistakes

Look back at the underlined phrases in your last German writing task. Write each mistake in the first column, try to work out what type of mistake it is by putting a tick in the right box, and try to write the correct version in the last column.

Write your mistake here	Silly spelling mistake	Adjectives don't agree	I mixed up my word order	I forgot to use capitals	Verb is in the wrong tense	Verb is not formed properly	I used the wrong word	Something else	Write the correct version here

What were your three most common types of mistake? Remember to check specifically for these in your next writing task!

1. _____
2. _____
3. _____

Example 5.3 Error correction activity

to add any common errors to their list of 'personal mistakes' which they were encouraged to consider when setting targets for and checking over subsequent tasks. This activity was initially modelled by the teacher using mistakes from a made-up text, and students completed a similar exercise in groups before being asked to try the task with their own work. In English, students were similarly encouraged to engage with feedback and to set targets for subsequent tasks. While the same principles applied, due to the nature of the tasks this more frequently tended to be at the level of content or structure for English rather than at word or sentence level.

Gradual removal of scaffolding

In line with other frameworks for LLSI (e.g. Chamot, 2005; Grenfell & Harris, 1999; Macaro, 2001; Mason *et al.*, 2011), the resources that explicitly guided students through a task were gradually removed and they were encouraged to select and combine the strategies they wanted to use more independently. After the students had been given the opportunity to practise their strategy use on several occasions using the guided task sheets, these were then replaced with summary sheets providing an overview of strategies. The students were encouraged before each task to take a moment to reflect on which strategies they would use and what they found useful afterwards. This was then reduced further to a summary sheet similar to Figure 5.2, which the students kept in their books and which was referred to progressively less by the L1 and FL teachers. However, it was found that strategy development occurred at different stages for different learners (see Chapter 8); while strategic writers were quickly able to manage their writing process relatively independently, other students, particularly lower or middle proficiency learners, required more scaffolding and practice. As such, there was a need for long-term and differentiated instruction over time to enable students to develop their strategy use and writing.

Step 4: Evaluation of the effectiveness of strategies used and transfer of strategies to new tasks

The aim is that the gradual removal of scaffolding and support on the part of the teacher during Step 3 will, in time, lead to more autonomous and proceduralised strategy use. Step 4, therefore, is important for encouraging students to evaluate the effectiveness of their strategy use and to take ownership of their learning. As such, teachers have an important role to play here 'in promoting student learning through enhancing their metacognition' (Lee & Mak, 2018: 2). This can be done by building in opportunities for reflection and also by providing students with feedback on their strategy use, i.e. on the *process* of completing the task rather than just on the final product. Such metacognitive engagement with their learning similarly facilitates students' transfer of strategies to different tasks and, ultimately perhaps, to different subjects.

In the X-LiST study, students were encouraged to reflect systematically on their strategy use through whole-class and small group discussions led by the teacher throughout the intervention, and also individually by means of the strategy evaluation sheets discussed above. In line with Graham and Macaro (2007), feedback was provided to the students, not just on the accuracy of the finished written product itself, but also on their strategic approach to writing tasks, with a view to helping them develop their strategy use; this took the form of verbal feedback to the students in class while they were working on a task and occasionally written comments on their work suggesting which strategies they should try. Such teacher feedback on strategy use is instrumental in helping learners to reflect more deliberately on their approach to writing with a view to helping them to gradually develop the metacognitive skills they need to engage with and expand on their strategy use more independently (Oxford, 2017). Schunk and Swartz (1993: 339) have similarly highlighted that 'strategy feedback promotes achievement outcomes and strategy use better than strategy instruction alone'. This was shown to be particularly important for average proficiency learners who initially relied heavily on teacher feedback and suggestions in order to assess the effectiveness of this strategy use (see example of Chris, 'the experimenter' in Chapter 8).

Conclusion

The aim of this chapter was to outline the process of developing the pedagogical intervention of LLSI at the heart of the X-LiST study. While many of the considerations and issues discussed above are indeed relevant to any form of LLSI (e.g. within the context of either L1 or FL classrooms), particular attention was given here to the design of a cross-linguistic, cross-curricular programme of LLSI. The key focus of the X-LiST study, after all, is on developing links between strategy use in the L1 and FL classrooms and, as such, on encouraging some form of collaboration between L1 and FL teachers. While De Angelis and Jessner (2012: 65) have called for a 'multilingual approach to the *study* of writing development' (my emphasis), I would extend this further and argue for a multilingual or cross-linguistic approach to the *teaching* of writing in schools. Writing, after all, is a crucial skill which permeates the entire school curriculum. As highlighted by Burley and Pomphrey (2003), both English and FL teachers are teachers of *language* and, as such, should aim to share some common aims and practices. There will undoubtedly be practical challenges to overcome, but the evidence from the X-LiST study presented in subsequent chapters suggests that this is indeed a worthwhile endeavour to pursue.

6 An In-Depth Exploration of Patterns of Strategy Development in Foreign Language and First Language Writing

The research reviewed in Chapter 3 provides evidence to suggest that strategy instruction within a classroom context can positively influence performance and strategy development in writing. However, as noted above, the vast majority of this research has taken place within a single context of either L1 or FL/L2 education and there has been less focus on the potential interactions between the two. Where links are made, they tend to suggest the one-way transfer of pre-existing skills and strategies *from* the L1 *to* the FL/L2. However, the X-LiST study was devised to explore whether the reverse may be equally (if not more) effective. Having provided an overview of the research design and intervention developed as part of the X-LiST study in Chapters 4 and 5 respectively, the focus of this chapter now shifts to the data. Whole-class trends will be explored over time to determine if and how the strategic writing approaches of students in the intervention group changed in German, French and English from Point 1 before any intervention took place, to Point 2 following a period of explicit LLSI in the German classroom only, to Point 3 following a further period of explicit, concurrent reinforcement of LLSI in both the English and the German classrooms. This chapter will consider evidence of planning strategies used *before* writing, problem-solving strategies used *while* writing and evaluation strategies employed to check work *after* writing. As a more objective measure of the effectiveness of strategy use, instances of errors and error correction will also be explored. This chapter draws primarily on data collected through the writing strategy task sheets (see Chapter 4) and builds further on ideas initially presented in Forbes and Fisher (2020).

Performance in Writing Tasks

Before examining the strategic approaches used by students, it is important first to consider any changes in their writing task performance over the course of the LLSI intervention. In order to explore performance in writing, each of the 336 writing tasks completed was given a mark out of 20 using a mark scheme that brought together key criteria used by both English and FL teachers (i.e. content, use of language and accuracy). In order to increase reliability, each task was double-marked and moderated by two experienced teachers of the respective language. As explained in Chapter 4, unfortunately it was not possible to collect comparison group data for French. Table 6.1 shows the mean task scores for each group, in each subject over time.

First, it is important to establish the comparability of the two groups at the beginning of the study. A Mann–Whitney test revealed no significant[1] difference in the distribution of scores between the intervention group and the comparison group at Point 1 in either German ($U = 221.000$, $z = -0.485$, $p = 0.628$) or English ($U = 196.000$, $z = -0.1.301$, $p = 0.193$). As such, the two classes can be considered reasonably comparable in terms of their written performance in these two subjects at this stage. However, it is acknowledged that there are other confounding variables that may influence writing development, such as vocabulary knowledge and general cognitive ability. As such, the MidYIS[2] scores of the students in each group were also taken into consideration. These standardised tests were taken by the students in the year prior to the start of this study and assessed four key cognitive areas of vocabulary, maths, non-verbal skills (such as spatial awareness) and general skills (such as proof-reading and perceptual speed). A Mann–Whitney test revealed no significant difference in the MidYIS scores of the pupils in the intervention group ($Mdn = 97$) and comparison group ($Mdn = 98$), ($U = 216.000$, $z = -0.365$, $p = 0.715$). This provides further evidence that the two groups were comparable at the beginning of the study.

At other points throughout the study, however, the difference between the scores of the two groups was significant, with the intervention group scoring higher than the comparison group. This was the case at Point 2 in German ($U = 152.000$, $Z = -2.115$, $p = 0.034$), Point 3 in German ($U = 114.500$, $Z = -2.845$, $p = 0.004$) and Point 2 in English ($U = 138.500$, $Z = -2.062$, $p = 0.039$). Over time, the mean scores of the intervention group improved consistently in each of the three subjects, particularly in the FLs.

Table 6.1 Mean scores for writing tasks

Language	Group	Mean score/20		
		Point 1	Point 2	Point 3
German	Intervention	11.79	13.67	13.69
	Comparison	11.04	11.43	10.34
French	Intervention	12.29	13.57	14.48
English	Intervention	12.50	13.05	13.35
	Comparison	13.70	10.73	13.95

This was not reflected among the comparison group where mean scores tended to fluctuate. A Wilcoxon signed ranks test[3] confirmed that the increase from Point 1 to Point 2 in German for the intervention group was significant ($Z = -3.019, p = 0.001$), as were the increases at both stages for French ($Z = -2.930, p = 0.002$ and $Z = -2.432, p = 0.013$, respectively).

The improvement shown here is in line with results from other studies that show the potential positive effects of strategy instruction on performance in writing (e.g. De Silva, 2015; De Silva & Graham, 2015; Macaro, 2001; Nguyen & Gu, 2013). However, of particular note here are the indications in the data that the benefits of the intervention of LLSI in the German classroom seemed to extend beyond just the German writing tasks to French and English as well. Nonetheless, due to the wide range of factors that contribute to writing scores, it is not possible to claim that any changes in performance that took place were necessarily the result of the intervention itself. It is therefore necessary to more closely examine the evolution of the students' strategic approaches over time. Given that strategies were grouped into planning, monitoring and evaluation strategies for the purpose of the intervention, findings will also be presented according to these groups.

Pre-Task Planning

The focus of this section will be on evidence of strategies used during any pre-task preparation completed by students, as identified on the first section of the writing strategy task sheets (see Appendix B). This planning phase covers a range of actions, for example: planning content items to include (e.g. bullet points of topics to be covered); language features (e.g. past tense, rhetorical questions); and drafting (e.g. at sentence/paragraph/text level). However, even though the students were encouraged to write down their pre-task thoughts and ideas, we have to bear in mind that some may have spent time thinking about their work without making any written notes which would therefore not have been captured on the task sheets. While it was not possible to capture such data at a whole-class level, this will be explored further in Chapter 8 which considers data gathered from the stimulated recall interviews of individual students. For the purpose of this chapter, however, planning was first analysed in terms of the students' engagement in planning, that is, whether any form of written planning was undertaken or not, and then in terms of the quality (i.e. the content) of their planning.

Engagement in planning

First, it is useful to consider the percentage of students who engaged in any form of written planning in each of the three languages over time, as shown in Table 6.2. The first point of note here is that at Point 1

Table 6.2 Percentage of students engaging in planning

Language	Group	Percentage of students		
		Point 1	Point 2	Point 3
German	Intervention	23%	81%	100%
	Comparison	39%	35%	27%
French	Intervention	33%	95%	77%
English	Intervention	95%	100%	85%
	Comparison	78%	68%	91%

students in both classes were much more likely to engage in planning in English than in German or French. This planning inevitably took various forms and plans in English were understandably longer than any of those in the FLs, but it seems fair to say that the students had developed and were using a range of planning strategies in their L1 which they did not automatically transfer to tasks in the FL classroom.

Looking at trends over time, in both FLs there was a dramatic increase in the number of students in the intervention group who engaged in planning following the LLSI. An exact McNemar's test confirmed that this increase was significant between Points 1 and 2 for both German ($p = 0.002$) and French ($p = <0.001$). The fact that very similar trends emerged for both FLs suggests that there was perhaps some form of implicit or automatic transfer taking place here, i.e. even though they were not being explicitly instructed to engage in planning strategies in their French lessons, many of them did so. Similar patterns were not, however, reflected in the comparison group where engagement in planning actually decreased over time in German. For English, there was less change in engagement with planning, perhaps due to this being very high to begin with. Yet, while there is evidence that the intervention group students were increasingly engaged in planning in the FLs over the course of the year, it is also worth asking whether there are any links between engagement in planning and performance, i.e. was their planning effective?

To explore this, a series of Mann–Whitney tests were conducted on the scores of those who did and did not plan their work. No significant differences emerged for English, probably due to the high percentage of students who planned at all time points. Yet there is some evidence to suggest that for German, the effectiveness of the intervention group students' planning improved over time. At Point 1 there was no significant difference between the scores of those who planned and those who did not. However, at Point 2 the median score for those who did plan was 14, versus 10 for those who did not ($U = 10$, $Z = -2.18$, $p = 0.031$). While there are undoubtedly many other factors that contribute to overall scores (some of which will be explored further below), this perhaps provides some indication of the potential benefits of effective planning. Nonetheless, it is also important to consider not only the number of students who planned, but also what and how they planned, i.e. the *quality* of their planning.

Quality of planning

The quality (or content) of planning was considered first in terms of the students' general approach to planning, for example, whether they chose to draft their work (at sentence/paragraph/text level). Then specific features of planning were also considered, such as the planning of content items, language features, structure, style, use of resources and goal-setting. It is acknowledged that the focus here is on the *evidence* of planning, which was identifiable through the writing strategy task sheets, and that the descriptors used here will often be underpinned by a combination of strategies used by each individual. For example, while 'goal-setting' could be considered as a strategy with a predominantly metacognitive function in itself, 'use of resources' will require a sequence or cluster of strategies e.g. students may first need to employ metacognitive strategies to decide which resource(s) to consult, followed by cognitive strategies to select and process the information they find. More in-depth examples of specific strategies used (as elicited through the stimulated recall interviews) are provided in Chapter 8. Table 6.3 illustrates the range of features of

Table 6.3 Features of planning (by number of students)

Language	German						French			English					
Group	Intervention			Comparison			Intervention			Intervention			Comparison		
Point	1	2	3	1	2	3	1	2	3	1	2	3	1	2	3
Drafting (paragraph)	2	0	0	1	0	0	1	1	0	5	5	3	5	0	0
Drafting (sentence)	1	10	9	1	3	2	2	10	5	6	4	1	2	0	2
Drafting (whole text)	0	1	2	0	0	0	0	4	2	4	1	3	0	0	0
Content items	4	14	16	6	6	4	5	7	11	15	19	16	17	15	20
Language features	2	12	8	1	4	0	0	11	8	2	2	9	5	0	4
Use of resources	0	3	10	0	1	2	0	1	2	0	4	1	0	2	0
Structure	0	6	7	2	0	0	0	9	2	3	15	10	2	6	2
Style	0	0	0	0	0	0	0	0	3	1	2	14	5	0	6
Translations	0	8	6	3	11	1	4	3	6	0	0	0	0	0	0
Goal-setting	0	2	9	0	0	0	0	1	4	0	1	8	0	0	1
Total	9	56	67	14	25	9	12	47	43	36	53	65	36	23	35

Source: Forbes and Fisher (2020: 333)

planning used by each class, at each point in time, in order to provide an overview of the number of students engaging in various planning strategies and the range of approaches used.

In terms of general trends, there is evidence that the explicit LLSI in the German classroom during Phase A of the intervention positively impacted the quality of planning among the intervention group students, not only in German but also in French and, to a lesser extent, in English. The most noticeable change over time occurred in the intervention group German tasks between Points 1 and 2, which was then maintained to Point 3. Similar trends were evident in the French tasks, which suggests that students were readily transferring a range of planning strategies from one FL context to another, without any explicit encouragement to do so.

For the English tasks at Point 1 it is evident that a higher number of students were using a larger range of strategies than in the FLs. This is not surprising when we consider that a much higher proportion of students were engaging in planning in English; however, it once again highlights the fact that students were not automatically using their pre-existing L1 planning strategies when writing in an FL. It is also interesting to note that after Phase A of the intervention in the German classroom there was evidence of an increase in both the frequency and type of planning used by the students in English. This is perhaps an indication of some level of FL to L1 transfer in relation to the *quality* of planning strategies. Overall, it seems as though the planning behaviours of the intervention group students in German, French and English were becoming more similar over time, particularly in relation to the planning of the content items, language features and goal-setting. However, while Table 6.3 provides a broad overview of a range of features of planning, it is worth exploring these more closely.

Drafting

A key feature of planning that was relatively common across the tasks was the use of drafting; this occurred variously at the level of the sentence, paragraph or the whole text. Drafting at sentence level (i.e. the inclusion of fully formed but isolated sentences on the pre-task planning sheet) was much more prevalent in the FL tasks. As a result of the more bottom-up approach to FL writing discussed in Chapter 2, the students were much more likely to approach writing in these languages at word and sentence level. Such drafting involved strategies such as planning which tenses to use and applying grammatical rules. Drafting at paragraph level often consisted of the drafting of an introduction or first paragraph of the final text and was much more prevalent in the English tasks. This involved additional strategies such as paying attention to style, and such an approach was often used in isolation. This suggests that these students may have initially intended to draft the entire text, yet after drafting the first one or two paragraphs decided simply to switch to working on the final version, possibly due to time constraints. At a whole text level, some students used the planning phase to write out their text more or less in its entirety, which was much more prevalent in English. Where this approach was taken, generally no other written planning was evident. With only one exception, the final texts remained more or less unchanged from the planned draft; occasionally students changed a word or corrected a superficial error, but they did not use this process to substantially change either the content, structure or overall quality of their work. As such, it could be argued that this was not necessarily a form of planning at all, but instead a rather time-consuming form of checking for accuracy.

Content items

The planning of content items in tasks generally took the form of bullet point lists of key topics to address. For example, when planning for the English travel writing task, one student noted that they would write about: 'Scotland: long walks, small roads, stormy sea, wet, wildlife, big estates …'. When planning for the first German writing task which involved introducing themselves, they wrote: 'Self + family (family members, me = hair, eyes etc.), live (England), Hobbies (sport – favourite sport), School'. Specific strategies employed here include thinking about relevance to the question and, in addition, elements of goal-setting. At Point 1 students were much more likely to plan content items in English than in the FLs. However, over time, the number of content items planned by intervention group students in both German and French increased gradually. This pattern was not mirrored among the comparison group students, where fewer content items were planned over time.

Language features

The planning of language features refers to explicit notes about particular grammatical structures or linguistic features that should be included in the text and, as such, also involves strategies related to goal-setting. For the English tasks examples of this include reference to 'rhetorical questions', 'first person' and 'metaphors', while for the FL tasks examples include 'reflexive verbs', 'connectives', 'past tense' and, for German specifically, 'weil [because] sentences'. At Point 1 this occurred very little in any subject; however, among the intervention group students the number of language features planned in both German and French rose significantly between Points 1 and 2 (with very similar trends in the two FLs). In fact, it seems as though patterns for the intervention group students in all three languages were gradually converging over time.

Use of resources

This includes where students indicated that they referred to books, textbooks, notes or dictionaries during the planning phase. This was usually in the form of explicit references to page numbers, use of direct quotations from books or, in the case of the FL planning, including translations of key items of vocabulary. As noted above, such actions will have involved the orchestration of a sequence or cluster of strategies such as, for example, deciding which resource to use, thinking about the most appropriate words and phrases to select, inferring meaning and applying grammatical rules. It is not surprising that the students used resources much more in planning the FL tasks compared to the English tasks given that they were more likely to encounter difficulties with language in particular. In German, the use of resources during the planning stage increased relatively consistently over time among the intervention group students, while it decreased over time in the comparison group.

Structure

Planning of structure was coded where students indicated what would be included in a particular section (e.g. the introduction or conclusion), made a note of the order in which points would be addressed, or structured their planning under headings (e.g. paragraph 1, paragraph 2, etc.). As with the planning of language features, at Point 1 this occurred very little in any subject; however, for the intervention group this rose after Phase A of the intervention across all languages, and particularly in English. Even though instances for English and French both dropped by Point 3, the peak at Point 2 may be indicative of students experimenting with their planning.

Style

Attention to style during the planning phase generally involved an awareness of the reader or the genre, such as adding humour or writing in an informal tone. It is not surprising that this was much more prevalent in the English tasks, yet there were a small number of examples in the FL tasks, such as 'write in first person "je"'. Instances of planning for style increased sharply among the intervention group students in English after Phase B of the intervention, suggesting that this may have been the result of the explicit LLSI in the English classroom.

Goal-setting

As mentioned above, there were elements of goal-setting strategies underpinning several of the other features. However, goal-setting was coded more broadly where there was evidence of students setting more global targets for themselves for the particular task at hand. For example, in the English diary-writing task one student sought to 'get the characters right for the diary to make sure they match the book', while a common goal in the FL tasks was to 'use different tenses'. At Point 1 this was not evident in any subject for either group. However, over time instances increased among the intervention group in all three languages, with changes being most notable following Phase B of the intervention; very similar patterns emerged across all subjects. As goal-setting could be considered as a more higher order planning strategy, the students perhaps required more time to become confident in setting appropriate goals and targets for themselves.

In relation to the features of planning discussed above, there is some evidence, therefore, to suggest that the planning behaviours of the intervention group in German, French and English were becoming more similar, or converging, over time, particularly concerning the planning of content items, language features and goal-setting.

Problem Solving While Writing

The focus of this section is on particular actions taken by students during the writing process which were often in response to problems that arose, such as using resources or asking for help from peers or the teacher. Such actions were self-reported by the students on the writing task sheets by underlining words or using the 'notes' section in the margin. As above, each of these actions is underpinned by the use of one or more strategies. For example, asking someone for help could perhaps be defined as a social strategy in itself; however, it may also involve a combination of strategies: it may require affective strategies to deal with the frustration of not being able to solve a problem, followed by metacognitive strategies activated to decide whether to ask for help and who to ask. Once the answer has been given, strategies with a cognitive function may also come into play as students process the response and make a judgement on how they can implement it into their writing. However, to avoid confusion, the broader label of 'strategy' is used below, with the caveat that for some individuals such actions will have involved a combination of strategies which were not necessarily captured at a whole-class level on the task sheets. Table 6.4 illustrates the instances of such strategies reported in each class, at each point of time. Instances of strategy use in this section and the following section are presented as the average number of instances per 1000 words, rather than the total number of coded references. This is to allow for more appropriate comparisons to be drawn between the various subjects, given that the FL tasks were, on average, around 120 words in length, while the English tasks averaged 450 words.

At all stages, the students engaged in such problem-solving strategies much more in the FLs than in the English tasks; this is to be expected considering that they were much less proficient in German and French and therefore much more likely to encounter problems when writing. However, it is also interesting to consider the trends that emerged within each language over time, particularly in the case of both FLs among the intervention group where the use of problem-solving strategies dropped between Points 1 and 2, and again between Points 2 and 3. This seemed surprising at first, as it would be expected that, as the academic year and

Table 6.4 Instances of problem-solving strategies (per 1000 words)

Language	German						French						English					
Group	Intervention			Comparison			Intervention			Comparison			Intervention			Comparison		
Point	1	2	3	1	2	3	1	2	3	1	2	3	1	2	3	1	2	3
Resources (other)	2.78	4.92	4.14	7.36	1.88	4.58	0.49	0.61	2.1	0	0.81	1.25	0.61	2.28	1
Resources (dictionary)	14.6	7.03	5.51	13.13	5.17	13.18	14.66	7.58	3.39	0.26	0.07	0.28	0.61	0.61	0.5
Resources (thesaurus)	0	0	0	0	0	0	0	0	0	0	0	0.14	0.2	0.15	0
Monitoring grammar	2.09	9.84	0.34	1.77	4.23	0.57	0.49	3.94	2.34	0	0.44	0	0	0.15	0
Avoidance	0.35	0.7	1.03	0.35	0.47	0	0.49	0	0	0	0	0.28	0	0	0
Ask help (peer)	1.04	0	1.38	2.84	0.94	1.15	1.24	0	0	0.45	0.15	0	0	0.15	0
Ask help (teacher)	5.91	0	0	4.61	4.7	1.15	3.02	0	0	0.34	0.37	0.14	0.71	0.15	0.2
Total	26.77	22.49	12.4	30.06	17.39	20.63	20.39	12.13	7.83	1.05	1.84	2.09	2.13	3.49	1.7

Source: Forbes and Fisher (2020: 334)

the level of difficulty increased, the instances of problem-solving strategies would also have increased or at the very least remained relatively consistent. However, upon closer examination, it seems as though the drop in the use of resources while writing corresponded to an increase in the use of resources while planning. This perhaps suggests a pre-empting of potential difficulties on the part of the students and a shifting of problem-solving behaviours, such as dictionary use, to the pre-writing stage, allowing more time to concentrate on fluency and accuracy during the writing process itself.

It also emerged that at Point 1 the students in the intervention group and comparison group were equally likely to ask a peer or a teacher for help in both German and English, but at Points 2 and 3 in German and Point 3 in English the intervention group students were less likely to ask for help and more likely to use resources to find the answer. This is perhaps indicative of the intervention group students becoming more independent learners in all languages over the course of the year – a key aim of LLSI. While similar patterns emerged once again in both German and French, suggesting a high level of FL–FL transfer, transfer to English was not particularly evident in the monitoring strategies examined. One possible explanation for this is the comparatively low occurrence of any form of monitoring strategies in the English tasks. This may simply be due to the fact that students, on the whole, tend to encounter fewer problems when writing in their L1 compared to an FL; however, it could also be evidence of proceduralisation of strategy use. As a result, it is not necessarily the case that the students were less engaged in monitoring while writing in English, but as they are much more experienced and proficient in this language, they may no longer be consciously aware of the strategies they are using and therefore may be unable to report on them.

Evaluation of Written Work

This section explores actions taken by students to check over their work either during or after writing and their focus while doing so as identified on the writing task sheets. In order to gather data about students' approaches to evaluation, there were several questions at the end of each task sheet which asked them to indicate whether they checked their work, how they checked it and what they checked for. This gives an indication of some of the specific evaluation strategies employed, such as checking spelling. It is acknowledged that analysis of evaluation strategies therefore relied more heavily on self-report data and, as such, may be considered to be less robust. The students may, for example, have felt inclined to give what they perceived to be the 'right' answer ('yes Miss, *of course* I checked over my work before I handed it in!'). However, when considered alongside more objective evidence (e.g. relating to accuracy as explored in the following section), it provides a valuable indication of students' perceptions of their evaluation strategies. It is also possible to some extent to check their responses; for example, if a student reported that they corrected spelling mistakes, then it is possible to check back to the task in order to establish whether this was indeed the case. Similar to the planning section above, evaluation was first analysed in terms of students' engagement in evaluation and then in terms of the quality (or focus) of their evaluation.

Engagement in evaluation

First, it is worth considering the percentage of students who reported that they engaged in some form of evaluation of their work, as shown in Table 6.5. One of the most striking features here is the very high proportion of students who reported having checked over their work, which is relatively consistent across all languages and time points. A series of McNemar tests confirmed that there were no significant differences between the proportion of students who reported engaging in any form of evaluation between Points 1 and 2 and Points 2 and 3 in any subject.

In terms of their approach to evaluation, around two-thirds of students at the beginning reported waiting until they had finished writing to check over their work. However, in both German and French the intervention group students became increasingly likely over the course of the year to check their writing as they went along either in addition to or instead of only doing so at the end. By Point 3, over three-quarters of students in German and French were taking this approach. Therefore, while the overall number of students engaging in evaluation may not have changed much, it seems that their approaches to checking their work did shift over time, implying a change in their strategy use. However, as stated above, it is possible that students may have indicated that they checked their work simply because they felt this was the 'right' answer. It is therefore necessary to further examine their use of evaluation strategies to establish any possible effects of the LLSI.

Table 6.5 Percentage of students who report engaging in evaluation

Language	Group	Percentage of students		
		Point 1	Point 2	Point 3
German	Intervention	74%	89%	86%
	Comparison	96%	86%	65%
French	Intervention	75%	94%	80%
English	Intervention	85%	89%	85%
	Comparison	96%	77%	68%

Quality of evaluation

The quality of evaluation was primarily considered in terms of what the students reported focusing on while checking over their work. Rather than providing a checklist (which might bias or restrict the students' responses), an open-ended question was included at the end of the writing task sheet. Table 6.6 illustrates the range of evaluation foci identified for each task by the number of students who identified them. It is interesting to note in the first instance that at Point 1 a higher number and wider range of evaluation foci were identified by both groups in English compared to German or French, even though the students were undoubtedly aware that they were more likely to make errors when writing in an FL. However, one notable commonality at this point was the predominance of checking for the more superficial features of spelling, punctuation and grammar. In fact, across all languages at Point 1 these three features alone accounted for around 70% of what the students said they checked for in their work.

In terms of change over time, as with the planning strategies, one of the most notable shifts that occurred was in the number and range of foci

Table 6.6 Focus of evaluation (by number of students)

Language	German						French			English					
Group	Intervention			Comparison			Intervention			Intervention			Comparison		
Point	1	2	3	1	2	3	1	2	3	1	2	3	1	2	3
Spelling	10	11	12	15	12	7	11	10	9	11	10	10	16	14	11
Punctuation	2	3	2	3	3	2	2	2	2	6	6	6	7	8	6
Grammar	3	9	10	6	6	6	3	7	7	6	7	6	13	7	4
Vocabulary	1	3	0	2	0	0	1	0	2	1	1	2	1	0	1
Content	0	0	3	0	1	0	0	2	2	1	1	3	1	0	0
Word order	2	3	4	0	4	2	1	3	0	0	0	0	0	0	0
Back-translating	0	0	3	0	0	0	0	0	0	0	0	0	0	0	0
Read through	1	1	1	5	3	3	2	0	0	2	1	0	1	1	2
Makes sense	0	2	4	5	1	2	1	5	4	4	4	4	4	4	3
Relevance	0	0	0	0	0	0	0	0	0	0	0	1	0	1	0
Structure	0	0	0	0	0	0	0	1	0	0	0	0	0	0	0
Checked by a peer	0	0	1	0	0	0	0	0	0	0	0	0	0	0	0
Checklist	2	1	12	2	0	0	0	1	4	1	1	7	1	0	0
Focused checking	1	1	3	0	0	0	0	0	3	1	2	4	0	0	0
Making improvement	0	0	2	0	0	1	0	1	1	0	2	4	1	0	1
Total	22	34	57	38	30	23	21	32	34	33	35	47	45	35	28

Source: Forbes and Fisher (2020: 336)

identified by the intervention group in German. This increased not only after Phase A of the intervention, but also continued to increase after Phase B. While the number of references to spelling, punctuation and grammar remained relatively static, the main increases related to what could perhaps be considered as more 'higher level' evaluation strategies. These include, for example, engaging in more focused checking where students identified particular areas where they had been prone to making errors (e.g. word order in German) and had checked specifically for those. Similarly, some students moved beyond simply checking what they had already written and sought to improve this further, for example, by adding additional sentences or replacing commonly used words with synonyms to broaden their use of vocabulary. It seems that, at least to some extent, the effects of Phase A of the intervention also transferred to French, which highlights once again the potential for FL–FL transfer. For the intervention group in English, an increase can also be observed; however, this occurred between Points 2 and 3, which would suggest that it was a result of the explicit LLSI in the English classroom during Phase B of the intervention rather than any implicit transfer from German. Yet, in English there was a small increase at Point 2 in the number of students engaging in more focused checking which suggests, perhaps, that transfer did occur for some, particularly given that such changes were not reflected among the comparison group students.

Evaluation of goals

Another feature that emerged as part of some students' evaluation process was an evaluation of the goals they had set for the task. Such comments were not mentioned in relation to the question about what they checked for, as examined above, but rather emerged in their responses to the final question on the task sheet which asked how they felt they had done in the task. Initially, this was designed to simply capture whether students felt positively or negatively about the work they had just produced. However, without being explicitly asked to do so, it also prompted some students to justify their success by evaluating the extent to which they had achieved their goals for the task; this could once again be considered as a 'higher order' evaluation strategy. While such comments were practically non-existent at Point 1, this rose to eight comments for German and five for each of French and English among the intervention group.

Many of the comments that constituted evaluation of goals involved a justification of how well individuals felt they had done in the task, often based on particular goals they had set during the planning phase. For example: 'I think I have done quite well as I have included many different structures like *weil* (because) and *wenn es* (when it is), also I have used connectives' (Intervention group student, German task 2). Other comments revealed students engaging in a more critical evaluation of their work by reflecting on ways it could have been improved further and implicitly setting goals for their next task, for example: 'I included some key points but

I overused *beaucoup* (a lot). I could have written some more' (Intervention group student, French task 2). It seems, therefore, that in addition to encouraging the intervention group students to check specific features of the task they had just completed, such as spelling or focusing on particular errors, the intervention of LLSI also encouraged some students to reflect more holistically on whether they achieved the goals they had set for themselves at the beginning of the task and, although perhaps less explicitly, to metacognitively set targets for their future writing.

Errors and Error Correction

While this section does not report on specific strategies per se, it provides a more objective measure of the *effectiveness* of a range of strategies used by students to improve the accuracy of their work, such as monitoring for accuracy, applying grammatical rules while writing and using resources such as dictionaries to check spelling. Errors that remained in the text were coded in four categories – grammar, punctuation, spelling and vocabulary – and instances where a student self-corrected an error themselves were coded under the same categories. It is certainly the case that any corrections could have been made at the time, as a result of monitoring while writing, or afterwards as part of the evaluation process. For the purpose of this section the exact point at which errors were corrected is not necessarily important in itself; rather, these corrections act as an explicit manifestation of students' (effective) strategic engagement with their writing.

Errors

Figure 6.1 shows the average number and type of errors made per 1000 words for each group in each language. This considers only those errors that remained uncorrected in the final text and not those that were made and then corrected by the student, which will be discussed in the next section. Given that the students were in the early stages of FL learning, it is to be expected that they would make considerably more errors when writing in French and German compared to in English. It is therefore not appropriate to make comparisons between the L1 and FLs here, but it *is* worth considering differences between the two groups and trends over time.

In terms of the difference between groups, results of a series of Mann–Whitney tests confirmed that there were no significant differences in the distribution of errors made by each class at Point 1, which suggests that both groups were comparable at the beginning of the study in terms of the level of accuracy of their work (German: $Z = -0.153$, $p = 0.879$, $r = -0.02$; English: $Z = -1.022$, $p = 0.307$, $r = -0.15$). However, at Point 3 in German ($Z = -3.183$, $p = 0.001$, $r = -0.49$) and at Points 2 and 3 in English ($Z = -2.115$, $p = 0.034$, $r = -0.33$ and $Z = -2.947$, $p = 0.003$,

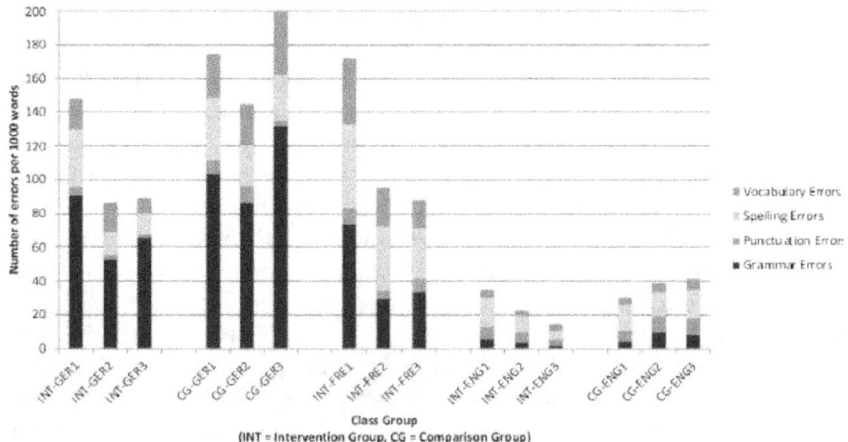

Figure 6.1 Frequency and type of errors (per 1000 words)
Source: Forbes and Fisher (2020: 325)

$r = -0.45$, respectively) the result is significant (with medium-large effect sizes), indicating that the intervention group made significantly fewer errors than the comparison group students in these tasks. To further explore trends over time, a series of Friedman's ANOVA tests were conducted, as shown in Table 6.7.

Results revealed that in all three languages for the intervention group there was a significant difference (i.e. reduction) in the number of errors made over time, which was not reflected in the comparison group. This was further investigated by conducting a series of post hoc Wilcoxon signed rank tests to look for differences between Points 1–2 and Points 2–3 and also to allow for calculation of effect size. The most striking changes among the intervention group in all three languages occurred between Points 1 and 2, following Phase A of the intervention, with large effect sizes (German: $Z = 3.493$, $p = < 0.001$, $r = -0.76$; French: $Z = -3.424$, $p = <0.001$, $r = -0.75$; English: $Z = -3.099$, $p = 0.002$, $r = -0.69$).

Table 6.7 Results of Friedman's ANOVA on errors made over time

Subject	Group	Friedman's ANOVA		
		F_r	df	p
German	Intervention	16.095	2	**<0.001**
	Comparison	4.023	2	0.134
French	Intervention	20.988	2	**<0.001**
English	Intervention	16.900	2	**<0.001**
	Comparison	2.455	2	0.293

Source: Forbes and Fisher (2020: 325)

Once again, the patterns for German and French were very similar, suggesting that the effects of a focus on accuracy as part of the LLSI in the German classroom were readily transferred to French. However, for English a drop in the number of errors also occurred after Phase A and this dropped further following Phase B. This suggests that this may be a key area where the students had transferred strategies for monitoring accuracy and checking their work, which were introduced initially in the German classroom, to their English writing, without explicit encouragement to do so. Errors then reduced further as the strategy instruction was reinforced explicitly in the English classroom. Given that the data collection took place over the course of an academic year, it may be argued that the accuracy of the students' work would have been expected to have improved over time as a result of normal classroom progression; however, the fact that such changes were not found among the comparison group suggests that the intervention of LLSI may have contributed, at least in part, to this improvement.

Error correction

In addition to considering the number of errors that remained in the final version of the writing tasks, it is also valuable to consider the extent to which students self-corrected their errors without guidance from the teacher. This may act as an indicator of students' level of metacognitive engagement with the text – i.e. if they were noticing and correcting errors themselves, either immediately after making them or while checking their work at the end, then this would indicate that that they were consciously evaluating the accuracy of what they had written. Once again, it is important to highlight that 'error correction' cannot be considered as a single strategy in itself, but rather it can represent the successful use of a combination of strategies. For example, a student may reflect on a verb they have just written, feel it may be incorrect, look it up in a dictionary or their grammar notes to find out how it is conjugated, and then apply the particular grammatical rule to their verb in order to correct it.

What emerged is that while the number of errors made by the intervention group decreased over time, the number of errors being self-corrected increased. Table 6.8 shows the percentage of errors corrected for both groups over time. Once again it is evident that students in both groups were relatively comparable at Point 1 and that students were more likely to notice and correct errors in English than in an FL. However, while the proportion of errors corrected by the comparison group decreased over time, it increased among the intervention group students to the point where they were able to self-correct over half of all errors made in English and around a quarter of all errors made in German and French.

It seems, therefore, that while previous sections of this chapter provided evidence that students in the intervention group developed their

Table 6.8 Percentage of errors corrected for each class over time

Subject	Group	Percentage of errors corrected		
		1	2	3
German	Intervention	14.80%	22.26%	26.70%
	Comparison	15.75%	16.98%	10.51%
French	Intervention	11.53%	18.02%	23.13%
English	Intervention	22.11%	30.80%	50.89%
	Comparison	33%	18.61%	21.86%

Source: Forbes and Fisher (2020: 326)

strategy use over time at each phase of the process (i.e. in relation to planning, monitoring and evaluation), this in turn correlated with an increase in task scores and an improvement in the accuracy of their writing. This provides evidence at a whole-class level to suggest that the intervention of LLSI was not only effective in the German classroom where it was initially implemented, but that the effects also transferred to French and English.

Conclusion

Evidence from the X-LiST study has been presented in this chapter which suggests that, at a whole-class level, the intervention group students developed both the quantity and quality, or effectiveness, of their strategy use over the course of the LLSI intervention. Although this occurred to some extent in all three languages, it was most evident in German, which is not surprising given that this was the context in which the LLSI was in place for the longest period of time. This overall development of writing strategies as a result of explicit LLSI is in line with findings from other studies (e.g. De La Paz & Graham, 2002; De Silva & Graham, 2015; Macaro, 2001; Nguyen & Gu, 2013).

As in the study by Nguyen and Gu (2013), the intervention group students in this study developed their strategy use particularly in relation to planning. There was a significant increase in planning among these students in both German and French after Phase A of the LLSI and in both FLs there was also an increase in the planning of content items, language features and goal-setting following Phase A. Similar changes were evident in English following Phase B, particularly in relation to the planning of language features and goal-setting. Similar improvements in the quality of planning following a period of LLSI were also reported by Sasaki (2002) and De La Paz and Graham (2002) in FL and L1 contexts, respectively. In the current study, there was similarly evidence of the intervention group students shifting problem-solving behaviours to the pre-writing stage, rather than disrupting the writing process by engaging in this while writing.

Another key area where the LLSI impacted students' writing was in relation to the number of errors made and corrected. The intervention group made significantly fewer errors over time in all subjects and this was significantly less than the comparison group in German at Point 3 and in English at both Points 2 and 3. This corresponds to an improvement in accuracy found by Macaro (2001) in a similar FL classroom context. Although not a strategy in itself, such an improvement in levels of accuracy provides an objective measure of a range of monitoring and evaluation strategies used successfully by the students. In particular, they took an increasingly thorough and more focused approach to checking over their work, especially following Phase A in the FLs and Phase B in English (in line with Sengupta, 2000). The findings presented in this chapter in relation to students' strategy development therefore not only provide further evidence of the positive effects of the intervention of LLSI across languages, but also pave the way for a more in-depth exploration of cross-linguistic transfer which forms the focus of the next chapter.

Notes

(1) A significance level of 0.05 was used for all statistical analyses.
(2) MidYIS (Middle Years Information System) is a baseline assessment designed to measure developed ability and underlying potential, rather than what has been taught in school (Forster & Metcalfe, 2010).
(3) A Wilcoxon signed-ranks test is an appropriate non-parametric test to examine differences between two related samples (Field, 2009).

7 Exploring the Cross-Linguistic Transfer of Strategies

As discussed in Chapters 3 and 6, there is evidence in the wider literature on language learning strategies and also in the X-LiST study to suggest that strategy instruction can be beneficial both to students' development of strategies and to their performance in writing. However, given that the key area of interest of both the X-LiST study and of this book as a whole is on the potential *transfer* of such strategies between L1 and FL contexts, this chapter is devoted to an in-depth exploration of this issue and builds on data presented initially in Forbes and Fisher (2020). Indeed, as suggested by Skehan (2008: 411), '*any* significant theory of second language acquisition has to account for transfer, and for transitional stages'. To this end, it is first necessary to explore the phenomenon of cross-linguistic transfer within the literature. This chapter, therefore, begins with an overview of language transfer from the L1 to the FL, as it was originally conceived, and then considers this in light of more recent developments relating to multicompetence which have led to an increasing interest in reverse transfer from the FL to the L1. Multiple directionalities of transfer are then further explored by drawing on the empirical findings from the X-LiST study, namely, the transfer of existing writing strategies from the L1 to the FL, between the two FLs, and from the FL to the L1.

The Phenomenon of Cross-Linguistic Transfer

Originally derived from within a behaviourist paradigm, language transfer (Odlin, 1989) was first conceptualised in the field of L2 acquisition as the influence, or more accurately the interference, of a learner's pre-existing L1 knowledge and habits on their L2/FL learning and performance. Such links between the L1 and additional languages have long been recognised: Vygotsky (1962: 110), for example, commented that a child 'can transfer to the new language the system of meanings he already possesses in his own'; transfer was identified by Selinker (1972) as one of the five central processes characteristic of interlanguage; and Cummins

(1979: 222) proposed a linguistic interdependence hypothesis whereby the development of certain competencies in the L2 'is partially a function of the type of competence already developed in L1'. He hypothesised an underlying proficiency which is common across languages and which allows for the transfer of literacy-related skills provided a certain level of proficiency has been reached. Although in principle Cummins' interdependence hypothesis does not preclude transfer from the L2/FL to the L1, he attributed the lack of transfer in this direction to the absence of motivation and exposure to an L2/FL environment (Cummins, 1981). Similarly, for many years within the literature on transfer and cross-linguistic influence, the focus also remained predominantly on the influence (or interference) of the L1 on the L2. Even though there was some acknowledgement of the possibility for 'the effects of L2 on the L1' (Sharwood Smith & Kellerman, 1986: 1), this was primarily depicted in terms of L1 attrition following a prolonged period of time living and working in an L2 environment.

In exploring some of the factors that influence such transfer, Kellerman (1977, 1979) identified the importance not only of the learners' knowledge of the target language and the structure of their L1, but also of their perceptions of the (typological) distance between their L1 and the target language, which he referred to as psychotypology. While attempts to more 'objectively' determine typological distance between languages in themselves have been made by linguists who undertook an analysis of structural similarities and differences, psychotypology instead focuses on how languages are perceived by their users or learners and how this, in turn, influences learning – that is, it is the *perceived similarity* (rather than the genetic relationship) that influences the learner's processing and production of the target language (Rast, 2010). This is of particular relevance to the X-LiST study, given the different perceptions of L1 (English) and the FLs (German and French) held by both teachers and learners as discussed in Chapter 2. While the focus here was not on *typological* distance per se, nonetheless this raises interesting questions about the intersections of perceptions of similarity/difference and transfer.

Yet, most existing studies that explore the phenomenon of transfer tend to focus on the transfer of linguistic systems such as lexical items, syntax, morphology or phonology, rather than exploring possibilities for transfer at the level of strategy development and use. In fact, Kellerman (1991) initially dismissed the importance of teaching learning strategies at all in the L2/FL classroom, suggesting that learners would already have developed strategies from the learning of their L1 and could simply transfer these to the L2/FL. While there is indeed some evidence to suggest that such transfer can take place and that writing strategies developed in the L1 can be used in the L2 (e.g. Jones & Tetroe, 1987), it is important to bear in mind that strategies transferred from the L1 may not necessarily be effective. Vann and Abraham (1990), for example, found that unsuccessful L2 learners in their study used a wide range of strategies, although they were often applied inappropriately. Additionally, as explored by Flower and Hayes (1981) and Bereiter and Scardamalia (1987), many writers are considered to be 'unskilled' or 'novice' writers even in their L1 and therefore may not have developed effective strategies which they can transfer to the learning of a new language. Indeed, even skilled L1 writers may not '*automatically* transfer the strategies they learn in one context to a different situation' (Rubin *et al.*, 2007: 147).

Transfer from a multicompetence perspective

More recently, the original conceptualisation of transfer, as outlined above, has been felt to be too restrictive and focus has gradually shifted beyond a preoccupation with a unidirectional form of transfer from the L1 to the L2/FL, to a more dynamic and multidirectional notion of transfer incorporating L3 acquisition and multilingualism. Much of the early research into transfer, as discussed in the previous section, was developed in relation to the acquisition of a single L2, but this has since been extended to L3/LX contexts (e.g. Bardel & Lindqvist, 2007; Cenoz, 2001; De Angelis, 2005). As such, it has been recognised that learners often have knowledge not only of their L1 and the particular target language being learned, but also of other languages in their repertoire. This has not only opened up further opportunities to consider the ways in which transfer may *positively* influence language development, but has also allowed for the exploration of multiple directionalities of transfer. For example, if an L1 speaker of English already has knowledge of Spanish and is now learning Italian, there is perhaps more chance that they will transfer knowledge between Spanish and Italian than from English. Learning Italian, in turn, may also influence their processing of and performance in Spanish. Such a reinterpretation of transfer was supported by the advent of the concept of multicompetence, which advocates that L1 and L2 (and indeed any additional languages) are not separate systems delineated by clear boundaries, but are instead merged or overlapping systems which exist in one mind and are continuously developing (Cook, 2002, 2008). The assumption, therefore, is that someone who knows two or more languages perceives language differently from a monolingual speaker and, as such, has opened up new avenues of research into 'reverse transfer' from the L2/FL to the L1 and other forms of transfer (Cenoz *et al.*, 2001; Jarvis & Pavlenko, 2010). This is in line with recent developments in the field of translanguaging which similarly has at its core 'the fluid and dynamic practices that transcend the boundaries between named languages, language varieties, and language and other semiotic systems' (Li, 2018: 9). As mentioned in Chapter 1, while translanguaging does not constitute the framework in which the current book is situated, there are undoubtedly areas of intersection here that are worth acknowledging.

However, such developments call into question the use of the term 'language transfer'. Such a notion has been criticised by Cook (2002: 18) for implying that something is moved 'from one place to another', a sentiment echoed by Hall *et al.* (2006: 232), who instead conceive of constantly developing language knowledge as 'reorganisation, redirection, expansion and transformation'. This has led several L2 writing researchers, such as James (2008) and Kobayashi and Rinnert (2012) to instead situate their work within a 'transfer of learning' framework. Transfer of learning originated in the fields of cognitive and educational psychology and occurs when learning in one context either enhances learning in another, which could be considered as 'positive transfer', or undermines learning, which could be viewed as 'negative transfer' or interference. Through a multi-competence lens, Rinnert *et al.* (2015: 215) argue for a more dynamic view of transfer and advocate that 'the transfer of learning construct is appropriate when looking at transfer of writing features across languages because literacy (reading and writing) is acquired largely through instruction and practice, even in L1'.

Transfer of learning

Perkins and Salomon (1988: 25) developed a theory of transfer of learning which has been used to examine its role 'in the teaching of thinking' – there are therefore strong links to be made here to metacognition. They distinguished between two mechanisms for transfer, referred to as high-road and low-road. Low-road, or reflexive, transfer is characterised by the semi-automatic triggering of well-practised responses and routines in circumstances where there is considerable perceptual similarity to the original learning situation. This is most likely to occur where the contexts are very similar (near transfer), for example, when students taking an exam must respond to problems of a similar kind to those previously practised in class (Perkins & Salomon, 1988, 1994). High-road transfer, on the other hand, involves deliberate, reflective thought in abstracting skills or knowledge from one context and seeking connections with others and is therefore less likely to take place automatically. This is more likely to take place between contexts that, on appearance, seem remote from one another (far transfer) (Perkins & Salomon, 1988, 1994; Salomon, 2001). There are clear parallels here to Kellerman's (1977, 1979) work on psychotypology in relation to language transfer. He similarly suggested that learners are more likely to engage in transfer between contexts (or languages) that they perceive as being relatively similar.

Within a school environment, on the surface it might seem reasonable to consider the context of writing in the English classroom as being sufficiently similar to that of writing in the FL classroom to trigger low-road transfer. However, as considered in Chapter 2, not only did the students in the X-LiST study perceive these two contexts to be distinct, but they are often also positioned very separately within the curriculum. The perceptual difference here would suggest that any transfer that does take place could be considered as far transfer which can be difficult to stimulate. Within their framework, Perkins and Salomon (1994) highlight 'metacognitive reflection' as a key technique for encouraging high-road transfer. This link between metacognitive strategy use and transfer of learning is further advocated by James (2006: 157), who emphasises that 'when students think relatively deeply about their own learning process and outcomes, they are thinking in a way that is consistent with high-road transfer'.

As Rinnert *et al.* (2015) have observed, the vast majority of existing research into transfer of learning within the field of L2 writing involves the transfer of L2 writing knowledge and skills across different genres rather than across different languages. James (2008, 2009, 2010, 2012), for example, conducted a series of studies into the transfer of learning from English as a second language (ESL) and English for academic purposes (EAP) writing courses at a university in America to English writing in other academic courses. He found that while transfer within this context is possible, it is not inevitable; transfer can be influenced by perceived similarity of task type and level of difficulty and is also more likely to occur in some disciplines, such as the humanities and social sciences, than others such as the natural sciences. Similarly, while transfer from one L2 context to another L2 context can be inhibited by task differences, it can also be stimulated by factors such as an explicit instruction in a task prompt.

L2/FL to L1 transfer in writing

Applying the transfer of learning theory to the field of strategy research, it would therefore seem logical that FL teachers, who have the opportunity to focus more explicitly on language learning strategies and to develop the metacognitive reflection which facilitates high-road transfer, are in a strong position to contribute to the overall improvement of writing standards in both the FL and the L1. As stated by Pomphrey (2000):

> The very act of consciously learning a language in the classroom implies a distancing of the self from the usual unconscious habits of everyday communication. This means that explicit knowledge about language as a system is likely to be more easily extracted from the foreign language learning experience than from learning which takes place in the L1. (Pomphrey, 2000: 278)

However, as Rubin *et al.* (2007) state, there is limited research on transfer of strategies in L2 acquisition. One of the few studies that does addresses possible links between strategy use in different languages is that conducted by Mitits and Gavriilidou (2016). The researchers here compared the language learning strategies used by adolescent multilinguals in Greek (their L2) and English (which they were learning as an FL) using the Strategy Inventory for Language Learning (SILL) questionnaire (Oxford, 1990). They found statistically significant correlations between the strategies used by participants in both Greek and English and therefore suggest that 'multilinguals tend to transfer strategies between a second language and an additional language they are in the process of learning' (Mitits & Gavriilidou, 2016: 304). However, while the assumption here is that the participants transferred their L2 Greek strategies to FL English, it is also possible to question the extent to which the reverse may also have occurred or, indeed, the extent to which they may have used similar strategies in their respective L1s. Nonetheless, this study raises interesting questions about general strategy use across different languages.

There are very few studies, however, that explore links between strategy use across languages in relation to writing in particular and it is necessary, therefore, to look beyond the field of strategy research to a small number of studies that have been conducted into the L2/FL to L1 transfer of writing *features* more generally. In these studies, the focus for analysis is predominantly on the written product rather than the writing process, but they nonetheless provide interesting insights into to the notion of transfer. Berman (1994) conducted an intervention study to examine the bidirectional transfer of writing skills between Icelandic (L1) and English (FL) among 126 upper secondary school students in Iceland. His participants were allocated into three groups: one received explicit writing instruction in the L1 classroom over the course of six 50-minute lessons; one received equivalent instruction in the FL classroom; and a third comparison group received no such intervention. The students completed pre- and post-intervention essays in both languages which were scored according to their organisation, fluency and length. Interestingly, the analysis revealed that the students' transfer of essay writing skills was actually more evident from the FL to the L1 than from the L1 to the FL, and results suggest that the latter may have been limited by a lack of grammatical proficiency in the FL.

Kecskes and Papp (2000) similarly focused on secondary school aged learners and more specifically on the influence of learning an FL (English, French or Russian) on L1 (Hungarian) writing. They hypothesised that multilingual development, even in a classroom setting, can enhance L1 development and result in multicompetence. They grouped their participants according to intensity of FL instruction: the immersion group received instruction in other curriculum subjects through the medium of the FL; the specialised group received seven to eight hours of FL instruction per week; and the third comparison group received two to three hours of regular FL instruction per week. The students completed writing tasks in both the L1 and FL three times over a two-year period and the focus of analysis was on the use of syntactic structures, specifically the use of complex sentences and the frequency and type of subordinates. However, this was not designed as an intervention study; teachers conducted regular classroom instruction throughout the study with no enhanced focus on the development of writing skills in any of the language lessons.

The authors found that FL learning can facilitate L1 development significantly; however, they concluded that not all kinds of FL learning lead to the development of multicompetence. Just as Berman (1994) found that the transferability of writing skills requires a certain level of grammatical proficiency, Kecskes and Papp (2000: 52) similarly concluded that 'multicompetence seems to begin to develop only after a certain threshold in the subsequent language is reached'. In their study, gains were evident among both the immersion and specialised groups, who showed evidence of more sophisticated written planning, improved construction of subordinate clauses and more complex embedded sentences in the L1. However, this was not evident among the comparison group who had less intensive exposure to and lower proficiency in the FL. This led the authors to propose what they refer to as a 'common underlying conceptual base' which is 'when knowledge or skills acquired through one language system become ready to be used through the other language channel(s)' (Kecskes & Papp, 2000: xvi). To some extent, this is a broader reinterpretation of Cummins' common underlying proficiency hypothesis through a multicompetence lens which, in this case, presupposes bidirectionality of transfer, but which similarly suggests that a threshold of proficiency in the FL must be reached in order for the FL to affect the L1.

A series of studies were also conducted by Kobayashi and Rinnert (2007, 2008, 2012) and Kobayashi (2009) into the bidirectional transfer of argumentative writing competence of university-level EFL students in Japan, some of whom had also spent time studying overseas. The essays produced by the participants were analysed in terms of the use of rhetorical features, discourse types, organisational structure and discourse markers. The findings from these studies would seem to support the above hypothesis and suggest that the influence of writing training and experience 'is bidirectional across L1 and L2 writing' (Kobayashi & Rinnert, 2012: 113). They found that L2/FL to L1 transfer occurred particularly in relation to the overall argumentation structure of essays and the inclusion of specific features such as counter arguments. However, as with the studies examined above, the authors note that such transfer is not automatic and is heavily influenced by language proficiency and the amount and content of writing experience. They reported that participants who had spent time studying overseas in an L2 environment were more likely not only to transfer this training to their L1, but also to be more consciously aware of such transfer. Motivation and the affective traits of the writer similarly played a key role in facilitating transfer between languages.

Consequently, although these studies did not specifically consider instruction in learning strategies, they provide some evidence to suggest that certain writing skills developed in the L2 or FL classroom can potentially have a positive impact on L1 tasks. However, it is important to note that such transfer is not inevitable. As highlighted by the studies above, transfer can be influenced by individual factors such as the learner's language proficiency, experience of writing instruction and motivation, and by contextual factors such as the teaching environment and the writing tasks themselves. The importance of explicit and consistent instruction in encouraging transfer across languages has also been emphasised (Berman, 1994; James, 2006). This was instrumental in informing the explicit instruction at the heart of the development of the X-LiST intervention, as explored in Chapter 5.

Evidence of Strategy Transfer from the X-LiST Study

In light of the research discussed above, one of the key aims of the X-LiST study was therefore to explore the cross-linguistic transfer of writing strategies which were explicitly developed in the German FL classroom to both a second FL (French) and the L1 (English). Data regarding strategy development at a whole-class level were reported in full in Chapter 6; however, a brief summary is provided below which highlights the various forms of transfer that emerged in the study.

Transfer of planning strategies

- Taking into consideration both engagement in planning and the quality of planning produced by the students, it was evident at the beginning that the students were much more likely to plan (and to produce longer plans) in English. At Point 1 in English, for example, most students planned content items related to the task. Yet, they did not transfer such behaviours to their German and French writing where there was little or no evidence of any planning strategies used at Point 1.
- The intervention of LLSI seemed to have had the greatest impact on the FLs in terms of both the number of students engaging in planning and the quality of their planning. For example, students increasingly planned content items and language features to include in their work (which involved an element of goal-setting) and also increasingly made use of resources during the planning phase. While effects were most noticeable in German, which is not surprising given that this was the context in which the intervention took place, there was also evidence of a high level of transfer to French across almost all of the features of planning explored.
- In English, although the LLSI did not seem to affect students' engagement with planning which was already high to begin with, it did seem

to impact the quality (or content) of students' planning. This was particularly evident in relation to increased instances in the planning of language features, style and goal-setting. Even though most of these changes in English seemed to occur after the explicit phase of LLSI in the English classroom, it seems that even after Phase A (which only took place in the German classroom), students were beginning to use a wider range of strategies which is perhaps indicative of some level of FL to L1 transfer.

Transfer of problem-solving strategies

- At the beginning of the study there was little commonality between problem-solving patterns in English and the FLs given that students were much more likely to encounter problems when writing in German and French.
- Changes in German over the course of the LLSI mostly consisted of a shift of problem-solving behaviours (such as dictionary use) to the pre-writing stage, rather than disrupting the process by engaging in this during the writing task itself. Similar patterns emerged once again in both German and French, suggesting a high level of FL to FL transfer.
- There was little evidence of FL to L1 transfer of problem-solving strategies. One possible explanation for this is the comparatively low occurrence of any form of monitoring strategies in the English tasks. This may simply be due to the fact that students, on the whole, tended to encounter fewer problems while writing in their L1 compared to an FL; however, it could also be evidence of proceduralisation of strategy use.

Transfer of evaluation strategies

- The intervention did not seem to greatly impact the number of students who engaged in checking over their work, but did seem to influence the quality of evaluation as those who did check their work were increasingly taking a more thorough and focused approach.
- Following Phase A of the intervention in the German classroom the largest gains occurred in German, and once again there was some evidence to suggest that transfer occurred quite readily to French, albeit to a slightly lesser extent. For example, in both FLs students increasingly identified specific areas where they felt they were likely to make errors and used strategies to check for those (for example, word order in German or adjective agreement in French).
- In relation to English, most changes in the quality of students' evaluation strategies occurred after Phase B of the intervention, which would suggest that it was the result of the explicit LLSI in the English

classroom. However, there is perhaps some evidence to suggest that some FL to L1 transfer did occur for a small number of students. One student, for example, in the second English task specifically mentioned checking back to her plan and goals as a strategy while evaluating her work by using this as a 'checklist'.

Transfer of strategies relating to errors and error correction

- Patterns of errors and error correction were examined in order to provide evidence of the effectiveness of a range of strategies used by students to improve the accuracy of their work, and also as an indicator of their metacognitive engagement with the text either while writing or after writing.
- Analysis revealed that this seems to be a key area where a range of strategies introduced in the German classroom during Phase A not only increased levels of accuracy in German, but effects also seemed to transfer to both French and English. Over the course of the year the number of errors made by the intervention group across all subjects decreased, while the number and range of errors self-corrected by students increased.

Multiple Directionalities of Transfer

Based on the data from the X-LiST study, it is possible to identify multiple directionalities of transfer with regard to students' strategy development and use. As shown in Chapter 6, at the beginning the students took different approaches to writing in English and the FLs and, as such, it seems as though they were not necessarily transferring their pre-existing L1 writing strategies automatically to an FL. What did emerge throughout the study, however, were very similar patterns of strategy development for both German and French, suggesting a high level of transfer *between* the two FLs. There were also instances of reverse transfer (from the FL to the L1), particularly in relation to the quality of planning and strategies relating to improving levels of accuracy. Each of these are explored in turn below in order to highlight the dynamic interactions between strategy development and cross-linguistic transfer.

Limited transfer of pre-existing strategies from the L1 to the FL

As outlined above, transfer between languages was originally conceptualised as the predominantly monodirectional transfer of pre-existing L1 linguistic systems or skills to the L2/FL. At one point this led some scholars (e.g. Kellerman, 1991) to dismiss the importance of explicitly teaching strategies in the L2 or FL classroom, suggesting that learners would simply transfer their existing L1 strategies. While such a viewpoint has since been rejected, there are a number of studies that report a similarity in the writing process for individual learners between the L1 and FL (e.g. Cumming, 1989; Jones & Tetroe, 1987; Pennington & So, 1993). Yet, this was not particularly evident in the findings of the X-LiST study. Given the differences between the students' baseline approaches to writing in English and the FLs at Point 1, it seems as though learners were not necessarily transferring their L1 writing strategies automatically to an FL. This was particularly evident in relation to the planning phase; the students were much more likely to engage in any form of planning in English than in German or French, and to produce much longer plans and use a wider range of planning strategies in English (in line with Albrechtsen, 1997). To some extent this could be explained by the difference in task type and expectations, i.e. in English the students were expected to generate longer texts which, by extension, may entail the need to think more explicitly about structure and argument in advance. Nonetheless, there are still a range of planning strategies that are appropriate to the FL tasks and that could have been used in this context, such as, for example, planning bullet points of content items, planning to use particular items of vocabulary or grammatical structures, setting targets, etc.

Differences also emerged in relation to problem-solving strategies as the students used more problem-solving strategies when writing in the FLs (in line with Roca de Larios *et al.*, 2006). This is not surprising given that they were more likely to encounter problems in the FLs. Yet, it is also important to consider the possibility that the students were similarly engaging in a substantial number of problem-solving strategies when writing in English. However, these may have become proceduralised over time and, as a result, may not have been self-reported during the data collection process. If this were the case, then the students' lack of awareness of their L1 problem-solving strategies would not only have inhibited them from self-reporting such strategy use, but would also have made it difficult for them to consciously transfer them to an FL context. Such proceduralisation is also evident in comments made by students in the initial set of interviews that they have to 'think more' when writing in German than in English (see Chapter 2) or, more accurately, that they are more consciously aware of their thought processes when doing a task in an FL.

It was in relation to the use of evaluation strategies that the students seemed to take a more similar approach across languages at the beginning. At Point 1 the students were almost equally likely to report checking over their work in English and the FLs and to take a similar approach to checking over their work. However, in terms of the focus of checking, a higher number and wider range of evaluation foci were identified by students in English than in the FLs, particularly strategies related to checking for accuracy. The students were therefore utilising a range of strategies in their L1 that they were not necessarily transferring independently to an FL context.

One possible explanation for this is that such L1 to FL transfer could be considered as 'far' transfer (Perkins & Salomon, 1988, 1994) as a result of students' distinct conceptualisations of writing in the two language contexts. This is in line with Kellerman's (1977, 1979) work on psychotypology which suggests that learners are more likely to engage in transfer between contexts (or languages) which they perceive as being relatively similar. As outlined in Chapter 2, English was viewed as a 'core' subject and therefore was seen as more important than the FLs at the beginning of the study. Task types and expectations were also thought to be very different. The students' perceptions of the two language contexts as being superficially distinct therefore perhaps hindered them from engaging in the deliberate and explicit connection making required to facilitate highroad transfer at this stage.

The ease of FL to FL transfer

The predominant focus of the X-LiST study, however, was on the transfer of strategies explicitly developed in an FL context to both another FL and the L1 following an intervention of LLSI. This allows for a more multidirectional discussion of the phenomenon of transfer. The most evident form of transfer to emerge from this study was undoubtedly the FL to FL transfer, where students readily transferred strategies explicitly developed in the German classroom to their French writing. This occurred relatively consistently throughout the year and across all categories of strategies. For example, in both German and French, students increasingly used planning strategies related to planning content items, language features and the structure of their work over time. In both FLs, strategies related to problem-solving while writing, such as dictionary use and asking for help, also showed similar trends in their decline over time. It was suggested that the first of these indicated a pre-empting of problems and a shift of related strategies to the planning phase, while the latter suggests that students were becoming more independent learners in both FLs. Even though the development of strategy use over time was perhaps more marked in German, patterns for French followed a very similar trend. Given that the students did not receive any explicit LLSI in the French classroom, nor were they explicitly instructed in the German classroom to transfer their strategies to French, this process seemed to occur relatively automatically.

In addition to similar trends in strategy use, students' conceptualisations of writing in German and French also evolved in a similar way throughout. Even though the two subjects involved writing in different languages about different topics, the students considered the teaching approaches and activities to be more comparable and seemed to associate German and French as 'FLs' and therefore as distinct from writing in English. Due to the similarity in the ways in which the two FL contexts were perceived and the relative ease with which students seemed to be able to transfer strategies between them, from a transfer of learning perspective this could be considered as 'low-road' or 'near' transfer. This is defined by James (2007: 99) as 'an unconscious process that requires that the learning task and transfer task are superficially similar enough to trigger this unconscious transfer'.

Such findings regarding the ease with which the intervention group students seemed to implicitly transfer strategies between two FL contexts also provide evidence to support Cenoz's (2001: 8) suggestion that 'the processes used in third language acquisition may be very similar to those used by L2 learners'. This is of particular relevance for the X-LiST study where the students were at a relatively similar stage of learning in both FLs and there is therefore little or no chronological or hierarchical distinction to be made between the L2 and the L3 here. It is not known, however, the extent to which such FL to FL transfer of strategies would hold true if the two FLs were at very different stages of proficiency or, indeed, if there was a greater typological distance between them.

The development of FL to L1 transfer

While there was little evidence of L1 to FL transfer at the beginning of the X-LiST study, as outlined above, the reverse was examined in two different forms: first, in relation to any FL to L1 transfer which took place *implicitly* following the intervention of LLSI in the German classroom only in Phase A; and secondly, whether a period of *explicit* reinforcement of the LLSI in the English classroom during Phase B facilitated such transfer.

Although the implicit FL to L1 transfer was not as evident as the implicit FL to FL transfer explored above, there was evidence to suggest that students did indeed transfer some strategies developed in the German classroom to English tasks without any explicit encouragement to do so. This was particularly evident in relation to the quality of planning, as indicated by an increase in both the frequency and range of planning strategies used by the intervention group, and an improvement in accuracy, as demonstrated by both a decrease in errors made and an increase in errors corrected. Following Phase A of the intervention, students also started to perceive planning and revising as being more important in English, as well as in the FLs. This suggests that the LLSI during Phase A may also have implicitly influenced their perceptions of the importance of certain criteria in English. Such examples of implicit FL to L1 transfer were also detected by Berman (1994), Kecskes and Papp (2000) and Kobayashi and Rinnert (2007) in relation to essay organisation skills, use of syntactic structures and transfer of rhetorical features, respectively. However, it is important to note that Kecskes and Papp (2000) only found such evidence of transfer among learners with a threshold proficiency in the

FL. The participants of the current study, on the other hand, were relatively beginner language learners. A possible explanation for this is that Kecskes and Papp's study did not involve a specific intervention of writing instruction. Therefore, perhaps their hypothesis may hold true for the *automatic* transfer of writing features between languages; however, the findings from the X-LiST study suggest that even relatively beginner or low-proficiency FL learners can be taught in such a way as to encourage transfer.

Similarly, it is important to consider why the X-LiST study provided stronger evidence of implicit transfer from the FL to the L1 than from the L1 to the FL, given that both can be considered as forms of 'far' or 'high-road' transfer due to the students' distinct perceptions of the two language contexts. High-road transfer, by nature, does not necessarily take place automatically (as shown by the limited L1 to FL transfer at the beginning), yet Perkins and Salomon (1988) highlighted metacognitive reflection as a key technique for encouraging it. It would seem, therefore, that the intervention of LLSI in the German classroom during Phase A not only helped to develop students' awareness and use of writing strategies in the FL context, but also facilitated metacognitive reflection when writing in English. This provides an indication that the FL classroom, where learners are more aware of being consciously and actively engaged in thinking about language, may be a key context for developing transferable metacognitive writing strategies which can also benefit the L1 (Forbes, 2018).

Yet, similarities between strategy use in the FLs and L1 were even more evident in the X-LiST study when the links were made explicit in *both* contexts. Following Phase B of the intervention, there was a further increase in the number and range of planning strategies used by the intervention group in English, further improvement in the accuracy of their writing and an increase in the number and range of evaluation foci identified by students. In addition to strategy use becoming more similar across the two contexts, evidence also suggests that, over time, the intervention group students' conceptualisations both of what they considered to be important and of their own performance in L1 and FL writing seemed to converge more closely over time, which in turn may have facilitated transfer. This is particularly striking when compared to the comparison group where strategy use and attitudes were more likely to remain static or, in some cases, to diverge over time.

However, given that the LLSI took place in both the English and German classrooms during Phase B of the study, it is important to acknowledge the possibility of bidirectionality of transfer here. Even though fewer changes took place in German and French at a whole-class level following Phase B of the intervention, there were indeed a few examples of L1 to FL transfer in the final tasks. For example, there were a few instances of students planning aspects of style in relation to the final French task, which was an element of the LLSI focused on predominantly

Table 8.1 General characteristics of the writer profiles (Forbes, 2019b, p.452)

Writer profile	No. of students	General characteristics arising from the data
The strategic writer	7	• Consistently achieved well in both English and FL writing tasks; • Used a range of writing strategies effectively; • Demonstrated a self-awareness of their strategy use.
The experimenter	7	• Generally average achieving students in both English and FL writing tasks; • Showed evidence of experimenting with their strategy use over the course of the year and a willingness to try different approaches.
The struggling writer	6	• Consistently lower achieving students in both English and FL writing tasks; • Did not particularly enjoy writing and generally found it difficult; • Made use of a range of strategies, however, not necessarily effectively.
The multilingual writer	2	• Spoke an L1 other than English; • Showed evidence of using their L1 strategically when writing in a variety of ways.

their disposal and were also approaching English from a different perspective, it was of interest to explore the extent to which this influenced their trajectories through the LLSI. Consequently, a fourth category, 'the multilingual writer', was added with a view to exploring this further.

Table 8.1 provides an overview of the general characteristics of each profile along with the number of intervention group students associated with each. It is acknowledged that not all students neatly fitted into one of these categories and that some may have shifted over time. However, based on the evidence from the writing tasks and interviews, Table 8.1 provides a useful indication of the general characteristics arising from the data that were broadly shared by each group. The following sections will explore each of these profiles in turn, exemplified through an in-depth focus on one student who tended to typify that profile. In line with the presentation of data in Chapters 6 and 7, this chapter will similarly reflect on the strategies used by each student during pre-task planning, while monitoring their writing (including problem-solving strategies) and when evaluating their work.

The Strategic Writer (Carissa)

The first type of writer that will be discussed is referred to as the 'strategic' writer. Such writers emerged as being relatively effective strategy users from the beginning. One typical example such writers is Carissa,[1] a native English speaking student in her third year of learning German and her fifth year of learning French at school. However, it is important to note that any French input received by students in primary school (which accounts for the first two years of instruction here) was minimal and delivered by non-specialist teachers. As such, it is fair to say that Carissa, like her peers, was at a relatively similar stage of learning in both French and German in spite of the apparent two-year disparity. She was a conscientious and consistently high-achieving student across all of her subjects in school and she was on the school's list of 'able, gifted and talented' students in languages. Her French teacher commented that she was a hardworking student and that her 'written and oral work is excellent if given the time to think of her answers'. Similarly, her German teacher spoke of her as an ambitious, confident student who 'wants to achieve top marks' and who would 'approach anything in her stride and just get on with it'. She was also portrayed by her English teacher as an independent student, and he praised her written work, saying that 'she's very thorough, writes at some length and she's got a good command of style, she clearly takes her time'.

In her writing tasks Carissa improved consistently over time in both FLs and maintained her high scores in English throughout. She said herself that she quite enjoyed writing in all three subjects, although she reported feeling more confident with writing in English. Unlike the majority of her peers, she preferred longer tasks in English, 'like essays and stuff' and seemed to find these easier than creative writing tasks. She liked the structure of more formal tasks and preferred being able to take her time when writing. When writing in German and French, she sometimes reported experiencing the frustration of 'wanting to say more than I can say' yet, conversely, she also seemed to enjoy the challenge of this, and felt a sense of accomplishment in seeing how much she was able to write. However, although she was very capable of writing in all subjects, at the beginning of the year she seemed to conceptualise L1 and FL writing in very distinct ways:

> I think I see them as quite different, cause like when I'm writing in, yeah, like when I'm writing in French and German like, I just feel like I'm being marked on like, like, spelling and like words and stuff, but with English it is more about what you're writing, so I do think they're quite different and I treat them differently.

Planning strategies

At the beginning of the study, Carissa was among the minority of students who engaged in written planning in all three subjects and, interestingly, she took a relatively similar approach across the languages by focusing on the main content items she would include. This may be an indication that she was already actively transferring strategies from one language context to another. However, while she did engage in planning in the FLs, she perceived this as being less important than planning in English, as she felt the focus was on 'the words and stuff rather than like, the plot', and admitted that the content items planned in German and French were largely based on what the teacher had mentioned when setting the task, rather than her own ideas.

In relation to her English planning, Carissa commented in the first interview that she had recently changed her approach. While for the first task she planned key content items and the overall structure in bullet point form, she said she had previously completed full drafts of her writing 'and then like, would go through it and change it'; these changes generally consisted of 'little things' like spelling, grammar and rephrasing sentences to make them sound better. However, she felt that this approach was very time consuming and therefore decided to change to be 'more organised'. Such a change in approach was entirely self-initiated and occurred before the start of the study, suggesting not only that she was aware of the strategies she used, but also that she was constantly evaluating their effectiveness and making deliberate changes when necessary – one of the key features of the 'strategic writer'.

In the second set of tasks Carissa spent more time planning in all of the subjects; however, the quality of her planning improved most in German where, in addition to content items, she also planned to include a range of language features and drafted some complex sentences. In addition, she commented that she referred back to her plan a lot more when writing. It is also worth noting that in French, Carissa chose on this occasion to draft the complete text in the FL, which is the approach she had previously taken in English. However, unlike some of her peers who adopted this approach, she did make changes and improvements to the draft before writing the final version. This once again suggests that she was able to actively transfer existing L1 approaches to an FL. In the second English task, planning was still mostly content driven, although it was much more detailed than before and she acknowledged that she not only 'spent more time planning', but 'couldn't have written it without the plan this time'.

In the final tasks, Carissa's approach to planning in all three subjects was very similar and included an even wider range of features and strategies than in previous tasks. Interestingly, she planned elements of style in both English and French, which involves using the strategy of considering tone and audience. For example, for the final English task she noted in her planning that the style should be 'informal, quite conversational' while for the French task she should write 'in first person "je"'. As style was more focused on in the second part of the intervention in English lessons, this may represent a further example of implicit L1 to FL transfer. At the end of the study, Carissa acknowledged that she felt she was becoming more effective in planning across all subjects and was increasingly referring back to her planning when writing. It seems, therefore, that in relation to planning, from the beginning Carissa not only utilised a range of strategies, but also evaluated and adapted these accordingly. However, over the course of the intervention she further developed and refined her strategy use, and seemed to be able to readily transfer these from one language context to another, particularly from the L1 to the FL.

Monitoring and problem-solving strategies

In relation to strategies used *while* writing, Carissa employed a range of monitoring strategies across all subjects relatively consistently over the course of the year. In terms of problem-solving, throughout all of the tasks she showed evidence of being an independent learner and was much more likely to look a word up in the dictionary or check her notes than to ask someone else for help, even at the beginning. When looking up a word she reported first deciding whether to use the bilingual dictionary or the glossary at the back of the textbook. She then used strategies to locate the word and looked at example sentences to ensure she had inferred the correct meaning. She then activated a combination of grammatical strategies to assess whether or not she needed to change the word to make it fit her sentence, for example, by conjugating a verb provided in the infinitive or adding a plural agreement to an adjective. She also frequently reported using avoidance as a problem-solving strategy; for example, in the final German task she could not remember how to say that computer games were hard, so instead opted for the alternative phrase '*ich bin nicht so gut*' (I am not so good) in order to convey the same message.

Carissa also reported closely monitoring the content of her writing as she went along by using the strategy of regularly looking back at her planning. For each task she crossed out or ticked planned items as she included them and seemed to be continuously thinking about how to include certain features; for example, in relation to the final English task she said: 'I made sure that I used the rhetorical questions that I wanted to use, but it was mostly as I was writing it that I was checking that I'd used them.' Carissa was also strategic in her language of thought for the FL tasks. In the first German task, for example, she mentioned that she had generally thought first about what she wanted to say in English and then tried to put that into German, but admitted that this may have been why 'there was some of the stuff that I didn't know how to say'. In the next task, therefore, she changed her approach and her starting point was to think first about the German she knew and then to build on that.

In addition to monitoring content, Carissa carefully monitored the accuracy of her work while writing; however, she admitted engaging with this to a much greater extent in the FLs. In German and French, she focused much more on the accuracy of 'the words and spelling', whereas in English she felt that 'you don't have to think about it as much, cause like, you already know it'. Yet, even though she may not have been as aware of monitoring the accuracy of her work in English, she was undoubtedly doing so throughout in all her subjects. In all tasks, the number of errors she made was well below the class average and, in addition, they decreased over time, suggesting that her monitoring strategies were becoming more effective.

Carissa also showed evidence of seeking to improve her work. In all tasks, but particularly in English, she engaged a lot in reformulating and rephrasing words and sentences, not because they were incorrect, but because she thought of a better way to say it; for example, in the first English task she changed the phrase 'the wondrous display' to 'the stunning display' because she thought it sounded better. This demonstrates engagement with the task while writing and an ongoing desire to improve her work. All in all, in terms of monitoring while writing, there is no evidence to suggest that the particular strategies she used changed significantly over the course of the year, but from the decrease in errors made over time, it seems as though she was increasingly using these strategies in a more focused and effective way.

Evaluation strategies

Carissa similarly emerged as a strategic learner in her approach to the evaluation of her work, which was very systematic from the beginning. Her general approach to checking over her work was to wait until she had finished writing in order to avoid interrupting the 'flow', which she did consistently across all of the tasks. Once again, this suggests that Carissa was readily transferring tried and tested strategies from one language context to another. However, although engagement in checking over her work remained consistent throughout, what did change somewhat was the focus of her evaluation. After the first tasks she tended to focus predominantly on checking for superficial spelling and grammatical errors because 'it's the sort of thing you can easily like, look over'. However, following the second set of tasks in all subjects she seemed to use more specific strategies to look for particular types of mistakes and to focus on more actively trying to improve the quality of what she had written. In German, for example, she checked particularly to make sure she had put the verb at the end of her 'because' sentences and also said that she wanted to see if she could 'say things better'. Similarly, following the English task she commented that, in addition to checking her spelling and grammar, she wanted to 'see if there were better ways to phrase the things I had written and to see if the writing flowed'. It seems, therefore, that this may be an area where Carissa demonstrated an ability to transfer strategies from the FL to the L1, without explicitly being encouraged to do so.

Carissa's refinement of her evaluation strategies continued through to the final task where, in all subjects, she not only checked for accuracy, but the process of checking over her work also led to changes to the content and structure. She felt that she checked through her German task 'more this time than usual' and, after reading through her English task 'to make sure it sounds right', decided to make some changes to the structure of her paragraphs in order to improve her work. It seems, therefore, that similar to her planning and monitoring, her evaluation strategy use did not change dramatically, yet seemed to become more refined and effective over the course of the year. It is also worth noting that Carissa's perceptions of her strategy use throughout seemed to align very closely with what she actually did; for example, not only did she say she checked over particular aspects of her work more thoroughly, but it is evident from the reduction in errors and from the type of corrections she made that she was in fact doing so. Such an astute sense of awareness regarding her strategy use is another characteristic feature of the 'strategic' writer.

Cross-linguistic transfer of strategies

While at the beginning of the year Carissa perceived L1 and FL writing to be very distinct, at the end of the year she acknowledged that, although she still thought about them differently: 'I think that the way that I approach them is probably more similar, like, I do more planning with French and German and stuff.' Her perception of having changed her approach more in relation to the FL tasks is also reflected in the consistent improvement in her FL scores over time. When asked further about the development of her writing, Carissa highlighted the influence of her L1 strategies on her FL writing, suggesting that: 'things that I've done in English have helped in French and German.' This was particularly evident in her approach to the first set of tasks, where she used similar strategies across all three subjects. Such L1 to FL transfer was also evident in her use of drafting in the planning of the second French task and in her consideration of style in the third French task. However, she said in the final interview that she felt this transfer worked 'both ways' and that some elements practised more in the FL classroom also helped her in English.

The Experimenter (Chris)

The next type of writer to emerge is referred to as 'the experimenter'. These writers tended to be average performing students who demonstrated a willingness to experiment with and try new strategies in order to improve their performance. An example of such a writer was Chris, a native English speaking student in his third year of learning German and fourth year of learning French. Throughout his first two years at secondary school he consistently scored around the average or just below average in class tests and exams in German, French and English. His English teacher said that he 'will ask for help where he needs it, but often that will be more to do with things like spellings and so on rather than help with structuring and style'. He was also described by his French teacher as a 'typical middle ability child' and his German teacher commented that he was quite confident and had potential, but was often distracted, tended to rush his work and to 'get in a muddle very quickly'.

Chris himself said that he quite enjoyed writing in English and felt reasonably confident with this, because 'you already know [the language], so English is fine to write in'. However, he preferred tasks that involved writing 'from your own point of view' and he did not enjoy writing essays based on a text 'cause you have to go back and look for quotations and stuff like that'. On the other hand, he perceived German and French as 'quite hard to write in' and said he often struggled to write longer texts. Like Carissa 'the strategic writer', he expressed frustration that 'you're always doing, like, write ups of yourself and you're not, you haven't got the ability to do, to write up your own experiences cause you don't know how to say everything'. The different task types and his limited language proficiency in German and French led him to conceptualise L1 and FL writing very differently at the beginning of the study and, as a result, he approached them in different ways. In terms of his performance in the three sets of writing tasks, Chris showed the most improvement in scores in German between Points 1 and 2, and he also improved consistently over time in English. The reasons behind such improvement will be explored further below.

Planning strategies

Over the course of the year, Chris experimented with and developed his use of planning strategies across all languages. For the first English task, which was completed before any form of strategy instruction took place, he engaged in some planning which consisted of 'just a few bullet points' related to the content of his writing. Yet, he did not consider this to be particularly important or useful and explained that: 'I didn't think there was much planning to do.' This was also evidenced by the fact that only half of his planned points were ultimately integrated into the final text. However, even though his planning in English was limited, it is important to note that he did not transfer his pre-existing L1 strategies to German and French, where he did not engage in any written planning at all for the first tasks. His belief was that 'planning's not really that useful for German'. It is also worth noting that his goals for both tasks were concerned purely with content rather than language, as he aimed to include details about his 'pets' in the German task about himself and his family and 'the journey' in the English task on travel writing.

However, by the second set of tasks following Phase A of the intervention in the German classroom, Chris had started to experiment with a range of different planning strategies introduced during the LLSI. This was particularly evident in German, where Chris's planning included a range of content items, language features and drafting of sentences in the target language. His goals shifted beyond the content itself, as he commented that he also aimed to include some particular grammatical structures they had recently covered in class. Interestingly, he described the overall structure for his text as 'kind of what I do in English … if I mention the points in the introduction I usually do a paragraph on each one', which suggests that he was starting to more actively make comparisons between writing in the different subjects and to transfer certain elements from one to another. Such evidence of an increasing level of metacognitive engagement with his approach to writing can be (at least to some extent) attributed to the intervention in the German classroom. It is also worth noting that Chris's planning for this task was mostly written in German, which he deliberately chose to do 'cause then it's already there in German and I didn't have to think what it was'. However, in French he experimented differently with his planning and this time used only English to write a draft of his text which he would later translate, although he did make a note of which tenses he would use throughout.

In the second English task Chris commented that he did 'much more planning' this time, and his plan was certainly more developed than in the first task. He included consideration of a wider range of features and this time all of the aspects he planned were integrated into the final text. Interestingly, he also specified that his English text should be written in the 'past tense' given that it was a diary entry. This is an aspect that students would perhaps be less likely to consciously plan in their L1. Given that the strategy instruction at this point was only taking place in the German classroom, this may therefore represent some FL–L1 transfer. In addition to engaging in more planning, Chris was also beginning to view this process as more important in each language. He felt that planning this time made it 'easier to write the actual piece, cause with no plan you haven't really got anything to go back and look at what your initial ideas were', and commented that 'planning helps to get a better mark at the end'. However, this comment also suggests that at this stage Chris seemed to evaluate the success of his strategy use according to the marks he received and, by extension, seemed to rely on the teacher to evaluate this for him, rather than engaging in self-evaluation as Carissa 'the strategic writer' had done.

Chris's experimentation with planning strategies continued to the third task where he showed evidence of using more similar planning strategies across all three languages, such as making a checklist of content items and language features. In German, he chose this time to draft his ideas using English, as he had previously done for the second French task. After having tried various approaches, he decided that this was what worked best for him: 'I think I found it easier cause I'd written it all in English before, it was easier to translate rather than thinking of it all in German without planning.' This provides evidence that he was starting to engage in more independent reflection on his strategy use and was adapting this accordingly.

Chris also made a more concerted effort to include particular language features 'like "because" sentences' and wanted to include a range of past tense sentences 'because Miss said that I needed to improve'. This shows that he was starting to use feedback from previous tasks in order to set himself goals for improving in future tasks. Similarly, for the final English task, Chris opted to make a checklist of bullet points which he said 'helped a lot' and, once again, all of his planning was integrated into the final text. At this point, he had received the LLSI in both the German and English classrooms which seemed to help to further facilitate the development and transfer of planning strategies between the languages.

Monitoring and problem-solving strategies

In relation to monitoring and problem-solving strategies, Chris demonstrated increasing levels of engagement with his writing over time. In the first set of tasks, when Chris encountered a problem his first reaction was to ask the teacher for help. This happened particularly in relation to translations of vocabulary in German and French and the spelling of words in English. However, if the teacher was not available, he would refer to a dictionary or his notes instead. Yet, it is worth noting that he reported difficulty at times with choosing the correct word, suggesting that his inferencing and grammatical strategies were perhaps not very effective at this stage. In the first German task he also commented that he aimed to make his work 'as simple as I can' in order to avoid possible problems. Yet, by the final tasks Chris was much more likely to try a range of strategies to solve a problem himself and would only ask the teacher as a last resort. In German, for example, he explained that he had to look up the word 'expensive' in the dictionary, because he did not know it 'and couldn't think of anything else to substitute it for'. It seems, therefore, that he was using a range of strategies to solve the problem independently, rather than just asking the teacher immediately.

He also increasingly engaged in monitoring the content of his writing throughout by looking back at his planning while writing, something which he admitted on several occasions to finding 'really helpful'. Additionally, in the final tasks he was making much more of a conscious effort to use strategies to vary his language and vocabulary use. For example, he was going to include the phrase '*Netflix ist interessant*' (Netflix is interesting) in his German task, but decided to change this to '*Netflix ist sehr nützliche*' (sic) (Netflix is very useful), as he realised that he had already used the word '*interessant*'.

Chris also became increasingly effective at monitoring his work and in noticing and self-correcting errors, particularly in German and English where the number of errors made decreased considerably for each task. In German and French, the biggest improvement in terms of accuracy took place between Points 1 and 2, which corresponds to the explicit LLSI in the

German classroom, and of particular note was his improvement in spelling. However, there was also a small improvement in the accuracy of his English writing following Phase A of the intervention, which may suggest some transfer of monitoring strategies from the FL. Yet, the biggest change for Chris took place in English following Phase B, which highlights the importance of explicit instruction and scaffolding for Chris in the development of his strategy use.

Evaluation strategies

Checking over his work was something that Chris said that he engaged in from the beginning in all subjects, yet he placed much more importance on this in English. This was in line with general class trends:

> In English I check much more…I think it's cause it's our main language so, and English they say is quite an important subject for you to have, so I see that as more important than checking over in German, although I do, I would check it over, I just wouldn't check it over as much as I would in English. (Interview 1)

However, his approach to checking over his work evolved over the course of the year. In the first set of tasks in all subjects he waited until the end to check, but for the second and third FL tasks he checked as he went along. It was not until the final task, however, that his approach changed in English and, instead of waiting until the end as he did for the first two, he checked both as he went along and again at the end.

The focus of his checking also evolved over the year. In the first tasks his prevailing concern in all languages was with surface-level accuracy and correcting 'silly mistakes', and in English also with the factual correctness of his writing. Yet, over time this became much more focused and he began to use the strategy of checking back to his plan to ensure he had included all the main points and taken on board feedback from previous tasks. In German, for example, he specifically checked his 'because' sentences, as he said that in his previous task he had 'lost marks from not doing a sentence structure right', while in English he looked for 'the sort of words that I'd spelt wrong before'. For German from the second task onwards and in English in the final task these changes in approach corresponded to a reduction in the errors being made, suggesting that his approach to checking his work was indeed becoming more effective over time. However, this highlights once again that, for Chris, the explicit phase of the LLSI was instrumental in encouraging him to experiment with his strategy use. Similarly, he attached increasing importance to the checking process and following the second German task he commented that 'once I've checked it over then usually I get a better mark than when I haven't checked it over'. For Chris, therefore, the correlation between strategy use and achievement was very explicit.

Cross-linguistic transfer of strategies

Given the difference in Chris's approaches to writing in English and the FLs at the beginning of the study, it seems as though he was not necessarily transferring his pre-existing L1 writing strategies automatically to German and French. Yet, it seems fair to say that the intervention of LLSI not only helped him to develop his metacognitive writing strategies over time, but also to transfer them between the FLs and L1. For Chris, the most notable changes in his strategy development took place in German and French after Phase A of the intervention and in English following Phase B. In comparison to some of the more 'strategic' writers in the class, he therefore seemed to rely more heavily on the explicit instruction and scaffolding and commented that he found the resources used in class valuable as a 'kind of prompt'.

However, even though the majority of changes in each subject took place following the explicit LLSI, there was also some evidence that he was beginning to transfer some strategies from German to English following Phase A of the intervention without being deliberately encouraged to do so, particularly in relation to the quality of his planning and evaluation strategies. In the interview following the second set of tasks, Chris hinted at this implicit transfer by stating:

> Well, I didn't use to do much planning but I do some now, and I didn't use to check it over in French and German but now I've started checking it over and it's started to work a lot more cause I'm getting better marks, so if I've done something and my marks have improved then I'd start to do that more [...] Then I was trying some of the things out in English as well, sort of reading through afterwards to check, make sure my spellings are OK and stuff like that. (Interview 2)

This comment is particularly striking given his much higher level of linguistic proficiency in English; it seems that his experience of engaging in metacognitive strategy use did, in fact, have a positive effect on his English writing strategies.

While at the beginning of the year Chris seemed to conceptualise the nature of L1 and FL writing, and likewise his approaches to L1 and FL writing, as being very distinct, by the end of the year he perceived them as being much more similar and he was beginning to view some aspects of writing as cross-linguistic, rather than as specific to L1 or FL contexts:

> I think they've got much closer now, doing these types of things, because you're planning more, you're using the same sort of sheets so it kind of shows you that they do relate to each other, so you can use the same things, so like reading through afterwards, checking for spelling and structures, they're all the same, they're all in French, German and in English. (Interview 3)

The Struggling Writer (Zoe)

The next type of writer to be discussed is referred to as the 'struggling' writer. Such writers tended to be lower performing students who generally did not enjoy writing and who found it difficult, particularly in the FLs. However, that is not to say that these students did not engage in strategy use; in fact, they often made use of a range of writing strategies, yet unlike the first two types of writer discussed above they did not necessarily do so effectively. A typical example of such a writer was Zoe, a native English speaking student who, like Chris 'the experimenter', was in her third year of learning German and her fourth year of learning French in school. She consistently scored below average in class tests and exams in German, French and English, but her results were particularly low in German. She was described by her English teacher as a student who didn't think things through for herself; she tended to ask 'a lot of questions about how to do it', yet often didn't manage to fulfil the demands of the task in the work she produced. Her French teacher commented that she was a student who wanted to do well but didn't quite know how to go about it, while her German teacher said that in lessons it seemed as though 'she'd sort of switched off' and did the minimum amount of work.

Zoe admitted herself that she felt she was 'not very good at languages' and, in particular, 'really bad at German'. She did not enjoy German and felt that it was 'hard to understand... much harder than French cause I've been doing it less than French'. She lacked confidence in her FL writing, especially German, and felt that 'everybody else gets it' while she struggled to understand. Like some of her peers, Zoe commented that the FL writing tasks were more restrictive and 'you have to do what you have to do, like in the subjects that they set you' using only a limited amount of language. On the other hand, she described writing in English as being 'OK', but she did not enjoy it as much as she previously had in her first two years of secondary school because 'it's got harder'. She preferred creative writing rather than essays because she liked to have the freedom to 'go wild with everything' and felt that there was less chance that she could 'get it wrong'. In relation to the writing tasks, Zoe's scores remained low in all three subjects throughout. Possible reasons for this will be explored below.

Planning strategies

In relation to planning, Zoe took an approach to the first set of tasks very similar to Chris 'the experimenter' by engaging in some planning in English but none whatsoever in German or French. For English, she listed a few bullet points of what she wanted to include but said that she did not refer to this while writing and, like Chris, did not integrate all of the planned points into her final text. She commented that her planning for English normally consisted of such 'lists' or 'spider diagrams'; however, she would only do this if she was writing 'a story or something' but not for other writing tasks or essays.

In the second set of tasks Zoe started to engage in some planning in German. However, like her English planning before, this consisted of general content-related bullet points which she said she did not develop further because 'it was hard to think about what to write'. In English her approach to planning changed to drafting the first two paragraphs of her text. She commented that she intended to draft the whole text, but when she got halfway through, she decided to start on the final version so she could finish more quickly. In the final version she made a small number of superficial changes to spelling and grammar from the draft, yet she did not use this process to make any significant improvements to her work. The drafting process in this case functioned more as a form of superficial error correction than planning. She said she took this drafting approach because she had 'always done it like that... I do it in rough and then change a few bits and do it neat'. Yet, evidence from her previous work suggests that this was not actually the case, which suggests a discrepancy between her perception of her strategy use and her actual strategy use. Similarly, the justification that she had 'always done it like that' may suggest that she was less willing to deliberately change her approach.

For the final set of tasks Zoe engaged in planning in all three subjects. In German, she continued to plan some key content items and also wrote down a number of translations; however, of the 12 vocabulary items she included, two were incorrect, two were misspelt and only five were integrated into the final text. This suggests that, although her planning had developed to include key content points and vocabulary, these seemed to consist more of isolated ideas, and she did not necessarily engage with this process strategically to think about how they would be incorporated into the final text. Her approach to planning in French was similar to German, although once again only a small proportion of the content items planned were integrated into the text itself. In English, she moved away from the drafting approach she used in the second task and instead made a 'checklist' of the key content points she wanted to include, reverting back to what she had done for the first task. However, unlike the first task, this time she integrated all of the points she planned into the text itself, suggesting that she gave more consideration to her planning and used the strategy of referring back to it while writing. This may indicate that, for English at least, her planning was beginning to become slightly more effective and useful.

Monitoring and problem-solving strategies

In relation to monitoring and problem-solving strategies while writing, Zoe also shared some of the same characteristics as Chris 'the experimenter' in her approach to the first set of tasks. It is unsurprising that Zoe encountered more problems when writing in German than in English or French as she did not enjoy the subject and found it difficult. Her approach throughout was to think first about what she wanted to say in English, yet she admitted that she then struggled with translating it into German. Like Chris at the beginning, her first reaction when she got stuck was to ask the teacher or a friend for help – in fact, in the initial tasks she made no attempts to find the answer herself.

However, in the second and third set of tasks, Zoe attempted to use a wider range of resources and problem-solving strategies. In the second German task, for example, she did not know how to say 'I walk my dog', so made the decision to look up 'walk' in the dictionary. She located the entry in the dictionary and at this point needed to activate a combination of strategies in order to select the correct entry by looking at examples and grammatical indicators (such as whether the word was a noun or a verb), and to incorporate it into her sentence. However, she acknowledged that she 'didn't know which one to put' so simply took the first translation provided which was the noun '*Spaziergang*'. The sentence she ultimately produced, '*ich Spaziergang mein Hund*' (*sic*), was therefore inaccurate. So, while Zoe was willing here to use the skill of using a dictionary in order to try to solve a problem independently, she lacked the strategies to carry this out successfully. Similarly, in the third task she asked a friend how to say 'do' in German. When her friend did not know, she then tried to look it up in the back of the book but couldn't find it, although it later transpired that she had been looking in the wrong place. Both of these examples indicate that, although Zoe was attempting to use resources to solve problems more independently in German, she did not fully understand how to do so. This highlights the importance of providing such students with more step-by-step guidance in the strategies needed for successful dictionary use.

In addition to trying to make use of resources to help when she got stuck, Zoe also frequently used avoidance as a problem-solving strategy; for example, when she couldn't work out how to say something in French, she said 'I just left it', and in German she 'didn't know so just went on to the next bit'. However, while Carissa 'the strategic writer' had also made use of avoidance as a strategy, she generally sought alternative ways to convey the same meaning by rephrasing a sentence. Zoe, on the other hand, seemed to use it as justification for giving up. This is a useful example of how the same strategy – in this case, avoidance – can be used successfully by one student in order to find a way to overcome difficulties and complete the task in a different way, yet unsuccessfully by another who uses it as a way to avoid completing a particular aspect of the task at all. There were also two occasions in the earlier FL tasks where Zoe did not know the word she wanted to use in German or French, so decided to 'just put the English'. This is an example of using her L1 as an avoidance strategy. However, although Zoe's attempts to use a range of more independent problem-solving strategies in German and French were not always effective, she seemed to have more success in English. As in the FLs, in the first English task Zoe relied heavily on asking others for help, particularly with the spelling of words; however, in the final task she commented that 'now I try to work it out myself or I get a dictionary'.

In relation to monitoring the overall accuracy of her work, Zoe did not notice or self-correct any errors in the first tasks in German or French and only a very small proportion of errors in English. However, in the second English task she made fewer errors and commented that she had made a deliberate effort 'to spell everything right' by more carefully paying attention when she was writing. Similarly, in the final English task she self-corrected a larger proportion of her mistakes and commented that she 'didn't want to spell anything wrong, so I kind of checked the words as I went along...the ones I was unsure about'. This seems to have been successful as in the final English task there was only one spelling error in her work. Yet, this was not evident to the same extent in the subsequent FL tasks where the overall number of errors remained comparatively high.

All in all, it seems as though any monitoring that Zoe engaged in while writing in all subjects was predominantly focused on superficial elements of the text, in particular, spelling. She seemed to engage little with monitoring the content of her work and even where she had made a plan, she often did not refer back to this while writing. As a result, she admitted in relation to both the English and German tasks that she often 'didn't write very much' and didn't manage to include everything she wanted to. It seems that in some cases, even though she was aware that she had missed particular points, she was not either willing or able to do anything to address this at the time.

Evaluation strategies

In relation to evaluating her work, Zoe commented that she did not check over her writing in German or French at all for the first two sets of tasks as she didn't think there was any point. However, she did say that she engaged in checking over her English writing as she went along in each of the tasks. The main focus of her checking for English tasks was spelling, as discussed above. However, in the second task she also seemed to be concerned with maintaining the fluency of her writing and found that checking her work as she went along was helpful, because 'sometimes if I lose track of what I'm writing I'd read over it again and then I'd try to get back on track'. She also commented that in the second English task she probably checked her work more as she went along 'because the tasks are getting harder... cause my grades are dropping and I don't want it to get lower'. It seems, therefore, that she was beginning to associate the use of evaluation strategies with achievement and as a way to help her to improve her marks.

Interestingly, in the third set of tasks Zoe started to engage in checking over her work as she went along in both German and French, which she had not done before. It seems that, for her, developing and recognising the benefit of particular strategies in English helped her to then try them out in the FLs. Following the final German task she said: 'I kind of checked it more as well, because before I used to just hand it in but now I don't, I check it.' In addition to checking her spelling, as she had done in English, she also checked to see if it made sense, yet quickly added that 'it probably doesn't, cause my making sense in German is not everybody's making sense in German'. The strategy of checking whether her work 'makes sense' suggests an attempt to distance herself from her writing and put herself in the position of an external reader. This is potentially a very useful strategy for ensuring clarity in a piece of writing. Yet, while there is certainly some evidence of Zoe attempting to engage in strategy use towards the end of the intervention of LLSI, it seems as though she still lacked the confidence, and perhaps also the competence, to do so effectively. More time and practice were needed to further develop her writing strategies.

Cross-linguistic transfer of strategies

At the beginning of the year Zoe perceived writing in each of the subjects to be quite difficult, although she particularly struggled with German, and at the end of the year this continued to be the case. Over the course of the year there was no perceptible improvement in terms of her marks or her confidence in any of the subjects. In fact, she felt that by the end of the year her German had 'kind of got worse, cause it's harder', while in English she had to 'concentrate much more' and felt it was 'harder to understand'. Even though there were some parallels that could be made between Zoe 'the struggling writer' and Chris 'the experimenter' at the beginning of the year, particularly in terms of their approach to planning, unlike Chris, Zoe did not seem to be willing to experiment with strategies or to deliberately change her approach to writing. Following the final English task when Zoe was asked whether she had tried out any of the other strategies introduced in class, she responded that she hadn't and didn't think they would be useful, 'because I've never done it before and I don't, I just don't think it would help me'.

Yet, even though Zoe did not perceive herself as having engaged much in strategy use, there is evidence to suggest that she did develop her approach to writing somewhat over the course of the year, albeit in English more than in the FLs. In both German and French, she gradually engaged in more planning, used a wider range of problem-solving strategies and started to check through her work as she went along. However, as discussed above, her attempts at strategy use in the FLs were not necessarily effective. She seemed to have had more success in English where her planning became more useful over time and she began to monitor and check her spelling more while writing, which in turn led to a gradual decrease in spelling errors in her work. It seems that for Zoe, Phase A of the intervention in the German classroom had little effect on her approach to writing, and most changes took place following Phase B in the English classroom. Her limited proficiency and lack of confidence in German may have acted as a barrier for the development of her strategy use in this context. Similarly, she may not have been as motivated to actively try to improve her work in a subject she did not enjoy.

It is also interesting to note that even though Zoe did take on board some new strategies, she often did not seem to be aware that she was doing anything differently and there seemed to be a discrepancy between what she thought she did and what she actually did. In the final interview, for example, she commented that in English she had approached writing all year 'in the same way' and, similarly, in German she did 'the same sort of thing' as always; she lacked the awareness and deliberateness displayed by Carissa 'the strategic writer' throughout and by Chris 'the experimenter' towards the end. Therefore, it is perhaps not only the particular strategies in themselves that make a difference, but also the learner's explicit awareness, self-evaluation and ultimately metacognitive engagement with these strategies which lead to successful strategy use. This highlights the importance of providing feedback to learners on their strategy use and building in time to encourage learners to reflect on the effectiveness of their approaches.

The Multilingual Writer (Mei)

As mentioned in the introduction to this chapter, there were three key profiles, or trajectories through the intervention of LLSI, that emerged among the X-LiST study participants. These were referred to as 'the strategic writer', 'the experimenter' and 'the struggling writer', and have been explained above through an in-depth consideration of an individual case representative of each. Yet, while all learners in the class aligned to some extent with one of these three categories, a fourth category also emerged which was particular to the EAL students in the group who had an L1 other than English. While these learners could equally be considered as being 'strategic writers', 'experimenters' or 'struggling writers', they also had additional linguistic resources at their disposal. A fourth category, referred to as 'the multilingual writer', was therefore added with a view to exploring how this might have influenced their negotiation of strategy use. One example of such a student is Mei, a native Mandarin speaking student who came to the UK with her mother approximately six years prior to the beginning of the study. When she first arrived she did not speak any English at all, but said that within her first year at primary school she was able to communicate relatively well. However, she commented that Mandarin remained the primary language spoken at home. She was considered by the school to be an advanced bilingual student and did not require any additional EAL support. Like many of her peers, she was in her third year of learning German and fourth year of learning French.

Mei, on the whole, was considered to be a middle-low performing student and generally scored around the class average in English tasks and below average in German and French tasks. Her written work was described by her English teacher as being reasonably accurate and 'very functional', but he felt that it often lacked 'flair'. He also commented that she tended to have more difficulty with critical pieces of writing, 'because that, in a sense, is analysing some quite subtle nuances of a language that she's only recently acquired'. Her French teacher, on the other hand, felt that Mei had a tendency to be 'quite lazy' in lessons and similarly her German teacher mentioned that she sometimes 'seemed to struggle' and did not always put in the effort that she needed to. Interestingly, at the beginning of the year, unlike the majority of her peers, Mei commented that she felt that the nature of her writing in English, German and French was 'quite similar', although admitted that she found writing in English easier 'cause I've been here for a long time and I've adapted to like, English'. She said that she quite liked writing in all three subjects, but particularly enjoyed creative writing tasks in English. She also admitted that she sometimes found writing in German and French difficult as she did not know 'the words or how to join it together'. In the writing tasks, Mei gradually improved her attainment in both English and French over time and there was a slight improvement in German between the first and final tasks.

Language of thought

Despite sharing some of the same initial characteristics as other students such as 'the struggling writer' and 'the experimenter' in terms of her attitude towards writing, what distinguishes Mei from her peers in terms of her strategy use is that she frequently employed her L1 as an additional resource when writing. Throughout the year, Mei consistently described Chinese as her primary language of thought and, as such, she inevitably engaged in a lot of translation between languages. When writing in English, Mei said that she always 'thought in Chinese first' and then translated into English, although she feared that because of this she would phrase sentences clumsily or wouldn't 'make sense at all' in her writing. Similarly, when writing in German she said that her thought process went from 'Chinese to English to German ... cause I think in Chinese before I go into English, I have to start there, cause it's, Chinese is my starting point for a language and then I just translate into that'.

As with English, when writing in the FLs Mei had a prevailing concern that her writing wouldn't make sense, but her added concern with

German and French was that, even if she realised that her work didn't make sense, she would not have the knowledge to fix it. Interestingly, when asked if she found it easier to think in German via Chinese or English, she commented that 'it's kind of the same, because my German skill level is the same'. It seems, therefore, that her high level of proficiency in both Chinese and English allowed her to use both as a resource for accessing and learning a new language. It is also worth noting that using Chinese as her principal language of thought extended beyond the three subjects focused on in this study, as she commented that 'in maths I think in Chinese as well actually...in all subjects I think'. As she was constantly engaging in translation between languages across all of her subjects, it is interesting to further examine how this influenced her use of strategies when planning, monitoring and evaluating her writing.

Planning strategies

Over the course of the year, Mei's approach to planning changed quite a lot across each of the languages. In the first English task her approach to 'planning' was to write a full draft 'and then edit it when I read through'. However, aside from the correction of one or two errors and the addition of two sentences at the end, her draft text was identical to the final version, suggesting that she essentially skipped the planning phase altogether. She said that although she would sometimes take this approach of drafting in English, it would 'depend what the task is' and for stories she would normally not plan at all and 'just go with the flow'. Like both Chris 'the experimenter' and Zoe 'the struggling writer', she did not engage in any planning whatsoever in the first German and French tasks. However, during the stimulated recall interview following the first German task, she commented that she should perhaps 'start planning to make sure it's not all over the place'. This provides some evidence to suggest that, even before the intervention of LLSI had started, Mei was already engaging in some evaluation of her strategy use (or lack thereof) and recognised herself that planning may be useful.

In the second set of tasks Mei did engage in some planning in German and French, which took the form of noting a few key content items, although it is interesting to note that her planning in both subjects was written directly in the target language. In English, however, she made a conscious decision to plan only bullet points rather than drafting her work: 'because I just thought instead of spending all the time just writing out the original one and then rewriting it neat, I thought maybe I should write like, little notes which would be better, quicker.' Like Chris 'the experimenter', she was engaging in deliberate experimentation with strategy use in order to find what worked best for her. In the final English task, however, Mei did not engage in any written planning, yet she indicated on the task sheet that she had spent ten minutes on planning. When asked about this she said that she spent this time thinking about 'how it was going to be arranged', what she was going to write about and how she could include rhetorical questions. She admitted that she 'never used to see the point' in planning, but now felt it was useful to 'start to think about it a bit more before going in and writing stuff'.

However, it is interesting to note that while her approach to planning in English shifted from drafting, to planning content-related bullet points, to thinking about key ideas and language features, Mei's approach in German and French took the opposite trajectory – from no planning whatsoever, to planning some key ideas, to drafting the whole text. Yet, what is noteworthy about her planning for the final FL tasks is that her draft was entirely written in English, and therefore she seemed to be somewhat playing to her strengths of being able to translate from one language to another. This type of planning therefore acted as a stepping-stone, allowing her to strategically think first in Chinese, then translate into English and then translate further into German or French. She was also conscious of the fact that her vocabulary in the FLs was much more limited than in English and she considered first what she already knew in the FL, then 'simplified that in English to make it easier to put in German'. She felt that this approach helped her to be more organised and by the end of the year she certainly valued planning as a strategy more than she had done previously:

> I think planning at the beginning helps so you make sure you plan before you actually write, because you don't know how you're going to write it, like if you structure one thing and then you want to structure another thing but it doesn't fit with the first one you kind of go into a mess and then you kind of get stressed and then you lose the confidence you had before. (Interview 3)

Monitoring and problem-solving strategies

In relation to monitoring her work while writing, Mei increasingly engaged in this over the course of the year in all languages and generally to a greater extent than the majority of her peers. This, at least partly, seems to have been driven by her prevailing concern with 'making sense' in her writing, especially given that she was often operating through multiple languages. As she wrote, she frequently engaged in the strategy of rephrasing sentences or substituting words for synonyms, not because what she had written initially was incorrect, but because she felt the alternative would 'make more sense'. For example, in the second German task she changed '*ich liebe Sport*' (I love sport) to '*ich mag Sport*' (I like sport) as she had already used '*ich liebe*' elsewhere in her text, and in the final English task she changed 'they agree' to 'they go along with' as she felt it sounded better. She frequently expressed a concern that her teacher would 'misunderstand what I'm trying to put across'. She was therefore using the strategy of putting herself in the mindset of an external reader to improve the clarity of her work.

In addition to reformulating her work as she was writing, Mei also engaged in problem-solving by using a range of strategies. Interestingly, the most common type of problems she encountered seemed to be cross-linguistic in nature and were often related to either vocabulary or punctuation. She also seemed to take a similar approach to solving these problems across all three languages. In the first set of tasks she generally made more vocabulary-related errors than most of her peers, specifically using the wrong word in a particular context, or in the case of German and French using a word in the other language. At the beginning, she occasionally used a dictionary in the FL tasks if she got stuck although she was more likely to guess a word and 'hope it was right', or in English if she wasn't sure of a word she tended to ask a friend. However, over time she increasingly made use of dictionaries and resources and as a result commented that she 'felt more confident' when writing in German. In the final German task, for example, if she got stuck, her first strategy would be to 'try to change it for another word' using the dictionary to help, and if she was unable to do that she would 'ignore it and move on'. As a result, she felt that in this particular task there was nothing that she could not resolve. Similarly, in English she tended to encounter vocabulary problems more frequently than many of her peers, but used a similar approach to resolve this, for example: 'I forgot the word for it [subconscious]…I couldn't phrase that word so I just went with "may not realise what you're doing".'

In addition, Mei commented throughout that she found it difficult to use punctuation when writing in all three languages: 'I'm never sure, I always misplace the commas and the full stops and starting a new paragraph and everything, and I just don't have the same problem in Chinese.' Similarly, she used the same strategy across all subjects to help monitor and improve her use of punctuation; as she was writing, she would 'just read it through in my head and see what bits need a comma and space and stuff like that'. As a result, in both German and English, Mei was self-correcting a higher percentage of errors in each task and her work, on the whole, was becoming more accurate over time.

Evaluation strategies

In relation to evaluating her work, like Zoe 'the struggling writer', Mei did not check over her writing in the first set of tasks in either German or French as she said she was 'in a rush to get it finished'. However, she did check through her first English task and once again focused on whether it 'made sense'. Yet, for the second set of tasks Mei commented that she checked through her work in all subjects. Interestingly, the reason she gave for doing so was that she 'wanted to get a higher mark' and she said that the process of checking through her work more thoroughly 'made me a bit more confident mentally cause I know what I've written down and I've read through it'. Like Chris 'the experimenter', it seems as though Mei also started to associate the use of particular strategies with achievement. Her primary concern in all subjects was once again checking that her work made sense, but in German she took a different approach to this and used back-translating as a strategy: 'I translated it into English in my head, just to make sure I wasn't going on about some random things.' Once again, she decided to play to her strengths and use translation strategically in order to try to improve her work.

In the third set of tasks, Mei continued to check over her work in all languages and the fact that she made fewer errors and self-corrected more errors in each subject, as indicated above, would perhaps suggest that her evaluation strategies were becoming increasingly effective. She also experimented with additional strategies this time and asked a friend to read over her German writing to check whether it 'made sense or not'. She seemed to engage more actively in the evaluation process in German this time and commented that she 'took on board feedback from other writing tasks and tried to improve that'. Similarly, in the final English tasks she checked specifically to see if she had 'swapped some words the wrong way' as she knew she had done so previously.

Cross-linguistic transfer of strategies

Mei's journey through the intervention of LLSI undoubtedly shared some of the same qualities as that of Carissa, Chris and Zoe and, similarly, there is some evidence to suggest that her strategy use developed over time, particularly in relation to her approach to planning and her engagement in increasingly focused monitoring and evaluation of her work. However, what differentiates her from her peers is the fact that she had an additional language at her disposal. For Mei, her native language was omnipresent and largely constituted her primary language of thought when writing in any subject. As a result, she became very adept at translating from and through Chinese. Yet, when asked if she thought that speaking another language was helpful in learning German and French, she said: 'probably not, I think it's just added more on ... it's complicated cause it's Chinese, English, German, French and it's just translating all of it, it's hard but at the same time I guess I'll learn from it.' It seems as though, rather than considering her ability to speak Chinese as an asset in learning additional languages, she viewed it more as an obstacle to be overcome.

However, perhaps it was the fact that she seemed to position herself primarily as a Chinese speaker learning English, German and French that led her to conceptualise these three subjects as being more similar than many of her classmates. She reported experiencing some of the same problems across all subjects, such as her prevailing concern with 'making sense', which seems to be directly related to her constant translations through Chinese, using the right vocabulary and using the correct punctuation. Similarly, she often approached these problems in a similar way across the various languages. When asked whether she often made connections or comparisons between them she replied, 'I think about it sometimes, but then sometimes I just do it naturally, without even knowing it', suggesting perhaps that being a multilingual writer has helped her to more easily transfer strategies across and between various languages. This could also be explained by drawing on theories related to transfer of learning (Perkins & Salomon, 1988, 1994) and psychotypology (Kellerman, 1977, 1979). It seems as though she perceived English (her L2) and German and French (her FLs) as being more similar than her L1 English speaking peers which may have enabled her to more effectively make connections and transfer strategies between these languages.

Conclusion

This chapter has explored the various trajectories through the intervention of LLSI of four students, who each represented one of the distinct writer profiles that emerged. The key characteristics of each of these students is summarised in Table 8.2.

Of course, as mentioned above, it is by no means expected that all students would fit neatly into one of these profiles; it is likely that they will share characteristics of more than one 'type' of writer and that this will shift over time. It is also important to acknowledge the limitations of focusing on just one student as representative of each profile. The in-depth cases presented here nonetheless reveal some interesting insights into the role of individual differences in the development and transfer of students' strategy use between languages. One factor that seemed to largely influence students' strategy use and their ability to transfer their strategies was their general proficiency level. That is not to say that middle or lower performing students are unable to develop their repertoire of strategies; Chris 'the experimenter', for example, shared more characteristics at the beginning with struggling writers such as Zoe, but through experimentation moved towards being a more strategic writer nearer the end. However, it seems as though a certain level of proficiency aids the development of strategies in a particular language. Similarly, those students who enjoyed writing or who enjoyed the subject seemed more motivated to achieve and therefore more likely to view the use of strategies as a means to help them to do so. In addition, it seems as though those who improved most were those who were more aware of what they were doing and why they were doing it. Perhaps, therefore, it is not only the particular strategies in themselves that make the difference, but also the extent to which students are able to reflect on and self-assess the effectiveness of their own approaches. The role of these factors will be further discussed in the following chapter.

Table 8.2 Overview of the key characteristics of the four students

Student	Key characteristics
Carissa (the strategic writer)	• High-performing student; • Generally enjoyed writing in all subjects; • Used a range of strategies effectively from the beginning; • Evidence of the ability to transfer strategies independently from one language context to another, both from the L1 to the FL and from the FL to the L1; • Demonstrated a self-awareness and self-evaluation of strategy use, which led to: • Continuous development and refinement of strategy use over time.
Chris (the experimenter)	• Average performing student with a desire to improve the standard of his writing; • Quite enjoyed writing in English, but found FL writing difficult; • Displayed a willingness to experiment with and try out new strategies and approaches; • His strategy use developed most following a period of explicit LLSI with the aid of scaffolding and opportunities to practise; • He often judged the success of his strategy use according to marks given by the teacher rather than independently.
Zoe (the struggling writer)	• Lower performing student; • Did not enjoy writing and found it difficult in all languages; • Made use of a range of strategies, however, not necessarily effectively; • Her strategy use was slower to develop and required considerable scaffolding, guidance and practice; • Less willing to try out new strategies; • Demonstrated less awareness of strategy use, which often led to a discrepancy between what she thought she did and what she actually did.
Mei (the multilingual writer)	• Her overall conceptualisations of writing in English, German and French were more similar than many of her native English speaking peers; • The key problems and concerns encountered while writing tended to be more cross-linguistic in nature; • Strategic use of the L1 as an additional resource in language learning; • More likely to use translation between languages as a key strategy.

Note

(1) All names used are pseudonyms.

9 The Role of Learners' Individual Differences

As shown in the previous chapter, students' ability to develop and transfer strategies varied considerably across the group and was seen to be influenced by a complex and dynamic range of factors. Such a focus on the role of individual differences is underpinned by theories associated with humanism which give analytic primacy to the 'awareness of the learner as an individual' (Griffiths, 2018: 56); this is an important consideration both for language learning strategy research in general and LLSI studies in particular (Macaro, 2019). There is a distinction to be made, however, between individual differences over which the learner has little choice or control (such as gender and age) and those which are subject to change (generally associated with more psychological constructs such as attitudes). The focus here is on the latter, given that they have the potential to be more malleable. To this end, this chapter builds on ideas initially presented in Forbes (2019b) and aims to explore some of the key factors which were identified in the X-LiST study as being particularly influential in facilitating (or indeed hindering) students' ability to develop and transfer strategies within and between different languages. These are: their level of proficiency in both the L1 and FLs; their level of metacognitive engagement with the task; their attitude towards writing; and the extent of the multilingual repertoire they have at their disposal.

The Symbiotic Relationship between Proficiency and Strategy Use

The question of proficiency in LLSI research has long been an important one. One of the key aims of LLSI, after all, is to help students to become more proficient language learners. Indeed, as recent meta-analyses (e.g. Ardasheva *et al.*, 2017; Plonsky, 2019) have shown, strategy instruction can have positive effects on students' language development. This is in line with findings from the X-LiST study presented in Chapter 6 which similarly suggest that the intervention led to an improved performance in writing at a whole-class level. However, proficiency is not only of interest as an *outcome* of LLSI, but also as a *moderator* or an individual difference. This relationship between strategy use and proficiency, therefore, is a complex and mutually interdependent one: just as the development of strategies can positively influence performance, learners' proficiency level can also impact the extent to which they are able to develop and transfer strategies in different contexts. Such a symbiotic relationship was evident in two main forms in the X-LiST data: first, at an inter-language level, i.e. in relation to the difference between L1 and FL proficiency; and secondly, at an intra-language level, i.e. the way in which the general proficiency level of individuals within each language influenced their ability to develop and transfer strategies.

The effect of a difference in inter-language proficiency on the development and transfer of strategies

It is to be expected that language learners, at any stage, will have differing levels of proficiency in each of the languages they speak; in most, but not necessarily all, cases their L1 is likely to be their most proficient, and even bilinguals will often identify one language as being dominant. This difference in proficiency level between the L1 and the L2 or FL, particularly for beginner learners, will undoubtedly have a bearing on their ability to develop and transfer strategies in a particular context and, as such, is a factor that has been addressed in a number of studies (e.g. Berman, 1994; Kecskes & Papp, 2000; Kobayashi & Rinnert, 2007). However, perhaps one of the most influential concepts to emerge from such a consideration is Cummins' (1979) linguistic interdependence hypothesis, which allows for the transfer of literacy-related skills from the L1 to the L2/FL, but only after a certain level of language proficiency in the L2/FL has been reached.

This may provide some explanation for the lack of transfer of pre-existing L1 skills to the FL writing tasks at the beginning of the X-LiST study (as explored in Chapter 7), which was similarly evident in Berman's (1994) study of upper secondary level English learners in Iceland. In both studies, the students may have been limited in transferring their existing L1 strategies to the FL classroom by a lack of grammatical proficiency in the FL. Yet, a lack of FL proficiency does not fully explain the relative absence of L1 to FL transfer for the X-LiST participants; this would not necessarily have prevented them, for example, from engaging in some form of planning for their writing tasks, as they could have used English or identified key words in the target language with the help of a dictionary

The question of a difference in inter-language proficiency in studies involving *reverse transfer* (from the FL to the L1) has also been raised. Kecskes and Papp (2000), for example, focused on the influence of learning an FL (English, French or Russian) on L1 (Hungarian) writing among secondary school learners. They found that FL to L1 transfer was evident only among the immersion and specialised groups in their study who received at least eight hours per week of exposure to/instruction in the FL, but not among the comparison group who had less intensive exposure to, and consequently less proficiency in the FL (only two hours per week). Given their findings, the authors proposed a common underlying conceptual base which exists 'when knowledge or skills acquired through one language system become ready to be used through the other language channel(s)' (Kecskes & Papp, 2000: xvi). However, as with Cummins' linguistic interdependence hypothesis, their model presupposes that 'a relatively weak L2 will not affect L1 in any visible way' (Kecskes & Papp, 2000: 19).

Yet, the findings of the X-LiST study do not seem to fully comply with the threshold proficiency requirement proposed by both Cummins (1979) and Kecskes and Papp (2000). The participants in the current study were relatively beginner language learners and were most similar to the comparison group in the latter study as they received just two hours of instruction per week in the FL. Yet, as the study progressed there was evidence that the students were transferring strategies developed in the FL classroom to their L1 writing; this was particularly evident in relation to an improvement in the quality of their planning and a reduction in the number of errors made. This could be because previous studies did not involve a specific intervention of LLSI or writing instruction. Therefore, while the proficiency threshold of the linguistic interdependence hypothesis and the common underlying conceptual base may hold true for the *automatic* transfer of writing features between languages, findings from the X-LiST study suggest that even beginner or low-proficiency FL learners can be taught in such a way as to encourage transfer and the development of multicompetence.

The effect of a difference in intra-language proficiency on the development and transfer of strategies

While all of the participants in the X-LiST study had a much higher level of proficiency in English than in either German or French, it is also important to acknowledge the wide range of individual variation in proficiency among the learners within each language class and the ways in which this can facilitate or hinder their development and transfer of strategies. This is a key factor which has been taken into consideration in a number of existing studies into writing processes and strategies. Raimes (1987), Sasaki (2000) and De Silva and Graham (2015), for example, distinguish between the less skilled or 'novice' writers and the more skilled or 'expert' writers among their participants, a distinction which has been conceptualised by Bereiter and Scardamalia (1987) within the field of composition research as models of knowledge-telling and knowledge-transforming, respectively. Similar distinctions can be made among the X-LiST participants presented in the previous chapter.

There was evidence that Carissa, who was identified as a strategic, high-performing writer across all three languages, used strategies more effectively and deliberately than many of her peers, even from the beginning of the study. She shared many characteristics with Bereiter and Scardamalia's (1987) knowledge-transforming model and with skilled writers from other studies, such as engaging in more planning (Cumming, 1989; Raimes, 1987; Sasaki, 2000), using more complex strategies (Bereiter & Scardamalia, 1987) such as higher order reasoning and using combinations of strategies, and engaging in more editing and revision (Myhill, 2009; Skibniewski, 1990). Her approach to writing did not change dramatically over the course of the LLSI; however, she was engaged in continuous refinement of her strategy use and was aware of the occurrence of transfer between subjects. She succeeded in maintaining her high level of attainment in English, while improving slightly in both German and French over the course of the year. This provides further evidence in support of the correlation between strategy use and attainment which has long been acknowledged, for example, by O'Malley and Chamot (1990), Macaro (2001) and Cohen (2011).

Interestingly, however, out of the four students explored in Chapter 8, it was Chris 'the experimenter' rather than Carissa 'the strategic writer' who developed his strategy use the most and also improved his attainment in all three subjects over time. This was particularly evident in German and French following Phase A of the LLSI which took place in the German classroom. He was characterised as an average performing student with a desire to improve and, as a result, was willing to actively experiment with his strategy use as a means of achieving this. For Chris, the link between strategy use and attainment was very explicit, as he had a tendency to evaluate the success of the strategies he used according to the marks he received from the teacher.

Zoe 'the struggling writer', on the other hand, provides an example of a lower performing writer who seemed to benefit relatively little from the intervention of LLSI in terms of either strategy development or attainment. Although she employed a range of strategies, she did not necessarily use them effectively and, as a result, many characteristics of her strategy use are reminiscent of the knowledge-telling model and of less skilled or struggling writers in other studies. Throughout the LLSI she engaged in minimal planning (Bereiter & Scardamalia, 1987; Harris et al., 2010), spent little time revising and any revision that did take place focused on superficial errors (Bereiter & Scardamalia, 1987), and tended to view writing as a series of words and sentences rather than as a global text (Raimes, 1987; Zamel, 1983). There were no perceptible improvements in terms of her attainment in any of the three subjects over time and any changes in her strategy use were much more limited than in the case of Chris 'the experimenter' and seemed to take longer to develop.

Given Zoe's limited proficiency and lack of confidence in German from the beginning, it is important to acknowledge that this may, in turn, have acted as a barrier to the development of her strategy use, particularly during Phase A of the LLSI which took place in the German classroom. While a low level of FL proficiency in comparison to the L1 may not in itself prevent strategy development or transfer, as this was evident among other students, the case of Zoe 'the struggling writer' provides some evidence to suggest that, at an intra-language level, a certain level of underlying proficiency in the FL *does* help to facilitate the successful development and transfer of strategies in a particular context. However, it would seem that this level does not need to be as high as that suggested by Cummins (1979) and Kecskes and Papp (2000) and that, on the whole, beginner or low-proficiency FL learners *can* be taught in such a way as to encourage strategy development and transfer to the L1. The caveat here, of course, is that some learners will require more time, scaffolding and practice than others.

The points made in this section raise complex questions surrounding the issue of cause and effect relating to level of proficiency and the development and transfer of writing strategies: Does strategy development increase proficiency? Does a higher level of proficiency increase the potential for strategy development? Or, in what Griffiths (2018: 123) refers to as the 'Tornado effect', is the relationship a spiral one, 'with one factor augmenting the other'? Evidence from the X-LiST study would suggest that the two are, indeed, inextricably intertwined. However, what also emerged as a key factor in both the development and transfer of writing strategies in the X-LiST study was the extent of learners' metacognitive engagement with the task.

The Importance of Metacognitive Engagement

Researchers in the field of language learning strategies have long suggested that strategies in themselves are not inherently good or bad, but can be applied successfully or unsuccessfully by learners (e.g. Cohen, 2011; Grenfell & Harris, 1999). What is crucial, therefore, is learners' ability to engage metacognitively with their strategy use and, by extension, with the writing task they are undertaking. Metacognition similarly emerged in the X-LiST study as a key factor for determining the success of students' development and transfer of strategies. Carissa, for example, emerged as a strategic writer from the beginning and, as such, she independently and consistently engaged in a high level of self-reflection and evaluation in order to continuously develop her strategy use over time. Zoe 'the struggling writer', at the other end of the spectrum, was less successful in developing her strategy use, and one of the key inhibitory factors was her lack of metacognitive awareness and engagement with the tasks. This was manifest primarily in the discrepancies that emerged between what she thought she did and what she actually did and is in line with the findings of a case study by Vann and Abraham (1990) into two unsuccessful adult learners of English. Although both participants in the latter study emerged as active strategy users, like Zoe, they often applied these strategies inappropriately. The authors similarly identified that these learners 'lacked certain necessary higher order processes … which would enable them to assess the task and to bring to bear the necessary strategies for its completion' (Vann & Abraham, 1990: 191). This highlights the importance of the quality of strategy use over the quantity of strategy use and suggests that it is not necessarily the particular strategies in themselves that make a difference, but the learner's explicit awareness, self-evaluation and ultimately metacognitive engagement with these strategies which leads to successful strategy use. This is evident in the example provided in Chapter 8 of how both Carissa and Zoe used the strategy of avoidance in their writing. While Carissa used this as a way to overcome difficulties and successfully complete the task by selecting an alternative phrase, Zoe used this as a way to 'opt out' of this particular aspect of the writing task entirely.

However, it is important to recognise that such profiles of struggling and strategic writers are not static and consequently helping learners to develop the ability to reflect metacognitively is key to enabling them to progress from the former to the latter. As stated by Zhang and Zhang (2013: 114), 'metacognition should be treated as dynamic systems, and it should be construed as something embedded in language learners, which is intertwined with many modifiable variables, both cognitive and sociocultural'. Such dynamism is effectively captured in the case of Chris 'the experimenter'; although not a particularly high-achieving or strategic writer at the beginning, Chris actively developed an increasing awareness of his strategy use over time. However, while Carissa 'the strategic writer' engaged in such self-evaluation relatively independently, Chris had a tendency to rely on summative marks and teacher feedback in assessing the effectiveness of his strategy use. This highlights the importance of building in opportunities for students to engage in guided practice of a range of strategies, but also the importance of including time for feedback and reflection; as suggested by Myhill (2006a: 28), 'we may well develop better writers not by doing more writing but by generating more thinking about writing'.

Just as enabling learners to engage metacognitively with their writing is a key factor in the *development* of successful strategy use, it is similarly fundamental to facilitating the *transfer* of such strategies from one language context to another. There was evidence in the X-LiST study that the intervention of LLSI in the German classroom during Phase A of the study helped to develop the students' awareness and use of writing strategies in both the FL and L1 contexts. For example, at the beginning of the study Chris did not automatically transfer his pre-existing English strategies to his German writing. From a transfer of learning perspective (Perkins & Salomon, 1988), it may be that his initial perception of the two language contexts as being superficially distinct hindered him from engaging in the explicit connection-making required to facilitate such transfer. Yet, following the intervention there was evidence that he was able to transfer strategies developed in the FL to the L1. As this did not take place automatically, it seems that the metacognitive strategies introduced as part of the intervention played a key role in stimulating this reverse transfer. By extension, given that high-road transfer is a conscious process requiring abstract thinking in order to make connections between contexts that seem superficially distant (see Chapter 7), the FL classroom emerged as an environment which is highly conducive to the cultivation of language-related metacognitive engagement more generally. It is a context in which learners are more consciously aware of their thought processes, perhaps more so than the L1 classroom where such processes are more likely to have become automatic and proceduralised.

Attitudes towards Writing

In addition to the learners' level of proficiency and the extent of their metacognitive engagement with a task, the development and transfer of strategies in the X-LiST study was also shown to be affected by their attitude towards writing, both in general and in relation to each particular subject. Even though there was no evidence that the intervention of LLSI directly affected students' enjoyment of writing in any subject (as this seemed to be more related to factors such as task type and topic), there was some evidence to suggest that the reverse may be true, i.e. that the extent to which students enjoyed writing in a particular subject may have influenced their willingness to develop their strategy use.

Zoe 'the struggling writer', for example, commented that she would 'try really hard' if she enjoyed the particular topic she was writing about, particularly in English. The implication here is that she would invest more time and effort in such tasks and perhaps be more likely to seek strategies to help her to achieve (however, as discussed above, these strategies may not necessarily be used effectively). Yet, she disliked writing in German which is also likely to have hindered her from transferring strategies both to and from this FL context. Similarly, Annie, another 'struggling writer', explained that while she always checked over her written work in English, she never did in German 'cause I don't enjoy German and I enjoy English'. Her attitudes towards the subjects therefore influenced which strategies she would use in a particular context and, in turn, whether or not she transferred strategies from one context to another. Kobayashi and Rinnert

(2008: 19–20), in their study exploring the bidirectional transfer of writing competence among university-level EFL learners in Japan, likewise suggested that 'students' attitudes toward English writing could prevent their knowledge from being transferred to L1 writing'.

Although not examined directly as part of the X-LiST study, motivation and beliefs have also been shown to affect the development of language learning strategies (Griffiths, 2013, 2018; Yang, 1999), in that those learners who are more motivated to achieve tend to be more likely to view the use of strategies as a means of helping them to do so. This is evident in the case of Chris 'the experimenter', who was motivated to improve his marks in writing across all subjects and was willing to experiment with strategies in order to achieve this. However, a focus on the role of attitudes extends beyond simply exploring students' views of a single subject to consideration of how they view these subjects in relation to each other; this is particularly pertinent when reflecting on factors that may influence transfer. As explored in Chapter 2, the students in the X-LiST study on the whole tended to have very different attitudes towards English compared to the FLs. English, as a core subject and global language, was considered to be important and writing tasks were viewed as varied and creative. FL lessons, on the other hand, were seen as more challenging and rigid. As suggested in Chapter 7, the fact that students' attitudes towards and conceptualisations of writing in these two contexts were so different at the beginning of the study may consequently have inhibited their ability to make connections and transfer strategies between them at this point.

Strategic Multilingualism

Another important factor influencing the development and transfer of strategies that emerged from the X-LiST study was learners' strategic use of other languages throughout the writing process. As emphasised by Tullock and Fernández-Villanueva (2013: 421), 'perhaps one of the most important resources multilingual writers possess is their ability to refer to their full linguistic repertoire while composing'. This was most strikingly evident among the bilingual English as an additional language (EAL) learners who were able to draw on their native-speaker competencies in another language, in addition to English, when learning German and French. As noted in Chapter 8, there were only two such students in the intervention group and therefore the sample is very limited. Nonetheless, the data from these students provide useful insights into their strategic use of languages.

It is often posited that multilinguals have increased metalinguistic awareness and increased language learning awareness (Cenoz, 2003; Psaltou-Joycey & Kantaridou, 2009), and this was reflected to some extent in the current study among the EAL learners by the omnipresence of their L1 during all stages of the writing process and across all languages. In the case of Mei, which was outlined fully in Chapter 8, it was evident that she strategically used her native Mandarin Chinese as an additional resource while writing in English, German and French. Although she had lived in England for many years and spoke fluent English, she still reported that she always 'thought in Chinese first' and that this was her 'starting point for [another] language', regardless of whether that language was English, German or French. As a result, she engaged in a lot of translation back and forwards between languages. It seems, therefore, that for Mei Chinese constitutes what I referred to in Chapter 8 as her primary language of thought. However, it is important to acknowledge that this was determined purely on the basis of interview data and, as such, represents only her general perceptions. Given her high levels of proficiency in both English and Chinese and the fact that she was in an English speaking environment, it is possible (and indeed, likely) that her thought processes were, in fact, multilingual rather than monolingual. Yet, even though a general self-report of language of thought is all that can be captured here, it nonetheless provides an interesting insight into how she positions herself, i.e. primarily as a speaker of Chinese who uses English on a daily basis in school and who is learning German and French. This relates well to Kellerman's (1977, 1979) views on the importance of psychotypology. In this case Mei, to some extent, grouped English, German and French together in her mind as languages being learned in addition to her L1 and, as such, was more likely to perceive them as being similar. She reported experiencing some of the same problems across all subjects, such as her prevailing concern with 'making sense', using the right vocabulary and correct use of punctuation. Consequently, she often approached these problems in a similar way in the various subjects, perhaps suggesting that being a multilingual writer has helped her to more easily transfer strategies across and between her languages.

The other 'multilingual writer' in the intervention group, Kacper (a Polish speaker), like Mei considered himself as an English language learner, even though he had lived in England for around six years prior to the start of the study. Interestingly, he described his primary language of thought as English in the English classroom, but often Polish in the German or French classroom, which he attributed to his higher level of proficiency in Polish. He used his knowledge of Polish more specifically as a problem-solving strategy, particularly at word level, and stated that when he got stuck, then he would 'fall back into Polish and then translate into English'. He also used his knowledge of Polish strategically to look for cognates in German; he described the two languages as being 'quite similar' and felt that his additional language enabled him to 'pick out words easier than other people'. From a psychotypological perspective it seems as though Kacper perceived German as being closer to Polish than English which in turn facilitated his ability to make connections between them.

This provides some evidence in support of the hypothesis that bilinguals are 'capable of transferring skills from the two languages they know to a third language' (Cenoz, 2003: 77). It is also in line with findings from the STIR (Strategy Instruction Research) study by Grenfell and Harris (2015, 2017) into bilingual adolescent students learning French in two schools in London compared to their monolingual peers. The focus of this study was on the receptive skills of reading and listening rather than on writing; nevertheless, they found that bilingual students in their study brought valuable strategies to the learning of an L3, particularly in terms of their listening comprehension skills which they attribute, in part, to the role of code-switching in parental input.

Yet, even though having an additional language at their disposal was certainly a strategic asset for the EAL learners in this study, it did not necessarily make them more proficient FL learners, which seems to go against the commonly held view that the more languages learners speak, the more proficient they are at acquiring additional languages. However, in a review of several European studies into L3 acquisition, Cenoz (2003: 77) concluded that 'when monolingual speakers of the national language and bilingual immigrants are compared there are, in general terms, no differences in third language acquisition'. In the case of these particular students it would seem to hold true that the strategic advantage of bilingual learners 'is to be found at the metalinguistic level, which includes both communicative and learning strategies' (Bono & Stratilaki, 2009: 211), rather than at the level of academic attainment.

However, it is important to note that the English L1 speakers (as 'emerging multilinguals') similarly displayed an ability to use their knowledge of one language strategically when learning another, albeit to a much lesser extent than the EAL learners. While those in the early stages of learning a new language are generally not yet in a position to be able to think directly *in* the FL, they think *about* the FL through the medium of the L1, consequently making the FL writing process a 'bilingual event' (Wang & Wen, 2002: 239). This generally manifests itself as the use of the L1 as a strategy when writing in the L2/FL (e.g. Cohen & Brooks-Carson, 2001; Friedlander, 1990; Kobayashi & Rinnert, 1992; Wang & Wen, 2002), particularly in relation to the language of planning and the use of translation. This was evidenced in the current study, for example, by Carissa's strategic choice of language of planning. In the first German task she mentioned that she had generally thought first about what she wanted to say in English before trying to translate it into German, but admitted that this may have been why she could not say everything she wanted to. Consequently, in the next task she changed her approach and her starting point was to begin with the German she knew and then to build on that. It seems fair to say, therefore, that there is evidence to suggest that students with knowledge of more than one language, even if that knowledge is not particularly advanced, can use their emerging multilingual repertoire strategically.

Conclusion

Drawing on data from the X-LiST study alongside evidence from the literature, this chapter has demonstrated how both the development and cross-linguistic transfer of strategy use are influenced by a complex and dynamic range of factors relating to individual differences. Those which emerged as most salient within the X-LiST study were associated with the learners' proficiency level in each of the languages, their level of metacognitive engagement with the task, their attitude towards writing and their strategic use of other languages in their repertoire. However, it is important to acknowledge that this is by no means an exhaustive list and there are countless other factors that merit further investigation, such as the interactions between language learning strategies and other key constructs such as motivation, self-efficacy, personality, affect and identity, to name but a few. Yet, what it is important to recognise in any consideration of individual differences is the extent to which these are all dynamic and subject to change. If, for example, a student has a low level of proficiency in a language at the start of the academic year, this (one would hope) can improve over time; if a student lacks an explicit, metacognitive awareness of their strategy use, this can be developed. The evidence presented throughout this book suggests that LLSI can be a useful tool for helping learners to develop in precisely these areas and in supporting them to become more strategic and proficient writers across a range of languages.

10 Reflecting Back and Looking Forward: Implications and Conclusions

As set out in the Introduction, the primary aim of this book was to provide a timely exploration of the phenomenon of cross-linguistic transfer of writing strategies and, ultimately, to encourage more joined-up, cross-curricular thinking related to language in schools. To this end, evidence has been presented throughout from the classroom-based Cross-Linguistic Strategy Transfer (X-LiST) study. The questions at the heart of this study emerged from several sources. On the one hand, they stemmed from my own experiences as a learner and teacher of languages and from exploring the disparities between the ways in which the L1 and FLs are positioned in schools (as discussed in Chapter 2). While my starting point here was the education system in England, parallels also emerged with trends in other predominantly Anglophone countries. On the other hand, questions also emerged from the literature and the existing evidence base surrounding language learning strategies. While there are a growing number of studies in the fields of both L2 acquisition and composition research which suggest that effective strategy use can be of benefit to language learners across a range of skill areas (e.g. Ardasheva *et al.*, 2017; Graham *et al.*, 2012; Plonsky, 2019), much of this research has taken place within a single context of either L1 or FL education (as reviewed in Chapter 3). As such, there has been less focus on the potential for interactions and transfer between the two. Indeed, it is often the case in the literature that any reference to transfer between these two contexts tends to suggest the one-way transfer of pre-existing skills and strategies *from* the L1 *to* the FL.

The X-LiST study therefore emerged from a hypothesis that the reverse may be equally (if not more) valid. That is, if the use of writing strategies is explicitly developed within the FL classroom (where students are arguably more explicitly aware of themselves as *language* learners), then it seems logical that this knowledge could not only benefit FL writing tasks, but may also positively affect their writing in other languages, including their L1. Chapter 4 then outlined the research design of this quasi-experimental, mixed-methods study which aimed to explore how an explicit focus on strategy instruction in the FL German classroom influenced students' strategy development and performance in writing in German, and whether any such effects transferred to another FL (French) and/or to the L1 (English). Chapter 5 focused on issues surrounding the development of the cross-linguistic intervention of LLSI. Emphasis was placed here on the ways in which L1 and FL teachers can establish some common aims and practices in order to better support students' writing.

The remaining chapters focused on the findings that emerged from the X-LiST study. Chapters 6 and 7 explored the trends in performance, strategy development and transfer that emerged at a whole-class level. It was demonstrated that even beginner or low-proficiency FL learners can develop effective skills and strategies in the FL classroom which can also positively influence writing in other FLs and the L1. The focus of Chapters 8 and 9 then shifted to the level of the individual and examined the complex and interrelated factors which were shown to influence students' development and transfer of strategies. These were: their level of proficiency in both the L1 and FLs; their level of metacognitive engagement with the task; their attitude towards writing; and the extent of the multilingual repertoire they have at their disposal.

The aims of this concluding chapter are, first, to reflect back on and discuss the key findings that have been presented in this book, but also to look forwards and to identify future directions in the field. As such, this chapter will begin by revisiting the key questions that were posed in the Introduction in light of the data. Careful consideration will also be given to the limitations of the study in order to inform readers' interpretations of the findings. Key theoretical and pedagogical implications and recommendations stemming from the book will be presented and, finally, areas for future research will be identified.

Revisiting the Key Questions

In the Introduction to this book a number of key questions were identified as being the drivers for the X-LiST study. This section will revisit each of these in turn with a view to highlighting and discussing the main findings presented throughout this book.

How are L1 and FL learning positioned in schools?

As stated above, the starting point of this book was an exploration of the ways in which the L1 and FLs are positioned in schools. A review of curriculum documents from a range of predominantly Anglophone countries revealed that English and FLs are conceptualised differently and tend to be presented separately at the level of the curriculum. There are few explicit links drawn between the two and where these do exist, the onus seems to be solely on the FL teachers to make connections to the L1, with little recognition of the potential links that could be made by L1 teachers to the skills and strategies developed by students in their other languages. This schism which emerged at the level of the curriculum was replicated in the views and practices of the L1 and FL teachers; while L1 teachers tend to take a more top-down approach to language, FL teachers adopt a more conscious, bottom-up approach. This, in turn, seemed to influence students' perceptions of and approaches to writing in the L1 and FL classrooms. Given that such segregation between these language-related subjects might inhibit students' ability to make connections and transfer strategies between them, a clear need was therefore identified to encourage more joined-up, cross-curricular thinking in schools related to *language* more broadly.

While the focus of this book has been on exploring how this cross-curricular thinking can be done in a more bottom-up way (i.e. by encouraging collaboration between individual teachers within the same school), there are also implications here for school leaders and, indeed, even for curriculum designers. One way to perhaps stimulate more collaboration between L1 and FL teachers would be to build in more specific connections between these subjects within departmental schemes of work and, more broadly, at the level of the national curriculum. It is also important to reflect on the wider relevance of these issues, which is why consideration was given here to trends across a range of Anglophone countries around the world. FL learning in countries such as the UK, the United States, Australia and New Zealand has been in steady decline in recent years. This is, at least in part, due to the international status of English as a global lingua franca. Yet, it is vital to acknowledge that English alone is simply not enough. While there is provision in some of these countries for alternative models of education which place much more emphasis on language learning (e.g. bilingual or immersion settings), the reality is that for many students in these countries exposure to FL learning is restricted to timetabled lessons during a short window of compulsory provision (if, indeed, such provision exists). It is therefore hoped that the evidence presented here, which demonstrates that the skills and strategies taught in FL lessons can benefit learning in other curriculum areas, can perhaps contribute to the evidence base in support of FL learning in schools.

To what extent do the existing writing strategies used by students in L1 and FL classrooms differ?

This was considered by examining the baseline data which were collected at Point 1 of the study before any form of intervention took place. The rationale for this was to explore the existing strategies students used when writing in the L1 and FLs and to examine the extent to which their strategies and approaches were similar. The evidence presented from the X-LiST study demonstrated that students approached writing differently in the L1 and FL classrooms at this point. They did not, as some researchers would suggest, automatically transfer their pre-existing skills and strategies from the L1 to an FL and there were several key distinctions in their strategy use which emerged from the data. For example, when planning their work, students were much more likely to engage in any form of planning in English than in German or French, to produce much longer plans and to use a wider range of planning strategies. Similarly, they identified a wider range of evaluation strategies in English (which is interesting given that they knew they were more likely to make errors when writing in either of the FLs). This highlights the importance of the awareness-raising process that followed as part of the intervention of LLSI. It was clear at the beginning that many of the students were not particularly aware of the approaches or strategies they used while writing in *any* language. Given that explicit awareness and metacognitive reflection has been identified as a key factor in both developing and transferring strategies, the low levels evident at the beginning of the study would undoubtedly have hindered any such transfer from taking place.

What happens when L1 and FL teachers collaborate to develop parallel LLSI? What are the stages in developing such an intervention?

In light of the lack of strategic transfer evident at the beginning of the study, a cross-linguistic intervention of LLSI was designed and implemented – first, in the German classroom only, and then in *both* the German and English lessons of a Year 9 (age 13–14) class in a secondary school in England. The focus of Chapter 5 was devoted to the *process* of developing this intervention; a step-by-step guide was provided and exemplified throughout with reference to activities used in the X-LiST study. There were undoubtedly challenges to be overcome here, particularly in establishing some shared aims and practices among the L1 and FL teachers; building explicit connections between strategy use in these subjects was, after all, something very new to all of them. Yet, evidence suggests that the outcome of this collaboration was indeed mutually beneficial for the students' overall writing development in both classroom contexts.

Anecdotally, the teachers involved in the study also reported gaining a lot from the process in terms of their own thinking and professional development. It provided them with an opportunity to understand how colleagues in other departments understood and approached the teaching of writing and also made them more aware of the skills and strategies that students develop in other areas of the curriculum. Therefore, while implementing such a programme does involve time and commitment on the part of the teachers, there is certainly reason to believe that it is worthwhile. Perhaps if such links between L1 and FLs can be made more explicit at the level of departmental policies and even at the level of the curriculum, then this would provide further opportunities and incentives for developing such cross-linguistic pedagogies.

To what extent does an intervention of LLSI in the FL classroom influence performance in writing and strategy development in the FL, and do any such effects transfer to writing tasks in another FL or the L1?

To address this question, whole-class trends were explored over time to determine if and how the strategic writing approaches of students in the X-LiST study changed in German, French and English from Point 1 before any intervention took place, to Point 2 following a period of explicit LLSI in the German classroom only, to Point 3 following a further period of explicit and parallel LLSI in both the English and German classrooms. As explored in Chapter 6, the intervention group students developed both the quantity and quality of their strategy use over the course of the LLSI. Although strategy development was most evident in German, which is unsurprising given that this was the context in which students received the LLSI for the longest period of time, changes also occurred in relation to French and English. Such development in students' strategy use also corresponded to an improvement in performance in writing at a whole-class level.

However, of particular interest here were the multiple directionalities of transfer that emerged in the X-LiST study as explored in Chapter 7. The most evident form of transfer was undoubtedly the FL to FL transfer, where the intervention group students were able to readily transfer strategies developed in the German classroom to their French writing, without any explicit encouragement to do so. Even though French and German are very different languages, the students conceptualised them in a similar way, which likely facilitated such transfer. Exploration of transfer between L1 English and the FLs, however, proved to be more complex. Given the difference in students' views of and approaches to writing in English at the beginning of the study, there was evidence to suggest that they were not necessarily transferring their pre-existing L1 writing strategies automatically to an FL (as noted above). Yet, there was some evidence of reverse transfer of strategies from the FL to the L1 following Phase A of the LLSI, which took place only in the German classroom. This could perhaps be explained by the emphasis on developing students' metacognition in relation to language learning strategies. The FL to L1 transfer of strategies was particularly apparent in relation to the quality of planning, the reduction in the number of errors made and the increase in number of errors corrected. Further changes occurred in English following Phase B of the intervention where the LLSI was conducted in parallel in both the FL and L1 classrooms. Such findings not only highlight the important role of FL teachers in contributing to learners' overall writing development, but also suggest the potential benefits for students of cross-curricular collaboration among language teachers.

What are the key factors relating to individual differences which influence students' development and transfer of language learning strategies?

In order to allow for an in-depth investigation of students' individual trajectories through the intervention of LLSI, four cases were presented in Chapter 8. These students were selected to represent a range of writer 'profiles' which emerged from the X-LiST study, referred to as 'the strategic writer', 'the experimenter', 'the struggling writer' and 'the multilingual writer'. Analysis revealed that both the development and transfer of strategy use were influenced by a complex and dynamic range of factors which were examined in Chapter 9. One key factor that emerged was the symbiotic relationship between proficiency and strategy use at both an inter- and intra-language level; just as the development of strategies was shown to positively influence achievement, the learner's own proficiency level was also shown to influence the extent to which they were able to develop and transfer strategies in different writing contexts. Another crucial factor identified was the importance of a learner's metacognitive engagement with the task in determining the success of their development, application and subsequent transfer of strategies. If students are not aware of the strategies they are using in one language, then they are not necessarily able to draw on this to help them in other languages. The FL classroom, in particular, emerged as an environment that is highly conducive to the cultivation of such language-related metacognition. After all, it is a context in which learners are more consciously aware of their thought processes, unlike the L1 classroom where such processes are more likely to have become automatic and proceduralised.

Similarly, students with knowledge of more than one language, even if that knowledge was not particularly advanced, were able to use their emerging multilingual repertoire strategically. This was particularly evident among the EAL learners in the study who were able to draw on their native-speaker competencies in another language, in addition to English, when learning German and French. For example, this was evident in the case of Mei, for whom L1 Chinese was her primary language of thought, and in the case of Kacper, who used his knowledge of Polish to look for cognates in German. However, the L1 English students also showed that they were able to use their emerging multilingual repertoire strategically. Carissa, for example, was very deliberate in the language(s) she used in her written planning and drew on her knowledge of both German and English. Given that all of the students in the X-LiST study had knowledge of more than one language (even if that knowledge was not particularly advanced), they all had the potential to use these languages strategically.

The above findings are undoubtedly important in furthering our understanding of some of the key factors that influence students' development and transfer of language learning strategies. However, it is important to note that both these factors and the writer 'profiles' identified above were dynamic and subject to change. The teachers, therefore, play a key role in facilitating students' strategy development through effective modelling, scaffolding and feedback in order to help them to progress towards becoming more strategic and proficient writers.

Limitations of the X-LiST Study

While the X-LiST study provided some valuable insights into the phenomenon of cross-linguistic transfer of writing strategies, it is nonetheless crucial to reflect on the limitations of this study. While these have been acknowledged where relevant throughout the book, this section will bring these together in order to help readers to evaluate the implications of the study and also to inform future research. The limitations discussed here relate to aspects of the overall design, sampling, the intervention of LLSI and methods of data collection.

Overall design

First, it is important to acknowledge limitations related to the overall research design of the X-LiST study. Given that the study was conducted in an authentic classroom environment over the course of an academic year, it was neither feasible nor ethical to randomly allocate students to either the intervention or comparison group solely for the purpose of the study. As such, the research design is quasi-experimental rather than experimental. As random allocation was simply not an option, measures were taken to check that the students in the two groups were comparable in terms of performance in writing in each of the languages at the beginning of the year. Yet, while this must be acknowledged as a limitation, it is also perhaps a strength of the study. Given that it was conducted in an authentic classroom, the data generated may provide a more realistic representation of the complexities of the learning environment and, by extension, ensure the relevance and applicability of the findings to real-world practice.

Another limitation of the research design more broadly concerns the lack of comparison group data for French. As explained fully in Chapter 4, the X-LiST study was initially only designed to explore the interactions between strategy use in L1 English and a single FL (German). However, the opportunity arose to collect 'bonus' data in the French lessons of the intervention group. As the French teacher of the comparison group was absent for some time at the beginning of the year it was unfortunately not possible to gain consent to collect data from this group. It was not envisaged at the time that the French data would end up playing such a key role in allowing for exploration of FL to FL transfer and so this is certainly something to bear in mind for future studies.

Sampling

It is also important to acknowledge limitations relating to sampling, the first being the small sample size. Studies that involve any form of pedagogical intervention necessitate considerable investment of time and commitment on the part of the teacher(s), students and researcher(s) and therefore, in this case, it was only possible to conduct the X-LiST study with two groups (the intervention and comparison group). As a result, outcomes here can only be seen as reflecting the trends within these particular classes. Working with a small sample, however, also has its advantages as it allowed for a more in-depth exploration of the development and transfer of strategies both at a whole-class and also an individual level. Larger scale studies of such interventions in the future would be very welcome.

An additional point to raise with regard to sampling is that the student participants were predominantly L1 English speakers. This was unavoidable due to the need to work with intact groups and, in particular, with groups taught by teachers who were willing to participate in the study. There were a small number of EAL students in the classes who are given particular attention in Chapters 8 and 9; however, the sample did limit opportunities to explore trajectories among more linguistically diverse populations.

Intervention

In relation to the intervention itself, the focus of the X-LiST study was on L1 English, FL German and FL French; these are all Indo-European languages which share the same Latin script for writing. The decision to focus on these languages was mostly dictated by practical concerns: these were the FLs languages offered by the school (and indeed, along with Spanish, represent the most common FLs currently taught in schools in England), and these were also languages which I had knowledge of in order to develop the intervention resources. However, this also perhaps represents a limitation in terms of the extent to which such findings might be relevant to schools offering more typographically distant languages. Would, for example, the high level of transfer evident here between strategies in French and German hold true for students learning Spanish and Arabic as FLs?

Methods of data collection

One of the key limitations in relation to the methods of data collection used (and perhaps also one of the most difficult to overcome) relates to the mentalistic nature of metacognition and strategic thought processes. It is often not possible to observe strategy use and therefore we have to rely heavily on self-report data, either in written form via questionnaires or task sheets or verbally through (stimulated recall) interviews or think-aloud protocols. Given that students can only report on strategies that they are consciously aware of using, there is therefore a risk that some of their strategy use will have become proceduralised and will consequently be inaccessible for report. While steps were taken in the X-LiST study to ensure that the data collection procedures were as reliable as possible (for example, by conducting stimulated recall interviews as soon as possible after completion of the task), it is important to acknowledge that much of the data collected can only be considered as learners' *perceptions* of their strategy use.

Similarly, it is important to be aware of the possibility that the students who took part in the X-LiST study may have simply reported what they felt they were expected to report given the focus of the intervention and the particular prompts used in the writing task sheets and interviews. It could therefore be argued that any increase in their reported use of strategies was simply the result of raised awareness of use, or ideas being planted in the minds of the participants. Yet, as Cohen *et al.* (1998: 147) state, 'the power of suggestion alone is not usually enough to produce strategy use' and, furthermore, exactly the same prompts and elicitation techniques were used with the comparison group students.

Another limitation lies in the complexity of what it is possible to capture at a whole-class level versus what can be elicited at an individual level. As stated above, the writing strategy task sheets constituted the main source of data collection at a whole-class level. While there was some provision here for students to self-report the strategies they used, as noted above, this relied on them (a) being aware of what they were doing and (b) taking the time to note this down. As such, some of the claims which could be made about the data at a whole-class level were limited to evidence of strategy use having occurred (e.g. the production of written planning or errors having been corrected), yet this did not always provide insights into the specific strategies that led to such actions. The stimulated recall interviews were much more enlightening on this front. However, due to limitations of time and resources it was simply not possible to conduct such interviews with each student after each task.

A final limitation to note here relates to the difficulties in establishing comparable tasks in English and the FLs. As discussed in Chapter 4, it would not have been feasible to adapt the same topic to all three languages given the substantial variation in students' level of proficiency in English compared to the FLs. As such, narrative-style (rather than analytical) tasks were chosen in order to ensure some comparability in terms of genre. Each of the tasks allowed some scope for students to be creative, although it must be acknowledged that students' ability to express themselves creatively in the FL tasks was inevitably limited by their lower proficiency level and restricted range of vocabulary. In a context where students were more proficient in the FLs, perhaps it would be possible to create more parallel tasks. However, given that the focus here was on relatively beginner FL learners, this was not possible and must therefore be acknowledged as a limitation.

Implications for Research and Practice

The evidence reviewed throughout this book, along with the data presented from the X-LiST study, has important implications which relate to both theory and pedagogy. Such implications gain further significance when we consider that the majority of existing research into the development of language learning strategies in both L1 and L2/FL writing, and similarly in relation to the transfer of learning, has been conducted with adults or advanced learners and in the main deals with the learning of English as the L2/FL.

Theoretical implications

At a theoretical level, the findings from the X-LiST study shed light on our understanding of the construct of bidirectional strategic transfer between a learner's L1 and L2/FL. As discussed in Chapter 3, links between these two language contexts have long been acknowledged. Cummins (1979), for example, hypothesised an underlying proficiency which is common across languages and which allows for the transfer of literacy-related skills, but only after a certain level of language proficiency has been reached. Building on this, Kecskes and Papp (2000) later proposed a broader interpretation of Cummins' hypothesis through a multicompetence lens, which presupposed the bidirectionality of transfer, but which similarly suggested that a threshold of proficiency in the L2/FL must be reached in order for it to affect the L1.

Yet, the evidence presented from the X-LiST study throughout this book does not seem to comply with such a threshold proficiency requirement. The participants in this study were relatively beginner language learners, yet there was evidence of some FL to L1 transfer, even after Phase A of the intervention when the LLSI was conducted only in the German classroom. One possible explanation for this, as discussed in Chapter 7, is that the previous studies mentioned above did not involve a specific intervention of LLSI. Therefore, perhaps the proficiency threshold suggested by both Cummins (1979) and Kecskes and Papp (2000) may hold true for the *automatic* transfer of writing features between languages; however, the findings from the current study suggest that even relatively beginner or low-proficiency FL learners can be *taught* in such a way as to encourage transfer at a strategic level. This can be facilitated further when the LLSI is made explicit in both the L1 and FL contexts. However, it must also be acknowledged that some learners will require more time, scaffolding and practice than others for this to occur.

The data presented here also contribute to the growing body of evidence which highlights the importance of metacognitive engagement in facilitating students' ability to both develop and transfer their writing strategies. This was identified in Chapter 9 as one of the key factors that determined each individual's strategy use. While such metacognitive engagement and reflection was already evident among the higher proficiency learners, results indicated that this can also be actively developed among middle and lower proficiency learners, albeit to varying degrees of success. There was strong evidence, therefore, that the FL classroom, where students are more explicitly aware of and engaged in their thinking about *language* (as compared to the L1 classroom), provides an environment which is highly conducive to the development of valuable metacognitive skills that relate to language more broadly.

Pedagogical recommendations: Facilitating collaboration between L1 and FL teachers

The findings of the X-LiST study suggest that strategies that are explicitly taught by FL teachers can benefit students when writing in other languages (including their L1). However, the effects of LLSI are most powerful when there is collaboration between L1 and FL teachers. As described in Chapter 7, it was the explicit LLSI in *both* English and German classrooms during Phase B of the intervention study that proved most effective in facilitating connection-making and transfer. In line with this, Kobayashi and Rinnert (2008: 20) also commented with regard to their study on the effects of high school training on the essay writing of first year undergraduates that 'the interaction between intensive L1 and L2 training led to greater effects than either of the separate kind of training alone would have allowed us to predict, perhaps because of the greater confidence it generated for both L1 and L2 writing'. Gunning *et al.* (2016) similarly found that when the L1 and L2 teachers in their study collaborated in the teaching of reading strategies at an elementary school in Francophone Canada, the students became more effective at self-monitoring their reading in both languages. Even though such studies are few and far between, the evidence that does exist on the potential for such cross-curricular, cross-linguistic LLSI collaborations is certainly encouraging. This is not to deny the various barriers that teachers (and perhaps also students) may face when undertaking such an endeavour; however, some practical recommendations are provided below to provide guidance:

- In order to cultivate collaboration across a range of language-related subjects, it is first important to try to make some space and time for such collaboration, for example, through an occasional shared departmental meeting between L1 and FL teachers which would allow for the sharing of practice and ideas.
- Teachers can raise awareness of approaches to teaching writing across the different subjects and languages by, for example, exchanging curricula, assessment criteria or departmental schemes of work and looking for potential areas of intersection.
- Following on from the above, a valuable exercise for further understanding pedagogical practices in other language-related lessons is for FL teachers to observe their L1 colleagues (and vice versa) when there is a particular focus on writing.
- Establish some common terminology to use in relation to writing strategies in both L1 and FL departments, e.g. goal-setting, planning language features, etc. It is also useful to reflect on how these terms might be used in each classroom. For example, 'planning language features' in the L1 might involve thinking about the use of metaphors or rhetorical questions, whereas in the FL classroom this might mean using the imperfect tense or an 'if' clause.
- Create some common templates which could be adapted and used in a range of language classrooms to help students use strategies to plan, monitor and evaluate their work (such as the examples shown in Chapter 5). These will, of course, vary between L1 and FL tasks; however, if there are some common terms or formats that can be shared then this can help learners to make connections more easily.
- Establish an agreement that both L1 and FL teachers will encourage students to reflect on their writing *process* in addition to focusing on the final product.
- Involve students in the discussion; for example, when setting a task in the FL classroom the teacher could ask students how they approach such tasks in their L1 (and vice versa).
- It is beneficial to make LLSI *explicit* and to integrate this as much as possible into regular classroom activities over a period of time.
- Students will need time to develop their strategy use and benefit from opportunities to practise this across different tasks and in different contexts.
- It is useful for teachers to provide learners with feedback and suggestions on their strategy use in addition to the final written product. For example, if a student makes a number of errors related to adjective agreement, the teacher could suggest that this becomes a target for evaluation in the next task. Such feedback can help learners to develop the metacognitive skills they need to become more effective and independent learners.

Looking Forward: Areas for Future Research

One of the key aims of this book has been to explore the development and transfer of strategies within and between different languages; in the X-LiST study, these languages were English as the L1, and German and French as the instructed FLs. As discussed above, there was evidence of strategy transfer not only between the FL and L1, but also between the two FLs. However, we must bear in mind that the three languages at the heart of this study are all Western European languages which are written using the Latin script. It is also important to note that the learners were at a relatively similar stage of learning in French and German and these teachers adopted similar pedagogical approaches which may have also facilitated FL to FL transfer here. Further research is therefore needed to determine whether the results evident in the X-LiST study hold true in different contexts. This could include, for example, the extent to which writing strategies are transferable between two typographically distant languages, such as French and Mandarin, or Spanish and Russian. There is also a need to explore whether the FL to FL transfer, which was so prevalent in the X-LiST study, extends to contexts where students are at very different levels of proficiency in their FLs. An example of this could include non-Anglophone countries where English learning begins at a young age and an additional FL is introduced in secondary school. Such research is crucial for furthering our understanding of the optimum conditions and contexts in which to maximise the benefits of strategy transfer.

In addition, more studies are needed to determine the effects of a similar intervention of LLSI on students at different stages of learning. The X-LiST study focused on relatively beginner secondary school learners in their third or fourth year of learning an FL; however, there is scope to also explore opportunities for cross-linguistic LLSI at primary school level. If the same teacher is responsible for both L1 and FL instruction in primary classrooms, then there is perhaps even greater potential for integration and connection-making. It is also important to explore the possibilities for and implications of such pedagogies in more linguistically diverse classrooms. In some schools, for example, there may be a wide range of home languages represented within a single class. What are the opportunities here to more explicitly bring reflection on these additional languages into discussions of strategy use in L1 or FL classrooms?

Furthermore, the X-LiST study has solely focused on the development and transfer of writing strategies within and between language subjects. However, as stated in the Introduction, writing is a skill that permeates the entire school curriculum. As such, there is scope for exploring the extent to which students may transfer strategies learned in the FL classroom to their writing in other subject areas, such as writing essays in history or reporting the results of experiments in science lessons. Finally, it is important to note that while the X-LiST study focused on aspects relating to both teaching and learning, the majority of the data generated and analysed came from the learners. Additional research is therefore needed into the perspective of teachers in order to provide further insights into the opportunities and challenges of creating and implementing a cross-curricular, cross-linguistic approach to writing pedagogy.

Final Reflections

This book began with reference to the ubiquitous quote from Goethe which suggests that 'those who know nothing of foreign languages, know nothing of their own'. This is a quote that many FL teachers will be familiar with, and I have no doubt that it appears on countless classroom displays in schools around the world. Indeed, the sentiment at the heart of this quote has resonated with me in many ways over the years as a language learner, language teacher and then as a researcher and it effectively encapsulates the essence of what this book has sought to achieve, i.e. to shift our attention to the ways in which the skills and strategies developed in the FL classroom can contribute to improving students' use of language more broadly, including in their L1.

This conclusion chapter has highlighted a series of concrete theoretical and pedagogical implications which have arisen from this study; however, it is hoped that it will have wider ranging implications. On the one hand, the evidence presented in this book provides an empirical basis to further support the position of FLs in the curriculum. It suggests that even beginner or low-proficiency FL learners can develop effective skills and strategies in the FL classroom which can also positively influence writing in other languages, including their L1. Given the decline in uptake in FL learning in schools across the Anglophone world, evidence of the cross-curricular benefits of language learning that extend beyond the FL classroom itself will certainly be of interest to school leaders and policy makers. Another key message that emerged is that the positive effects of the LLSI were, in fact, most powerful when there was collaboration between FL and L1 teachers. Evidence therefore calls for a more cross-linguistic approach to the teaching of writing in schools, where L1 and FL teachers are both recognised as teachers of *language* and, as such, share some common aims and practices in order to support students' strategy development and facilitate transfer across the curriculum.

Appendix A: Student Questionnaire

Name: ....
Class: ....
Native language(s): ....

Please indicate any other languages you speak/have studied/are studying and for how many years? e.g. French – 5 years, German – 2 years.
....
....
....

1. How **confident** do you feel about writing in the following subjects? (circle number)

	Not confident at all	Not very confident	Quite confident	Very confident
English	1	2	3	4
French	1	2	3	4
German	1	2	3	4

2. How would you rate your **ability** in writing in the following subjects? (circle number)

	Poor	Fair	Good	Very good
English	1	2	3	4
French	1	2	3	4
German	1	2	3	4

3. How **difficult** do you find writing tasks in the following subjects? (circle number)

	Very difficult	Quite difficult	Quite easy	Very easy
English	1	2	3	4
French	1	2	3	4
German	1	2	3	4

4. How much do you **enjoy** doing writing tasks in the following subjects? (circle number)

	I don't like writing	*I'm not keen on writing*	*I quite like writing*	*I really enjoy writing*
English	1	2	3	4
French	1	2	3	4
German	1	2	3	4

Please consider the criteria below and indicate in the first column how **important** you think each one is in relation to writing, and in the last column how you would rate your own **performance** in each of these areas. Please answer by ticking the relevant boxes. There is a separate table for **English, French** and **German**.

5. **ENGLISH**

a. Importance				Criteria	b. Performance			
1 – Not at all	2 – Not very	3 – Quite	4 – Very		1 – Poor	2 – Fair	3 – Good	4 – Very good
				Planning your work				
				Thinking of creative/interesting ideas				
				Developing ideas				
				Organising/structuring a text clearly				
				Using a good range of vocabulary				
				Spelling				
				Punctuation				
				Grammar/sentence structures				
				Using appropriate style (e.g. formal/informal)				
				Fluency (i.e. how well your writing flows)				
				Using reference materials (e.g. dictionary, thesaurus)				
				Overall accuracy				
				Revising/editing your work				

6. FRENCH

a. Importance				Criteria	b. Performance			
1 – Not at all	2 – Not very	3 – Quite	4 – Very		1 – Poor	2 – Fair	3 – Good	4 – Very good
				Planning your work				
				Thinking of creative/interesting ideas				
				Developing ideas				
				Organising/structuring a text clearly				
				Using a good range of vocabulary				
				Spelling				
				Punctuation				
				Grammar/sentence structures				
				Using appropriate style (e.g. formal/informal)				
				Fluency (i.e. how well your writing flows)				
				Using reference materials (e.g. dictionary, thesaurus)				
				Overall accuracy				
				Revising/editing your work				

7. GERMAN

a. Importance				Criteria	b. Performance			
1 – Not at all	2 – Not very	3 – Quite	4 – Very		1 – Poor	2 – Fair	3 – Good	4 – Very good
				Planning your work				
				Thinking of creative/interesting ideas				
				Developing ideas				
				Organising/structuring a text clearly				
				Using a good range of vocabulary				
				Spelling				
				Punctuation				
				Grammar/sentence structures				
				Using appropriate style (e.g. formal/informal)				
				Fluency (i.e. how well your writing flows)				
				Using reference materials (e.g. dictionary, thesaurus)				
				Overall accuracy				
				Revising/editing your work				

Thank you very much
Merci beaucoup
Danke schön

Appendix B: Writing Strategy Task Sheet (Carissa, German Task 2)

Writing Task (German 2)

Title: Meine Hobbies

Planning

If you **want** to, you can use the space below to make a plan for your piece of writing. You can use it in whatever way you wish, or you can skip this section and turn over to start the task.

- Ich finde Hobbies fantastisch
  total super // interessant // absolut super //
- Lestes Jahr habe ich viel Tennis gespielt.
- Ich finde Tennis besser als Golf
- See p12 Logo webb for comparitives / superlatives
- (Leider habe ich nie so viel Zeit für meine Hobbies, weil ich natürlich immer total viele Hausaufgaben habe.)
- Weil sentences (verb to end)
- When it is... sentences   um... zu sentences

③ • Tanze x
⑥ • Lese x
⑤ • Ski (x Sport) x
④ • Fern sehen - Kino x
① • Music - das Konzert / Konzerte x
② • Wandern x
⑦ • Schwimmen, Baden x

How long (approximately) did you spend planning? ...ten......... minutes

Appendix B: Writing Strategy Task Sheet (Carissa, German Task 2) 179

Writing

Use the space below to write your answer to the question.

- If you make a mistake put a neat line through it like this
- Underline any words you looked up in a dictionary/glossary
- Use the 'notes' margin at the right hand side to note any relevant thoughts or problems as you write, e.g. something you wanted to say but couldn't find the right word for, if you got stuck, or if you used any other notes or resources to help, or asked the teacher/a friend.

Notes

Ich finde meine Hobbies absolut fantastisch! Mein LieblingsHobby ist tanzen weil es lustig und nützlich ist. Die Lehrerin ist total super, und ich habe viel Freunde wer tanzen. — not sure is correct
Es ist lustig, und es ist gesund. ~~Ich tanze~~ Wenn es Mittwoch oder Samstag ist, ich tanze. Ich bin nicht so sportlich, aber ich tanze und ich liebe Schwimmen. Ich finde Schwimmen lustig weil es einfach ist. Wenn es sonnig ist, ~~bade~~ ich manchmal am Strand, — dictionary
aber wenn es regnet gehe ich ins Hallenbad. Zu Schule ich spiele Netball und Hockey, aber ich hasse es. Schwimmen ist nützlicher und lustiger als Netball.
Auch, ich finde Ski fahren super. Letztes Jahr ~~Katze~~ ich nach Amerika ~~gege~~ Ski gefahren. Es war total fantastisch und sehr lustig.
Wenn ich faulenze bin, sehe ich Fern oder gehe ich ins Kino. Mein Lieblingsfilm ist "Juno", weil es sehr lustig ist. Auch ich — book
liebe Horrorfilme. Wenn ich in ~~die~~ der Stadt ~~gehen~~, gehe ich ins Kino oder gehe ich einkaufen. Ich liebe einkaufen aber meine

                                                                    Notes

Schwester hasst einkaufen, also ich gehe   sie hasst?
mit meine Freunde.
   Wenn es schön ist, ~~er~~ pausiere ich
draußen. Manchmal lese ich ein Buch oder
ich höre Musik. Mein lieblings Buch ist
"Harry Potte," ich finde das total ~~so~~ super.
Auch ich liebe Musik. Mein lieblingsgruppe   *
ist "Mumpord+ Sons. Ich liebe konzerte. ~~M~~
Manchmal in die Wochenende gehe ich zum   p12
ein Konzert. Meine lieblings konzerte ist Tom
Odell. Das war total super und sehr
lustig.
   Leider, ich immer mache Hausaufgaben, also
habe ich no so viel ~~echt~~ Freizeit.

How long (approximately) did you spend writing? ..40..... minutes

Evaluation

Did you check over your writing afterwards (please circle)?   Yes / No

If yes, which of the following statements is most true (please circle number):

1. I checked my work as I went along
2. I waited until the end and checked my work altogether

How long (approximately) did you spend checking your work? ...5... minutes

If you did check your work, what specifically did you check? Did you make many changes as a result of this?

Spelling mistakes, grammar

What did you find easy about the writing task?

I found some of the sentence structures easy as we have gone over them quite a lot

What did you find difficult about the writing task?

I found it quite hard to say all the things I wanted to say

How well do you think you have done? Why?

I think I have done alright but there were some words that I had no clue what to say.

References

Alamargot, D. and Fayol, M. (2009) Modelling the development of written composition. In R. Beard, D. Myhill, J. Riley and M. Nystrand (eds) *The Sage Handbook of Writing Development* (pp. 24–47). London: Sage.

Albrechtsen, D. (1997) One writer two languages: A case study of a 15-year-old student's writing process in Danish and English. *International Journal of Applied Linguistics* 7 (2), 223–250.

Allal, L. (2000) Metacognitive regulation of writing in the classroom. In A. Camps and M. Milian (eds) *Metalinguistic Activity in Learning to Write* (pp. 145–166). Amsterdam: Amsterdam University Press.

American Councils for International Education (2017) *The National K-12 Foreign Language Enrollment Survey Report*. Washington, DC: American Councils for International Education.

Anderson, J.R. (1985) *Cognitive Psychology and its Implications* (2nd edn). New York: Freeman.

Anderson, N.J. (2005) L2 learning strategies. In E. Hinkel (ed.) *Handbook of Research in Second Language Teaching and Learning* (pp. 757–772). Mahwah, NJ: Lawrence Erlbaum.

Ardasheva, Y., Wang, Z., Adesope, O.O. and Valentine, J.C. (2017) Exploring effectiveness and moderators of language learning strategy instruction on second language and self-regulated learning outcomes. *Review of Educational Research* 87 (3), 544–582. doi:10.3102/0034654316689135

Arndt, V. (1987) Six writers in search of texts: A protocol-based study of L1 and L2 writing. *ELT Journal* 41 (4), 257–267.

Australian Bureau of Statistics (2016) *2016 Census: Multicultural*. See https://www.abs.gov.au/ausstats/abs@.nsf/lookup/Media Release3 (accessed 19 October 2019).

Australian Curriculum Assessment and Reporting Authority (2018) *Learning Areas*. See https://www.australiancurriculum.edu.au/f-10-curriculum/learning-areas/ (accessed 19 October 2019).

Bai, B. (2015) The effects of strategy-based writing instruction in Singapore primary schools. *System* 53, 96–106. doi:10.1016/j.system.2015.05.009

Bandura, A. (1986) *Social Foundations of Thought and Action: A Social Cognitive Theory*. Upper Saddle River, NJ: Prentice Hall.

Bardel, C. (2015) Lexical cross-linguistic influence in third language development. In H. Peukert (ed.) *Transfer Effects in Multilingual Language Development* (pp. 111–128). Amsterdam: John Benjamins.

Bardel, C. and Falk, Y. (2012) The L2 status factor and the declarative/procedural distinction. In J. Cabrelli Amaro, S. Flynn and J. Rothman (eds) *Third Language Acquisition in Adulthood* (pp. 61–78). Amsterdam: John Benjamins.

Bardel, C. and Lindqvist, C. (2007) The role of proficiency and psychotypology in lexical cross-linguistic influence. In M. Chini, P. Desideri, M.E. Favilla and G. Pallotti (eds) *Atti del VI Congresso di Studi dell'Associazione Italiana di Linguistica Applicata* (pp. 123–145). Perugia: Guerra Editore.

Bense, K. (2014) 'Languages aren't as important here': German migrant teachers' experiences in Australian language classes. *Australian Educational Researcher* 41 (4), 485–497. doi:10.1007/s13384-014-0143-2

Bereiter, C. and Scardamalia, M. (1987) *The Psychology of Written Composition*. Hillsdale, NJ: Lawrence Erlbaum.

Berman, R. (1994) Learners' transfer of writing skills between languages. *TESL Canada Journal/Revue TESL Du Canada* 12 (1), 29–46.

Berninger, V.W. and Swanson, H.L. (1994) Modifying Hayes and Flower's model of skilled writing to explain beginning and developing writing. In E.C. Butterfield (ed.) *Advances in Cognition and Educational Practice, Vol. 2* (pp. 57–82). Bingley: Jai Press.

Bialystok, E. (1978) A theoretical model of second language learning. *Language Learning* 28 (1), 69–83.

Bono, M. and Stratilaki, S. (2009) The M-factor, a bilingual asset for plurilinguals? Learners' representations, discourse strategies and third language acquisition in institutional contexts. *International Journal of Multilingualism* 6 (2), 207–227. doi:10.1080/14790710902846749

Bouwer, R., Koster, M. and van den Bergh, H. (2018) Effects of a strategy-focused instructional program on the writing quality of upper elementary students in the Netherlands. *Journal of Educational Psychology* 110 (1), 58–71. doi:10.1037/edu0000206

Bowles, M.A. (2010) *The Think-Aloud Controversy in Second Language Research*. Abingdon: Routledge.

Boyle, A., August, D., Tabaku, L., Cole, S. and Simpson-Baird, A. (2015) *Dual Language Education Programs: Current State Policies and Practices*. Washington, DC: American Institute for Research.

Brisk, M.E. (2011) Learning to write in the second language: K-5. In E. Hinkel (ed.) *Handbook of Research in Second Language Teaching and Learning, Vol. II* (pp. 40–56). Abingdon: Routledge.

British Academy (2019) *The Cognitive Benefits of Language Learning: A Critical Synthesis for Policy, Practice and Research*. London: British Academy

British Educational Research Association (2018) *Ethical Guidelines for Educational Research*. London: British Educational Research Association.

Brown, A.L. (1987) Metacognition, executive control, self-regulation, and other more mysterious mechanisms. In F.E. Weinert and R.H. Kluwe (eds) *Metacognition, Motivation, and Understanding* (pp. 65–116). Hillsdale, NJ: Lawrence Erlbaum.

Burley, S. and Pomphrey, C. (2003) Intercomprehension in language teacher education: A dialogue between English and Modern Languages. *Language Awareness* 12 (3-4), 247–255. doi:10.1080/09658410308667080

Burley, S. and Pomphrey, C. (2015) Transcending language subject boundaries through language teacher education. In D.J. Rivers (ed.) *Resistance to 'the Known': Counter-Conduct in Language Education*. London: Palgrave Macmillan.

Canale, M. and Swain, M. (1980) Theoretical bases of communicative approaches to second language teaching and testing. *Applied Linguistics* 1 (1), 1–47.

Carter, M. (1990) The idea of expertise: An exploration of cognitive and social dimensions of writing. *College Composition and Communication* 41 (3), 265–286.

Cenoz, J. (2001) The effect of linguistic distance, L2 status and age on cross-linguistic influence in third language acquisition. In J. Cenoz, B. Hufeisen and U. Jessner (eds) *Cross-Linguistic Influence in Third Language Acquisition: Psycholinguistic Perspectives* (pp. 8–20). Clevedon: Multilingual Matters.

Cenoz, J. (2003) The additive effect of bilingualism on third language acquisition: A review. *International Journal of Bilingualism* 7 (1), 71–87. doi:10.1177/13670069030070010501

Cenoz, J. and Gorter, D. (2017) Minority languages and sustainable translanguaging: Threat or opportunity? *Journal of Multilingual and Multicultural Development* 38 (10), 901–912. doi:10.1080/01434632.2017.1284855

Cenoz, J. and Gorter, D. (2019) Multilingualism, translanguaging, and minority languages in SLA. *The Modern Language Journal* 103, 130–135. doi:10.1111/modl.12529

Cenoz, J., Hufeisen, B. and Jessner, U. (2001) Introduction. In J. Cenoz, B. Hufeisen and U. Jessner (eds) *Cross-Linguistic Influence in Third Language Acquisition: Psycholinguistic Perspectives* (pp. 1–7). Clevedon: Multilingual Matters.

Chamot, A.U. (2005) Language learner strategy instruction: Current issues and research. *Annual Review of Applied Linguistics* 25, 112–130.

Chamot, A.U. (2008) Strategy instruction and good language learners. In C. Griffiths (ed.) *Lessons From a Good Language Learner* (pp. 266–281). Cambridge: Cambridge University Press.

Chamot, A.U. (2009) *The CALLA Handbook: Implementing the Cognitive Academic Language Learning Approach* (2nd edn). White Plains, NY: Pearson Education.

Chamot, A.U., Barnhardt, S., El-Dinary, P. and Robbins, J. (1999) *The Learning Strategies Handbook*. White Plains, NY: Addison-Wesley.

Cohen, A.D. (1995) The role of language of thought in foreign language learning. *Working Papers in Educational Linguistics* 11 (2), 1–23.

Cohen, A.D. (1998) *Strategies in Learning and Using a Second Language* (1st edn). Harlow: Longman.

Cohen, A.D. (2007) Coming to terms with language learner strategies: Surveying the experts. In A.D. Cohen and E. Macaro (eds) *Language Learner Strategies: 30 Years of Research and Practice* (pp. 29–45). Oxford: Oxford University Press.

Cohen, A.D. (2011) *Strategies in Learning and Using a Second Language* (2nd edn). Harlow: Longman.

Cohen, A.D. (2014) The interface of styles, strategies, motivation, and age in second language learning. Paper presented at the conference on *Matters of the Mind: Psychology and Language Learning*, Graz, Austria.

Cohen, A.D. and Brooks-Carson, A. (2001) Research on direct versus translated writing: Students' strategies and their results. *The Modern Language Journal* 85 (2), 169–188. doi:10.1111/0026-7902.00103

Cohen, A.D. and Wang, I.K.H. (2018) Fluctuation in the functions of language learner strategies. *System* 74, 169–182. doi:10.1016/j.system.2018.03.011

Cohen, A.D. and Wang, I.K.H. (2019) Fine-tuning word meanings through mobile app and online resources: A case study of strategy use by a hyperpolyglot. *System* 85, 1–16. doi:10.1016/j.system.2019.102106

Cohen, A.D., Weaver, S.J. and Li, T.Y. (1998) The impact of strategies-based instruction on speaking a foreign language. In A.D. Cohen (ed.) *Strategies in Learning and Using a Second Language* (pp. 107–156). Harlow: Longman.

Cohen, A.D., Oxford, R.L. and Chi, J.C. (2005) Language strategy use inventory. See https://carla.umn.edu/maxsa/documents/LanguageStrategyInventory_MAXSA_IG.pdf (accessed 17 June 2020).

Collins, J.L. (1998) *Strategies for Struggling Writers*. New York: Guilford Press.

Commission on Language Learning (2017) *America's Languages: Investing in Language Education for the 21st Century*. Cambridge, MA: American Academy of Arts and Sciences. See https://www.amacad.org/multimedia/pdfs/publications/researchpapersmonographs/language/Commission-on-Language-Learning_Americas-Languages.pdf

Cook, V. (2002) Background to the L2 user. In V. Cook (ed.) *Portraits of the L2 User* (pp. 1–28). Clevedon: Multilingual Matters.

Cook, V. (2008) Multi-competence: Black hole or wormhole for second language acquisition research. In Z. Han (ed.) *Understanding Second Language Process* (pp. 16–26). Clevedon: Multilingual Matters.

Council of the European Union (2002) *Presidency Conclusions*. See http://data.consilium.europa.eu/doc/document/ST-6993-2002-INIT/en/pdf.

Cowan, J. (2019) The potential of cognitive think-aloud protocols for educational action-research. *Active Learning in Higher Education* 20 (3), 219–232. doi:10.1177/1469787417735614

Cramer, A.M. and Mason, L.H. (2014) The effects of strategy instruction for writing and revising persuasive quick writes for middle school students with emotional and behavioral disorders. *Behavioral Disorders* 40 (1), 37–51. doi:10.17988/0198-7429-40.1.37

Cumming, A. (1989) Writing expertise and second language proficiency. *Language Learning* 39 (1), 81–141.

Cumming, A. (1990) Metalinguistic and ideational thinking in second language composing. *Written Communication* 7 (4), 482–511.

Cumming, A. (2001) Learning to write in a second language: Two decades of research. *International Journal of English Studies* 1 (2), 1–23.

Cummins, J. (1979) Linguistic interdependence and the educational development of bilingual children. *Review of Educational Research* 49 (2), 222–251.

Cummins, J. (1981) The role of primary language development in promoting educational success for language minority students. In *Schooling and Language Minority Students: A Theoretical Framework* (pp. 3–50). Los Angeles, CA: Evaluation, Dissemination and Assessment Center, California State University.

De Angelis, G. (2005) Interlanguage transfer of function words. *Language Learning* 55 (3), 379–414. doi:10.1111/j.0023-8333.2005.00310.x

De Angelis, G. and Jessner, U. (2012) Writing across languages in a bilingual context: A dynamic systems theory approach. In R.M. Manchón (ed.) *L2 Writing Development: Multiple Perspectives* (pp. 47–68). Berlin: Walter de Gruyter.

De La Paz, S. and Graham, S. (2002) Explicitly teaching strategies, skills, and knowledge: Writing instruction in middle school classrooms. *Journal of Educational Psychology* 94 (4), 687–698.

Department of Education (2008) *Review of Irish-Medium Education Report*. Belfast: Department of Education.

Desautel, D. (2009) Becoming a thinking thinker: Metacognition, self-reflection, and classroom practice. *Teachers College Record* 111 (8), 1997–2020.

De Silva, R. (2015) Writing strategy instruction: Its impact on writing in a second language for academic purposes. *Language Teaching Research* 19 (3), 301–323. doi: 10.1177/1362168814541738

De Silva, R. and Graham, S. (2015) The effects of strategy instruction on writing strategy use for students of different proficiency levels. *System* 53, 47–59. doi:10.1016/j.system.2015.06.009

Devine, J., Railey, K. and Boshoff, P. (1993) The implications of cognitive models in L1 and L2 writing. *Journal of Second Language Writing* 2 (3), 203–225. doi:10.1016/1060-3743(93)90019-Y

DfE (2014) *The National Curriculum*. London: Department for Education. See https://www.gov.uk/national-curriculum/overview.

DfE (2019) *Schools, Pupils and their Characteristics: January 2019*. London: Department for Education. See https://assets.publishing.service.gov.uk/government/uploads/system/uploads/attachment_data/file/812539/Schools_Pupils_and_their_Characteristics_2019_Main_Text.pdf.

DfEE (1998) *The National Literacy Strategy*. London: Department for Education and Employment.

Dörnyei, Z. (2005) *The Psychology of the Language Learner: Individual Differences in Second Language Acquisition*. Mahwah, NJ: Lawrence Erlbaum.

Dörnyei, Z. (2007) *Research Methods in Applied Linguistics*. Oxford: Oxford University Press.

Dörnyei, Z. and Ryan, S. (2015) *The Psychology of the Language Learner Revisited*. London: Routledge.

Dörnyei, Z. and Skehan, P. (2003) Individual differences in second language learning. In C. Doughty and M.H. Long (eds) *The Handbook of Second Language Acquisition* (pp. 589–630). Oxford: Blackwell.

Dressler, R. (2018) Canadian bilingual program teachers' understanding of immersion pedagogy: A nexus analysis of an early years classroom. *Canadian Modern Language Review* 74 (1), 176–195. doi:10.3138/cmlr.3407

Duff, P.A. (2017) Commentary: Motivation for learning languages other than English in an English-dominant world. *The Modern Language Journal* 101 (3), 597–607. doi:10.1111/modl.12416

Edwards, S. (2012) Knowing the learner: What do New Zealand secondary mainstream teachers know about their English language learners, and why does it matter? *New Zealand Journal of Teachers' Work* 9 (2), 107–118.

Evans, M., Schneider, C., Arnot, M., Fisher, L., Forbes, K., Liu, Y. and Welply, O. (2020) *Language Development and the Social Integration of Students with English as an Additional Language*. Cambridge: Cambridge University Press.

Faerch, C. and Kasper, G. (1983) *Strategies in Interlanguage Communication*. Harlow: Longman.

Ferris, D.R. (2003) *Response to Student Writing: Implications for Second Language Students*. Mahwah, NJ: Lawrence Erlbaum.

Field, A. (2009) *Discovering Statistics Using SPSS* (3rd edn). London: Sage.

Flavell, J.H. (1979) Metacognition and cognitive monitoring. *American Psychologist* 34 (10), 906–911.

Flower, L. and Hayes, J.R. (1981) A cognitive process theory of writing. *College Composition and Communication* 32 (4), 365–387.

Flower, L. and Hayes, J.R. (1984) Images, plans and prose: The representation of meaning in writing. *Written Communication* 1 (1), 120–160.

Forbes, K. (2018) 'In German I have to think about it more than I do in English': The foreign language classroom as a key context for developing transferable metacognitive strategies. In Å. Haukås, C. Bjørke and M. Dypedahl (eds) *Metacognition in Language Learning and Teaching* (pp. 139–156). Abingdon: Routledge.

Forbes, K. (2019a) Teaching for transfer between first and foreign language classroom contexts: Developing a framework for a strategy-based, cross-curricular approach to writing pedagogy. *Writing and Pedagogy* 11 (1), 101–126. doi:10.1558/wap.34601

Forbes, K. (2019b) The role of individual differences in the development and transfer of writing strategies between foreign and first language classrooms. *Research Papers in Education* 34 (4), 445–464. doi:10.1080/02671522.2018.1452963

Forbes, K. and Fisher, L. (2020) Strategy development and cross-linguistic transfer in foreign and first language writing. *Applied Linguistics Review* 11 (2), 311–339. https://doi.org/10.1515/applirev-2018-0008

Forster, N. and Metcalfe, I. (2010) *Using MidYIS Individual Pupil Records to Inform Teaching and Learning*. Durham: Centre for Evaluation and Monitoring.

Friedlander, A. (1990) Composing in English: Effects of a first language on writing in English as a second language. In B. Kroll (ed.) *Second Language Writing* (pp. 109–125). Cambridge: Cambridge University Press.

Gass, S.M. and Mackey, A. (2017) *Stimulated Recall Methodology in Applied Linguistics and L2 Research* (2nd edn). Abingdon: Routledge.

Gillespie, A. and Graham, S. (2014) A meta-analysis of writing interventions for students with learning disabilities. *Exceptional Children* 80 (4), 454–473. doi:10.1177/0014402914527238

Goldenberg, C. and Wagner, K. (2015) Bilingual education: Reviving an American tradition. *American Educator*, Fall, 28–33. See https://www.aft.org/ae/fall2015/goldenberg_wagner.

Goethe, J.W. (1821) *Über Kunst und Alterthum*. Retrieved from: http://mdz-nbn-resolving.de/urn:nbn:de:bvb:12-bsb10913665-1 (accessed 17 June 2020).

Gordon, L. (2008) Writing and good language learners. In C. Griffiths (ed.) *Lessons From a Good Language Learner* (pp. 244–254). Cambridge: Cambridge University Press.

Gorter, D. and Cenoz, J. (2017) Language education policy and multilingual assessment. *Language and Education* 31 (3), 231–248. doi:10.1080/09500782.2016.1261892

Grabe, W. and Kaplan, R.B. (1996) *Theories and Practice of Writing*. Harlow: Longman.

Graham, S. (1997) *Effective Language Learning: Positive Strategies for Advanced Level Language Learning*. Clevedon: Multilingual Matters.

Graham, S. (2006) A study of students' metacognitive beliefs about foreign language study and their impact on learning. *Foreign Language Annals* 39 (2), 296–309. doi:10.1111/j.1944-9720.2006.tb02267.x

Graham, S. (2015) Writing instruction. In J. Wright (ed.) *The International Encyclopedia of Social and Behavioural Science* (pp. 767–772). London: Elsevier.

Graham, S. and Harris, K.R. (2003) Students with learning disabilities and the process of writing: A meta-analysis of SRSD studies. In H.L. Swanson, K.R. Harris and S. Graham (eds) *Handbook of Learning Disabilities* (pp. 323–344). New York: Guilford Press.

Graham, S. and Macaro, E. (2007) Designing Year 12 strategy training in listening and writing: From theory to practice. *Language Learning Journal* 35 (2), 153–173. doi:10.1080/09571730701599203

Graham, S. and Macaro, E. (2008) Strategy instruction in listening for lower-intermediate learners of French. *Language Learning* 58 (4), 747–783.

Graham, S., McKeown, D., Kiuhara, S. and Harris, K.R. (2012) A meta-analysis of writing instruction for students in the elementary grades. *Journal of Educational Psychology* 104 (4), 879–896. doi:10.1037/a0029185

Grenfell, M. and Harris, V. (1999) *Modern Languages and Learning Strategies: In Theory and Practice*. London: Routledge.

Grenfell, M. and Harris, V. (2013) Making a difference in language learning: The role of sociocultural factors and of learner strategy instruction. *Curriculum Journal* 24 (1), 121–152. doi:10.1080/09585176.2012.744326

Grenfell, M. and Harris, V. (2015) Learning a third language: What learner strategies do bilingual students bring? *Journal of Curriculum Studies* 47 (4), 553–576. doi:10.1080/00220272.2015.1033465

Grenfell, M. and Harris, V. (2017) *Language Learner Strategies: Contexts, Issues and Applications in Second Language Learning and Teaching*. London: Bloomsbury Academic.

Grenfell, M. and Macaro, E. (2007) Claims and critiques. In A.D. Cohen and E. Macaro (eds) *Language Learner Strategies: 30 Years of Research and Practice* (pp. 9–28). Oxford: Oxford University Press.

Griffiths, C. (2013) *The Strategy Factor in Successful Language Learning*. Bristol: Multilingual Matters.

Griffiths, C. (2018) *The Strategy Factor in Successful Language Learning: The Tornado Effect* (2nd edn). Bristol: Multilingual Matters.

Gu, P.Y. (2019) Approaches to learning strategy instruction. In A.U. Chamot and V. Harris (eds) *Language Learning Strategy Instruction in the Language Classroom: Issues and Implementation* (pp. 22–37). Bristol: Multilingual Matters.

Gunning, P., White, J. and Busque, C. (2016) Raising learners' awareness through L1–L2 teacher collaboration. *Language Awareness* 25 (1–2), 72–88. doi:10.1080/09658416.2015.1122022

Gunning, P., White, J. and Busque, C. (2019) Designing effective strategy instruction: Approaches and materials for young language learners. In A.U. Chamot and V. Harris (eds) *Language Learning Strategy Instruction in the Language Classroom: Issues and Implementation* (pp. 155–170). Bristol: Multilingual Matters.

Guo, X. and Huang, L.S. (2018) Are L1 and L2 strategies transferable? An exploration of the L1 and L2 writing strategies of Chinese graduate students. *Language Learning Journal* 1–23. doi:10.1080/09571736.2018.1435710

Hall, J.K., Cheng, A. and Carlson, M.T. (2006) Reconceptualizing multicompetence as a theory of language knowledge. *Applied Linguistics* 27 (2), 220–240. doi:10.1093/applin/aml013

Hammarberg, B. (2001) Role of L1 and L2 in L3 production and acquisition. In J. Cenoz, B. Hufeisen and U. Jessner (eds) *Cross-Linguistic Influence in Third Language Acquisition: Psycholinguistic Perspectives* (pp. 21–41). Clevedon: Multilingual Matters.

Harklau, L. (2011) Commentary: Adolescent L2 writing research as an emerging field. *Journal of Second Language Writing* 20 (3), 227–230. doi:10.1016/j.jslw.2011.05.003

Harris, K.R., Santangelo, T. and Graham, S. (2010) Metacognition and strategies instruction in writing. In H. Salatas Waters and W. Schneider (eds) *Metacognition, Strategy Use, and Instruction* (pp. 226–256). New York: Guilford Press.

Harris, V. (2006) Language learning strategies across the curriculum: Government policy and school practice. Paper presented at the *British Educational Research Association Annual Conference*, University of Warwick. Education-Line. See http://www.leeds.ac.uk/educol/documents/160889.htm.

Harris, V. (2019) Diversity and integration in language learning strategy instruction. In A.U. Chamot and V. Harris (eds) *Language Learning Strategy Instruction in the Language Classroom: Issues and Implementation* (pp. 38–52). Bristol: Multilingual Matters.

Haukås, Å. (2016) Teachers' beliefs about multilingualism and a multilingual pedagogical approach. *International Journal of Multilingualism* 13 (1), 1–18. doi:10.1080/14790718.2015.1041960

Hayes, J.R. (1996) A new framework for understanding cognition and affect in writing. In C.M. Levy and S. Ransdell (eds) *The Science of Writing: Theories, Methods, Individual Differences and Applications* (pp. 1–27). Mahwah, NJ: Lawrence Erlbaum.

Hayes, J.R. (2012) Modeling and remodeling writing. *Written Communication* 29 (3), 369–388. doi:10.1177/0741088312451260

Hayes, J.R. and Flower, L. (1980) Identifying the organization of writing processes. In L.W. Gregg and E.R. Steinberg (eds) *Cognitive Processes in Writing: An Interdisciplinary Approach* (pp. 3–30). Hillsdale, NJ: Lawrence Erlbaum.

Hyland, K. (2002) *Teaching and Researching Writing*. London: Pearson Education.

James, M.A. (2006) Teaching for transfer in ELT. *ELT Journal* 60 (2), 151–159. doi:10.1093/elt/cci102

James, M.A. (2007) Interlanguage variation and transfer of learning. *IRAL – International Review of Applied Linguistics in Language Teaching* 45 (2), 95–118. doi:10.1515/IRAL.2007.004

James, M.A. (2008) The influence of perceptions of task similarity/difference on learning transfer in second language writing. *Written Communication* 25 (1), 76–103. doi:10.1177/0741088307309547

James, M.A. (2009) 'Far' transfer of learning outcomes from an ESL writing course: Can the gap be bridged? *Journal of Second Language Writing* 18 (2), 69–84. doi:10.1016/j.jslw.2009.01.001

James, M.A. (2010) An investigation of learning transfer in English-for-general-academic-purposes writing instruction. *Journal of Second Language Writing* 19 (4), 183–206. doi:10.1016/j.jslw.2010.09.003

James, M.A. (2012) An investigation of motivation to transfer second language learning. *The Modern Language Journal* 96 (1), 51–69. doi:10.1111/j.1540-4781.2012.01281.x

Jarvis, S. and Pavlenko, A. (2010) *Crosslinguistic Influence in Language and Cognition*. London: Routledge.

Johns, A.M. (1990) L1 composition theories: Implications for developing theories of L2 composition. In B. Kroll (ed.) *Second Language Writing* (pp. 24–36). Cambridge: Cambridge University Press.

Jones, C.S. and Tetroe, J. (1987) Composing in a second language. In A. Matsuhashi (ed.) *Writing in Real Time* (pp. 34–57). New York: Addison-Wesley.

Kecskes, I. and Papp, T. (2000) *Foreign Language and Mother Tongue*. Mahwah, NJ: Lawrence Erlbaum.

Kellerman, E. (1977) Towards a characterisation of the strategy of transfer in second language learning. *Interlanguage Studies Bulletin* 2 (1), 58–145.

Kellerman, E. (1979) Transfer and non-transfer: Where we are now. *Studies in Second Language Acquisition* 2 (1), 37–57. doi:10.1017/S0272263100000942

Kellerman, E. (1991) Compensatory strategies in second language research: A critique, a revision, and some (non-) implications for the classroom. In R. Phillipson, E. Kellerman, L. Selinker, M. Sharwood Smith and M. Swain (eds) *Foreign/Second Language Pedagogy Research: A Commemorative Volume for Claus Faerch* (pp. 142–161). Clevedon: Multilingual Matters.

Kids Count Data Center (2018) *Children Who Speak a Language Other than English at Home in the United States*. See https://datacenter.kidscount.org/data/tables/81-children-who-speak-a-language-other-than-english-at-home?loc=1&loct=2&loc=1&loct=2#detailed/2/2-52/true/870,573,869,36,868/any/396,397 (accessed 15 October 2019).

Kim, Y.K., Hutchison, L.A. and Winsler, A. (2015) Bilingual education in the United States: An historical overview and examination of two-way immersion. *Educational Review* 67 (2), 236–252. doi:10.1080/00131911.2013.865593

Kobayashi, H. (2009) Task response and text construction across L1 and L2 writing: Japanese overseas high school returnees. *Bulletin of the Graduate School of Integrated Arts and Sciences (Hiroshima University)* 15, 11–27.

Kobayashi, H. and Rinnert, C. (1992) Effects of first language on second language writing: Translation versus direct composition. *Language Learning* 42 (2), 183–215.

Kobayashi, H. and Rinnert, C. (2007) Transferability of argumentative writing competence from L2 to L1: Effects of overseas experience. In M. Conrick and M. Howard (eds) *From Applied Linguistics to Linguistics Applied: Issues, Practices, Trends. Proceedings of the 2006 BAAL/IRAAL Conference (Cork, September)* (pp. 91–110). London: British Association for Applied Linguistics.

Kobayashi, H. and Rinnert, C. (2008) Task response and text construction across L1 and L2 writing. *Journal of Second Language Writing* 17 (1), 7–29. doi:10.1016/j.jslw.2007.08.004

Kobayashi, H. and Rinnert, C. (2012) Understanding L2 writing development from a multicompetence perspective: Dynamic repertoires of knowledge and text construction. In R.M. Manchón (ed.) *L2 Writing Development: Multiple Perspectives* (pp. 101–134). Berlin: Walter de Gruyter.

Kormos, J. (2012) The role of individual differences in L2 writing. *Journal of Second Language Writing* 21 (4), 390–403. doi:10.1016/j.jslw.2012.09.003

Koster, M., Tribushinina, E., de Jong, P.F. and van den Bergh, H. (2015) Teaching children to write: A meta-analysis of writing intervention research. *Journal of Writing Research* 7 (2), 249–274.

Kroll, B. (1990) Introduction. In B. Kroll (ed.) *Second Language Writing* (pp. 1–5). Cambridge: Cambridge University Press.

Lave, J. and Wenger, E. (1991) *Situated Learning: Legitimate Peripheral Participation*. Cambridge: Cambridge University Press.

Lee, I. and Mak, P. (2018) Metacognition and metacognitive instruction in second language writing classrooms. *TESOL Quarterly* 52 (4), 1085–1097. doi:10.1002/tesq.436

Lei, X. (2008) Exploring a sociocultural approach to writing strategy research: Mediated actions in writing activities. *Journal of Second Language Writing* 17 (4), 217–236. doi:10.1016/j.jslw.2008.04.001

Leonet, O., Cenoz, J. and Gorter, D. (2020) Developing morphological awareness across languages: Translanguaging pedagogies in third language acquisition. *Language Awareness* 29 (1), 41–59. doi:10.1080/09658416.2019.1688338

Li, W. (2018) Translanguaging as a practical theory of language. *Applied Linguistics* 39 (1), 9–30. doi:10.1093/applin/amx039

Lyster, R., Quiroga, J. and Ballinger, S. (2013) The effects of biliteracy instruction on morphological awareness. *Journal of Immersion and Content-Based Language Education* 1, 169–197.

Macaro, E. (2001) *Learning Strategies in Foreign and Second Language Classrooms*. London: Continuum.

Macaro, E. (2006) Strategies for language learning and for language use: Revising the theoretical framework. *The Modern Language Journal* 90 (3), 320–337. doi:10.1111/j.1540-4781.2006.00425.x

Macaro, E. (2019) Language learning strategies and individual differences. In A.U. Chamot and V. Harris (eds) *Language Learning Strategy Instruction in the Language Classroom: Issues and Implementation* (pp. 68–80). Bristol: Multilingual Matters.

MacArthur, C.A., Philippakos, Z.A. and Ianetta, M. (2015) Self-regulated strategy instruction in college developmental writing. *Journal of Educational Psychology* 107 (3), 855–867. doi:10.1177/0091552113484580

Manchón, R.M. and de Haan, P. (2008) Writing in foreign language contexts: An introduction. *Journal of Second Language Writing* 17 (1), 1–6. doi:10.1016/j.jslw.2007.08.002

Manchón, R.M., Roca de Larios, J. and Murphy, L. (2007) A review of writing strategies: Focus on conceptualizations and impact of first language. In A.D. Cohen and E. Macaro (eds) *Language Learner Strategies: 30 Years of Research and Practice* (pp. 229–250). Oxford: Oxford University Press.

Mason, L.H., Harris, K.R. and Graham, S. (2011) Self-regulated strategy development for students with writing difficulties. *Theory into Practice* 50 (1), 20–27. doi:10.1080/00405841.2011.534922

McCutchen, D. (2006) Cognitive factors in the development of children's writing. In C.A. MacArthur, S. Graham and J. Fitzgerald (eds) *Handbook of Writing Research* (pp. 115–130). London: Guilford Press.

McGee, A., Haworth, P. and MacIntyre, L. (2015) Leadership practices to support teaching and learning for English language learners. *TESOL Quarterly* 49 (1), 92–114. doi:10.1002/tesq.162

McGraw Hill Education (2017) *2017 English Learner Education Report* (November). See http://s3.amazonaws.com/ecommerce-prod.mheducation.com/unitas/school/explore/el-survey-results-2017.pdf.

Ministry of Education (2004) *British Columbia Language Education Policy*. See https://www2.gov.bc.ca/gov/content/education-training/k-12/administration/legislation-policy/public-schools/language-education-policy (accessed 19 October 2019).

Ministry of Education (2017) *The New Zealand Curriculum for English-Medium Teaching and Learning in Years 1–13*. Wellington: Ministry of Education. See http://nzcurriculum.tki.org.nz/The-New-Zealand-Curriculum#collapsible2.

Mitchell, R., Hooper, J. and Brumfit, C.J. (1994) Knowledge about language, language learning and the National Curriculum: Final report. Occasional Paper No. 19, University of Southampton.

Mitits, L. and Gavriilidou, Z. (2016) Exploring language learning strategy transfer between Greek L2 and English FL in case of early adolescent multilinguals. *International Journal of Multilingualism* 13 (3), 292–314. doi:10.1080/14790718.2016.1158266

Myhill, D. (2006a) Designs on writing (1). *Secondary English Magazine* 10 (1), 25–28.

Myhill, D. (2006b) Designs on writing (2). *Secondary English Magazine* 10 (2), 25–28.

Myhill, D. (2007) Designs on writing (3). *Secondary English Magazine* 10 (3), 25–28.

Myhill, D. (2009) Children's patterns of composition and their reflections on their composing processes. *British Educational Research Journal* 35 (1), 47–64. doi:10.1080/01411920802042978

Myhill, D. and Jones, S. (2007) More than just error correction: Students' perspectives on their revision processes during writing. *Written Communication* 24 (4), 323–343. doi:10.1177/0741088307305976

Myhill, D.A., Jones, S.M., Lines, H. and Watson, A. (2012) Re-thinking grammar: The impact of embedded grammar teaching on students' writing and students' metalinguistic understanding. *Research Papers in Education* 27 (2), 139–166.

Naimen, N., Fröhlich, M., Stern, H. and Todesco, A. (1975) *The Good Language Learner*. Clevedon: Multilingual Matters.

New Zealand Association of Language Teachers (2016) *Five Key Recommendations for Learning Languages to Thrive in New Zealand Schools*. See https://www.asianz.org.nz/assets/PDFs/594a8a8896/Five-key-recommendations-for-learning-languages-to-thrive-in-NZ-schools.pdf.

Newell, A. and Simon, H. (1972) *Human Problem Solving*. Englewood Cliffs, NJ: Prentice Hall.

Nguyen, L.T.C. and Gu, Y. (2013) Strategy-based instruction: A learner-focused approach to developing learner autonomy. *Language Teaching Research* 17 (1), 9–30. doi:10.1177/1362168812457528

Odlin, T. (1989) *Language Transfer: Cross-Linguistic Influence in Language Learning*. Cambridge: Cambridge University Press.

OFSTED (2012) *Moving English Forward: Action to Raise Standards in English*. London: OFSTED. See https://www.gov.uk/government/uploads/system/uploads/attachment_data/file/181204/110118.pdf.

OFSTED (2013) *Improving Literacy in Secondary Schools: A Shared Responsibility*. London: OFSTED. See www.ofsted.gov.uk/resources/120363.

Olivares-Cuhat, G. (2002) Learning strategies and achievement in the Spanish writing classroom: A case study. *Foreign Language Annals* 35 (5), 561–570.

O'Malley, J.M. and Chamot, A.U. (1990) *Learning Strategies in Second Language Acquisition*. Cambridge: Cambridge University Press.

Oxford, R. (1990) *Language Learning Strategies: What Every Teacher Should Know*. Boston, MA: Heinle & Heinle.

Oxford, R. (2011) *Teaching and Researching Language Learning Strategies*. Harlow: Pearson Education.

Oxford, R. (2017) *Teaching and Researching Language Learning Strategies: Self-Regulation in Context*. New York: Routledge.

Oxford, R. and Nyikos, M. (1989) Variables affecting choices of language learning strategies by university students. *The Modern Language Journal* 73, 291–300.

Oxford, R.L. and Schramm, K. (2007) Bridging the gap between psychological and sociocultural perspectives on L2 learner strategies. In A.D. Cohen and E. Macaro (eds) *Language Learner Strategies: 30 Years of Research and Practice* (pp. 47–68). Oxford: Oxford University Press.

Oxford English Dictionary (2019) Strategy.

Pennington, M.C. and So, S. (1993) Comparing writing process and product across two languages: A study of 6 Singaporean university student writers. *Journal of Second Language Writing* 2 (1), 41–63. doi:10.1016/1060-3743(93)90005-N

Perkins, D.N. and Salomon, G. (1988) Teaching for transfer. *Educational Leadership* 46 (1), 22–32.

Perkins, D.N. and Salomon, G. (1994) Transfer of learning. In T. Husen and T.N. Postelwhite (eds) *The International Encyclopedia of Education* (2nd edn) (pp. 6452–6457). Oxford: Pergamon Press.

Pittard, V. and Martlew, M. (2000) Socially-situated cognition and metalinguistic activity. In A. Camps and M. Milian (eds) *Metalinguistic Activity in Learning to Write* (pp. 79–102). Amsterdam: Amsterdam University Press.

Plonsky, L. (2011) The effectiveness of second language strategy instruction: A meta-analysis. *Language Learning* 61 (4), 993–1038. doi:10.1111/j.1467-9922.2011.00663.x

Plonsky, L. (2019) Language learning strategy instruction: Recent research and future directions. In A.U. Chamot and V. Harris (eds) *Language Learning Strategy Instruction in the Language Classroom: Issues and Implementation* (pp. 3–21). Bristol: Multilingual Matters.

Pomphrey, C. (2000) Language transfer and the Modern Foreign Languages curriculum. In K. Field (ed.) *Issues in Modern Foreign Languages Teaching* (pp. 269–282). London: RoutledgeFalmer.

Pomphrey, C. (2004) Professional development through collaborative curriculum planning in English and Modern Languages. *Language Learning Journal* 29 (1), 12–17.

Pomphrey, C. and Burley, S. (2009) Teacher language awareness education and pedagogy: A new discursive space. *Language Awareness* 18 (3–4), 422–433. doi:10.1080/09658410903197314

Pomphrey, C. and Moger, R. (1999) Cross-subject dialogue about language: Attitudes and perceptions of PGCE students of English and Modern Languages. *Language Awareness* 8 (3–4), 223–236.

Prior, P. (2006) A sociocultural theory of writing. In C.A. MacArthur, S. Graham and J. Fitzgerald (eds) *Handbook of Writing Research* (pp. 54–66). London: Guilford Press.

Psaltou-Joycey, A. and Kantaridou, Z. (2009) Plurilingualism, language learning strategy use and learning style preferences. *International Journal of Multilingualism* 6 (4), 460–474.

Pufahl, I. and Rhodes, N.C. (2011) Foreign languages in U.S. schools: Results of a national survey of elementary and secondary schools. *Foreign Language Annals* 44 (2), 258–288. doi:10.1111/j.1944-9720.1988.tb01059.x

QCA (2007) *The National Curriculum*. London: Qualifications and Curriculum Authority. See http://archive.teachfind.com/qcda/curriculum.qcda.gov.uk/uploads/QCA-07-3340-p_MFL_KS3_tcm8-405.pdf

Raimes, A. (1987) Language proficiency, writing ability, and composing strategies: A study of ESL college student writers. *Language Learning* 37 (3), 439–468.

Rast, R. (2010) The use of prior linguistic knowledge in the early stages of L3 acquisition. *IRAL – International Review of Applied Linguistics in Language Teaching* 48 (2–3), 159–183. doi:10.1515/iral.2010.008

Rees-Miller, J. (1993) A critical appraisal of learner training: Theoretical bases and teaching implications. *Teachers of English to Speakers of Other Languages* 27 (4), 679–689.

Rinnert, C., Kobayashi, H. and Katayama, A. (2015) Argumentation text construction by Japanese as a foreign language writers: A dynamic view of transfer. *The Modern Language Journal* 99 (2), 213–245. doi:10.1111/modl.12210

Robson, C. and McCartan, K. (2016) *Real World Research* (4th edn). Chichester: John Wiley.

Roca de Larios, J. and Murphy, L. (2001) Some steps towards a socio-cognitive interpretation of second language composition processes. *International Journal of English Studies* 1 (2), 25–45.

Roca de Larios, J., Manchón, R.M. and Murphy, L. (2006) Generating text in native and foreign language writing: A temporal analysis of problem-solving formulation processes. *The Modern Language Journal* 90 (1), 100–114.

Rubin, J. (1975) What the 'good language learner' can teach us. *TESOL Quarterly* 9 (1), 41–51.

Rubin, J., Chamot, A.U., Harris, V. and Anderson, N.J. (2007) Intervening in the use of strategies. In A.D. Cohen and E. Macaro (eds) *Language Learner Strategies: 30 Years of Research and Practice* (pp. 141–160). Oxford: Oxford University Press.

Salomon, G. (2001) School learning for transfer. In N.J. Smelser and P.B. Battes (eds) *International Encyclopedia of the Social and Behavioural Sciences* (pp. 13576–13579). Oxford: Pergamon Press.

Sasaki, M. (2000) Toward an empirical model of EFL writing processes: An exploratory study. *Journal of Second Language Writing* 9 (3), 259–291. doi:10.1016/S1060-3743(00)00028-X

Sasaki, M. (2002) Building an empirically-based model of EFL learners' writing processes. In S. Ransdell and M.-L. Barbier (eds) *New Directions for Research in L2 Writing* (pp. 49–80). Dordrecht: Kluwer Academic.

Scardamalia, M. and Bereiter, C. (1986) Research on written composition. In M.C. Wittrock (ed.) *Handbook of Research on Teaching* (3rd edn) (pp. 778–803). New York: Macmillan.

Schoonen, R., van Gelderen, A., de Glopper, K., Hulstijn, J., Simis, A., Snellings, P. and Stevenson, M. (2003) First language and second language writing: The role of linguistic knowledge, speed of processing, and metacognitive knowledge. *Language Learning* 53 (March), 165–202. doi:10.1111/1467-9922.00213

Schunk, D.H. and Swartz, C.W. (1993) Goals and progress feedback: Effects on self-efficacy and writing achievement. *Contemporary Educational Psychology* 18, 337–354.

Schutz, D. (2011) *The Common Core State Standards for English Language Arts and Literacy in History/Social Studies, Science, and Technical Subjects.* Washington, DC: Common Core State Standards Initiative. doi:10.2139/ssrn.1965026

Scottish Government Languages Working Group (2012) *Language Learning in Scotland, a 1 + 2 Approach: Report and Recommendations.* Edinburgh: Scottish Government Languages Working Group.

Selinker, L. (1972) Interlanguage. *IRAL – International Review of Applied Linguistics in Language* 10 (1–4), 209–232.

Sengupta, S. (2000) An investigation into the effects of revision strategy instruction on L2 secondary school learners. *System* 28 (1), 97–113. doi:10.1016/S0346-251X(99)00063-9

Sharwood Smith, M. and Kellerman, E. (1986) Crosslinguistic influence in second language acquisition: An introduction. In E. Kellerman and M. Sharwood Smith (eds) *Crosslinguistic Influence in Second Language Acquisition* (pp. 1–9). Oxford: Pergamon Press.

Silva, T. (1990) Second language composition instruction: Developments, issues and directions in ESL. In B. Kroll (ed.) *Second Language Writing* (pp. 11–23). Cambridge: Cambridge University Press.

Skehan, P. (2008) Interlanguage and language transfer. In B. Spolsky and F.M. Hult (eds) *The Handbook of Educational Linguistics* (pp. 411–423). Malden: Blackwell. doi:10.1002/9780470694138.ch29

Skibniewski, L. (1988) The writing processes of advanced foreign language learners in their native and foreign languages: Evidence from thinking aloud protocols. *Studia Anglica Posnaniensia* 21 (3), 177–186.

Skibniewski, L. (1990) The writing processes of advanced foreign language learners in their native and foreign languages: Evidence from thinking aloud and behaviour protocols. *Papers and Studies in Contrastive Linguistics* 25, 193–202.

Smyth, J. and Terry, C.T. (2011) Self-report. In N.J. Salkind (ed.) *Encyclopedia of Measurement and Statistics* (p. 878). Thousand Oaks, CA: Sage. doi:10.4135/9781412952644

Statista (2019) *Market Size of the Global Language Services Industry from 2009 to 2021 (in billion U.S. dollars)* [Graph]. See https://www.statista.com/statistics/257656/size-of-the-global-language-services-market/ (accessed 12 October 2019).

Statistics Canada (2016) *Data Tables (2016 Census).* See https://www12.statcan.gc.ca/census-recensement/2016/dp-pd/dt-td/Rp-eng.cfm?APATH=3&DETAIL=0&DIM=0&FL=A&FREE=0&GC=0&GID=0&GK=0&GRP=1&LANG=E&PID=109980&PRID=10&PTYPE=109445&S=0&SHOWALL=0&SUB=0&THEME=118&Temporal=2016&VID=0&VNAMEE=&VNAMEF=) (accessed 19 October 2019).

Steele, J.L., Slater, R.O., Zamarro, G., Miller, T., Li, J., Burkhauser, S. and Bacon, M. (2017) Effects of dual-language immersion programs on student achievement: Evidence from lottery data. *American Educational Research Journal* 54 (1S), 282S–306S. doi:10.3102/0002831216634463

Stern, H.H. (1975) What can we learn from the good language learner? *Canadian Modern Language Review* 31, 304–318.

Stratman, J.F. and Hamp-Lyons, L. (1994) Reactivity in concurrent think-aloud protocols: Issues for research. In P. Smagorinsky (ed.) *Speaking about Writing: Reflections on Research Methodology* (pp. 89–112). Thousand Oaks, CA: Sage.

Stutchbury, K. (2017) Ethics in educational research. In E. Wilson (ed.) *School-Based Research: A Guide for Education Students* (3rd edn) (pp. 82–95). London: Sage.
Taber, K. (2007) *Classroom-Based Research and Evidence-Based Practice: A Guide for Teachers*. London: Sage.
Tavakoli, M., Ghadiri, M. and Zabihi, R. (2014) Direct versus translated writing: The effect of translation on learners' second language writing ability. *Journal of Language Studies* 14 (2), 61–74.
Teddlie, C. and Tashakkori, A. (2009) *Foundations of Mixed Methods Research: Integrating Quantitative and Qualitative Approaches in the Social and Behavioural Sciences*. London: Sage.
Tinsley, T. and Doležal, N. (2019) *Language Trends 2019: Language Teaching in Primary and Secondary Schools in England*. London: British Council.
Torgerson, D., Torgerson, C., Ainsworth, H., Buckley, H., Heaps, C., Hewitt, C. and Mitchell, N. (2014) *Improving Writing Quality: Evaluation Report and Executive Summary*. London: Education Endowment Foundation. See https://files.eric.ed.gov/fulltext/ED581140.pdf.
Tullock, B.D. and Fernández-Villanueva, M. (2013) The role of previously learned languages in the thought processes of multilingual writers at the Deutsche Schule Barcelona. *Research in the Teaching of English* 47 (4), 420–441.
Uzawa, K. (1996) Second language learners' processes of L1 writing, L2 writing, and translation from L1 into L2. *Journal of Second Language Writing* 5 (3), 271–294.
Vann, R.J. and Abraham, R.G. (1990) Strategies of unsuccessful language learners. *TESOL Quarterly* 24 (2), 177–198.
Vygotsky, L. (1962) *Thought and Language*. Cambridge, MA: MIT Press.
Wang, W. and Wen, Q. (2002) L1 use in the L2 composing process: An exploratory study of 16 Chinese EFL writers. *Journal of Second Language Writing* 11 (3), 225–246. doi:10.1016/S1060-3743(02)00084-X
Welsh Government (2015) *Global Futures: A Plan to Improve and Promote Modern Foreign Languages in Wales 2015–2020*. Cardiff: Welsh Government.
Wenden, A. (1987) Conceptual background and utility. In A. Wenden and J. Rubin (eds) *Learner Strategies in Language Learning* (pp. 3–13). New York: Prentice Hall.
Whalen, K. and Ménard, N. (1995) L1 and L2 writers' strategic and linguistic knowledge: A model of multiple-level discourse processing. *Language Learning* 45 (3), 381–418.
What Works Clearinghouse (2017) *WWC Intervention Report: Self-Regulated Strategy Development*. See https://ies.ed.gov/ncee/wwc/InterventionReport/680
White, C., Schramm, K. and Chamot, A.U. (2007) Research methods in strategy research: Re-examining the toolbox. In A.D. Cohen and E. Macaro (eds) *Language Learner Strategies: 30 Years of Research and Practice* (pp. 93–116). Oxford: Oxford University Press.
Williams, J. (2012) The potential role(s) of writing in second language development. *Journal of Second Language Writing* 21 (4), 321–331. doi:10.1016/j.jslw.2012.09.007
Wolfersberger, M. (2003) L1 to L2 writing process and strategy transfer: A look at lower proficiency writers. *Teaching English as a Second or Foreign Language* 7 (2). See http://tesl-ej.org/ej26/a6.html.
Yang, N.-D. (1999) The relationship between EFL learners' beliefs and learning strategy use. *System* 27 (4), 515–535. doi:10.1016/S0346-251X(99)00048-2
Yin, R.K. (2012) *Applications of Case Study Research* (3rd edn). London: Sage.
Zamel, V. (1983) The composing processes of advanced ESL students: Six case studies. *Teachers of English to Speakers of Other Languages* 17 (2), 165–187.
Zhang, L.J. and Zhang, D. (2013) Thinking metacognitively about metacognition in second and foreign language learning, teaching, and research: Toward a dynamic metacognitive systems perspective. *Contemporary Foreign Language Studies* 396 (12), 111–121.

Subject Index

Attitudes, 3, 5–6, 19–26, 34–35, 59–61, 68, 122, 155–156, 161
Autonomy, 30, 48, 53, 74–75, 78, 88–89, 120, 128, 133, 138–139, 171
Awareness-raising, 78–81, 163

Behaviourism, 109

Cognitive academic language learning approach (CALLA), 77, 79
Cognitive process model, 38–39
Cognitive psychology, 33
Cognitive strategies, 33–38, 51, 82, 94, 98
Common underlying conceptual base, 115, 151
Communication strategies, 33
Conceptualisations of writing
 among students, 22–26, 42, 60–61, 120, 122–123, 126, 135, 146, 148, 156, 161–162, 164
 among teachers, 19–21, 161–162
Curriculum, 2–3, 7, 10–12, 18–21, 27, 73, 78, 89, 113, 161–164, 172, 173
 Australia, 16–17
 Canada, 15–16
 New Zealand, 17–18
 UK, 12–14
 USA, 14–15

Declarative knowledge, 33, 78
Dictionary use, 27, 52, 64, 82, 99–100, 106, 117, 120, 128, 133, 138–139, 145, 150
Drafting, 27, 38, 40–42, 49, 65, 92–96, 127, 130, 132, 137, 143, 144

English as an additional language (EAL), 77, 124, 141–142, 156, 158, 165, 167

English language, status of, 2, 11–13, 18–19, 73, 156, 162
Errors/error-correction, 26, 39, 65, 84, 87–88, 102–108, 117–118, 121, 129–130, 133–134, 137, 139, 141, 145–146, 151–152, 163–164
Ethics, 68–70

Feedback, 38, 41, 84, 88–89, 133–134, 141, 146, 154, 166, 171

Goal-setting, 38, 48, 94–98, 107, 116, 117, 171

Individual differences, 5–6, 31, 41, 69, 74, 124, 147, 149–159
Interview (see also stimulated recall interview), 6, 22–26, 31–32, 43, 59–61, 70, 119, 124, 127, 134–135, 141, 144, 157, 168

Knowledge-telling model, 39, 151–152
Knowledge-transforming model, 39, 152

Linguistic interdependence hypothesis, 110, 151

Metacognition, 10, 25, 35–42, 45, 48, 51, 74, 78, 81, 88–89, 94, 106, 113, 118, 122, 153–155, 159, 163–165, 168, 170–171
Metacognitive strategies, 25, 34–40, 48, 51–53, 82, 89, 94, 98, 104, 113, 135, 163, 165
Mixed-methods, 6, 58–61, 69, 160
Motivation, 34–35, 38, 41, 47, 50, 115–116, 159
Multicompetence, 9, 109, 111–112, 114–115, 151

Multilingualism, 4, 6, 9, 12–13, 17, 21, 46–47, 89, 111, 114, 125, 141–149, 156–158, 165

Procedural knowledge/proceduralisation, 33, 53, 60, 76, 78, 88, 100, 119, 155, 165, 168
Proficiency, role of, 3–6, 9, 19–23, 25, 43–47, 61, 74–75, 78, 110, 114–116, 121–123, 149–153, 157, 159, 161, 163, 169–170
Psychotypology, 110, 120, 147, 157

Quasi-experiment, 13, 48, 55–56, 59, 69, 160, 166
Questionnaires, 6, 22, 25–26, 52, 57–61, 64, 78, 114, 174–177

Scaffolding, 75, 83–84, 88, 134–135, 153, 166, 170
Self-regulated strategy development programme (SRSD), 48–50, 77, 80
Self-regulation, 29, 34, 41, 48–51, 79–80
Social cognitive theory, 40–41, 59, 83
Social strategies, 31, 34–37, 98
Stimulated recall interview (see also interview), 6, 42, 52, 57, 59, 65–68, 82, 92, 94, 124, 143, 168

Strategic multilingualism, 156–159, 165–166
Strategic self-regulation model (S^2R), 34–35, 79

Teacher collaboration, 10–11, 14, 20–21, 73–74, 89, 162–165, 170–171, 173
Teacher, role of, 2–4, 19–21, 40–41, 72–89, 162–165, 170–171
Transfer
  FL to FL, 117, 120–121, 123, 164, 167, 172
  FL to L1, 7, 90, 110–111, 113–118, 121–123, 150–151, 155, 164, 169–170
  L1 to FL, 90, 118–120, 127, 130, 150
Transfer of learning, 76, 112–113, 121, 147, 155, 169
Translation, 34, 46, 65, 68, 94, 133, 137–138, 142–148, 165

Writing
  As a skill, 3, 7, 11, 14, 37, 50, 75, 89, 160–161
  Task performance and strategy use, 47–54, 90–92, 149–153, 164–165
  Task selection, 61–63, 75–76, 168
Writing strategy task sheet, 63–65, 100, 102, 103, 143, 178–181

Author Index

Abraham, R.G., 110, 154
Alamargot, D., 40
Albrechtsen, D., 44, 119
Allal, L., 41
American Councils for International Education, 14
Anderson, J.R., 33, 77
Anderson, N.J., 30
Ardasheva, Y., 3, 51, 149, 160
Arndt, V., 44
Australian Bureau of Statistics, 12
Australian Curriculum Assessment and Reporting Authority, 24–25

Bai, B., 52–53
Bandura, A., 41
Bardel, C., 6, 111
Bense, K., 16
Bereiter, C., 39–40, 43, 111, 151–152
Berman, R., 114–116, 121, 150
Berninger, V.W., 40
Bialystok, E., 30
Bono, M., 158
Bouwer, R., 49
Bowles, M.A., 67
Boyle, A., 15
Brisk, M.E., 47
British Academy, 2
British Educational Research Association, 68
Brooks-Carson, A., 46, 158
Brown, A.L., 34
Burley, S., 13–14, 20–21, 23, 89

Canale, M., 33
Carter, M., 40
Cenoz, J., 4, 16, 47, 111, 121, 156, 158
Chamot, A.U., 3, 33–34, 36–39, 76–77, 79, 88, 152

Cohen, A.D., 3, 29–31, 35–36, 46–47, 64, 78–79, 82–83, 152–153, 158, 168
Collins, J.L., 39, 49, 83
Commission on Language Learning, 2, 14–15
Cook, V., 111–112, 123
Council of the European Union, 13
Cowan, J., 66
Cramer, A.M., 50
Cumming, A., 37, 43, 45, 66, 119, 152
Cummins, J., 109–110, 115, 150–151, 153, 169–170

De Angelis, G., 89, 111
de Haan, P., 47
De La Paz, S., 48–49, 83, 107
De Silva, R., 52–53, 92, 107, 151
Department of Education (Northern Ireland), 13
Desautel, D., 34
Devine, J., 44
Department of Education (UK), 12, 14
Department of Employment and Education (UK), 40
Doležal, N., 13
Dörnyei, Z., 29, 34–35, 56, 124
Dressler, R., 16
Duff, P.A., 11

Edwards, S., 12
Evans, M., 12

Faerch, C., 33
Falk, Y., 6
Fayol, M., 40
Fernández-Villanueva, M., 156
Ferris, D.R., 42
Field, A., 108
Fisher, L., 90, 109

Flower, L., 38–40, 66, 111
Forbes, K., 25, 72, 90, 109, 122, 124, 149
Forster, N., 108
Friedlander, A., 45, 158

Gass, S.M., 66–67
Gavriilidou, Z., 113–114
Gillespie, A., 50
Goethe, J.W., 1, 10, 173
Goldenberg, C., 15
Gordon, L., 38
Gorter, D., 4, 16, 47
Grabe, W., 39, 42
Graham, Steve, 3, 37, 48–50, 77, 83–84, 107, 160
Graham, Suzanne, 32, 36, 52–53, 56, 75, 89, 92, 107, 151
Grenfell, M., 4, 18–19, 21, 23, 26, 29–32, 36, 56, 58, 71, 73, 76–77, 80, 83, 88, 153, 158
Griffiths, C., 30, 36, 47, 50, 72, 76, 83, 149, 153, 156
Gu, P.Y., 33, 72, 74, 76
Gu, Y., 52–53, 92, 107
Gunning, P., 4, 21, 72–74, 77, 81, 83, 170
Guo, X., 3–4, 44

Hall, J.K., 112
Hammarberg, B., 6
Hamp-Lyons, L., 67
Harklau, L., 47
Harris, K.R., 39, 48, 50, 77, 152
Harris, V., 4, 18–19, 21, 23, 26, 30, 36, 47, 56, 58, 71, 73, 76–77, 80, 83, 88, 153, 158
Haukås, Å., 21
Hayes, J.R., 38–40, 66, 111
Huang, L.S., 3–4, 44
Hyland, K., 39, 41

James, M.A., 112–113, 116, 121
Jarvis, S., 111
Jessner, U., 89
Johns, A.M., 40
Jones, C.S., 44–45, 66, 110, 119
Jones, S., 41–42

Kantaridou, Z., 156
Kaplan, R.B., 39, 42
Kasper, G., 33

Kecskes, I., 7, 18–19, 26, 114–115, 121–122, 150–151, 153, 169–170
Kellerman, E., 76, 110, 112, 118, 120, 147
Kids Count Data Center, 12
Kim, Y.K., 15
Kobayashi, H., 46, 56, 112, 115, 121, 150, 155, 158, 170
Kormos, J., 124
Koster, M., 48
Kroll, B., 44

Lave, J., 41
Lee, I., 36, 88
Lei, X., 66
Leonet, O., 11
Li, W., 4, 111
Lindqvist, C., 111
Lyster, R., 73

Macaro, E, 29, 31–33, 35, 37, 47, 51–52, 56, 61, 63, 67, 75, 80, 84, 88–89, 92, 107, 108, 149, 152
MacArthur, C.A., 48
Mackey, A., 66–67
Mak, P., 36, 88
Manchón, R.M., 37, 47
Martlew, M., 40
Mason, L.H., 48, 50, 80–81, 88
McCartan, K., 68
McCutchen, D., 38
McGee, A., 12
McGraw Hill Education, 15
Ménard, N., 44–45, 66
Metcalfe, I., 108
Ministry of Education (British Columbia), 16
Ministry of Education (New Zealand), 17–18
Mitchell, R., 19
Mitits, L., 113–114
Moger, R., 20–21
Murphy, L., 40
Myhill, D., 41–42, 152, 154

Naimen, N., 32, 39
New Zealand Association of Language Teachers, 17
Newell, A., 66
Nguyen, L.T.C., 52–53, 92, 107
Nyikos, M., 72

O'Malley, J.M., 33–34, 36, 38–39, 76, 152
Odlin, T., 109
OFSTED, 13–14
Olivares-Cuhat, G., 52–53
Oxford English Dictionary, 29
Oxford, R. L., 2–3, 29–31, 33–35, 40–41, 46, 58–59, 69, 72, 78–79, 89, 114

Papp, T., 7, 18–19, 26, 114–115, 121–122, 150–151, 153, 169–170
Pavlenko, A., 111
Pennington, M.C., 39, 44, 119
Perkins, D.N., 73, 76, 112–113, 120, 122, 147, 155
Pittard, V., 40
Plonsky, L., 3, 50–51, 149, 160
Pomphrey, C., 13–14, 19–21, 23, 89, 113
Prior, P., 41, 83
Psaltou-Joycey, A., 156
Pufahl, I., 14

QCA, 14

Raimes, A., 42–44, 151–152
Rast, R., 110
Rees-Miller, J., 76
Rhodes, N.C., 14
Rinnert, C., 46, 56, 112–113, 115, 121, 150, 155, 158, 170
Robson, C., 68
Roca de Larios, J., 40, 44–45, 119
Rubin, J., 31–32, 34, 39, 111, 113
Ryan, S., 124

Salomon, G., 73, 76, 112–113, 120, 122, 147, 155
Sasaki, M., 52–53, 66–67, 83, 107, 151–152
Scardamalia, M., 39–40, 43, 111, 151–152
Schoonen, R., 44–45
Schramm, K., 29, 40, 59
Schunk, D.H., 89
Schutz, D., 14
Scottish Government Languages Working Group, 13
Selinker, L., 32, 109
Sengupta, S., 51–53, 108
Sharwood-Smith, M., 110
Silva, T., 40

Simon, H., 66
Skehan, P., 29, 34, 109, 124
Skibniewski, L., 44, 152
Smyth, J., 58
So, S., 39, 44, 119
Statista, 2
Statistics Canada, 12
Steele, J.L., 15
Stern, H., 31–32
Stratilaki, S., 158
Stratman, J.F., 67
Stutchbury, K., 69–70
Swain, M., 33
Swanson, H.L., 40
Swartz, C.W., 89

Taber, K., 60
Tashakkori, A., 61
Tavakoli, M., 46
Teddlie, C., 61
Terry, C.T., 58
Tetroe, J., 44–45, 66, 110, 119
Tinsley, T., 13
Torgerson, D., 49
Tullock, B.D., 156

Uzawa, K., 44, 66–67

Vann, R.J., 110, 154
Vygotsky. L., 37, 40, 109

Wagner, K., 15
Wang, I.K.H., 31, 35–36, 82
Wang, W., 46, 158
Welsh Government, 13
Wen, Q., 46, 158
Wenden, A., 29–30
Wenger, E., 41
Whalen, K., 44–45, 66
What Works Clearinghouse, 50
White, C., 30
Williams, J., 37
Wolfersberger, M., 44–45

Yang, N.-D., 156
Yin, R.K., 59

Zamel, V., 42–44, 152
Zhang, D., 35, 154
Zhang, L.J., 35, 154

For Product Safety Concerns and Information please contact our EU Authorised Representative:

Easy Access System Europe

Mustamäe tee 50

10621 Tallinn

Estonia

gpsr.requests@easproject.com